SEQUENTIAL PROGRAM STRUCTURES

Prentice-Hall International
Series in Computer Science

C. A. R. Hoare, Series Editor

Published

BACKHOUSE, R. C., *Syntax of Programming Languages: Theory and Practice*
de BAKKER, J. W., *Mathematical Theory of Program Correctness*
BJORNER, D. and JONES, C., *Formal Specification and Software Development*
CLARK, K. L. and McCABE, F. G., *micro-PROLOG: Programming in Logic*
DROMEY, R. G., *How to Solve it by Computer*
DUNCAN, F., *Microprocessor Programming and Software Development*
GOLDSCHLAGER, L. and LISTER, A., *Computer Science: A Modern Introduction*
HENDERSON, P., *Functional Programming: Application and Implementation*
INMOS LTD., *The Occam Programming Manual*
JACKSON, M. A., *System Development*
JONES, C. B., *Software Development: A Rigorous Approach*
JOSEPH, M., PRASAD, V. R., and NATARAJAN, N., *A Multiprocessor Operating System*
MacCALLUM, I. *Pascal for the Apple*
REYNOLDS, J. C., *The Craft of Programming*
TENNENT, R. D., *Principles of Programming Languages*
WELSH, J., and ELDER, J., *Introduction to Pascal,* 2nd Edition
WELSH, J., ELDER, J. and BUSTARD, D., *Sequential Program Structures*
WELSH, J., and McKEAG, M., *Structured System Programming*

SEQUENTIAL PROGRAM STRUCTURES

JIM WELSH
University of Queensland, Australia

JOHN ELDER
Queen's University of Belfast

and

DAVID BUSTARD
Queen's University of Belfast

Prentice/Hall PHI **International**

ENGLEWOOD CLIFFS, NEW JERSEY   LONDON   NEW DELHI   RIO DE JANEIRO
SINGAPORE   SYDNEY   TOKYO   TORONTO   WELLINGTON

Library of Congress Cataloging in Publication Data
Welsh, Jim, 1943–
    Sequential program structures.

    Bibliography: p.
    Includes index.
    1. Modular programming.   2. PASCAL (Computer program language)
I. Elder, John, 1949–   . II. Bustard, Dave, 1949–   . III. Title.
QA76.6.W4639 1984   001.64'2   83-19070
ISBN 0-13-806837-2
ISBN 0-13-806828-3 (pbk.)
British Library Cataloguing in Publication Data
Welsh, Jim
    Sequential program structures
    1. PASCAL (Computer program language)
    I. Title. II. Elder, John, 1949–   . III. Bustard, Dave
    001.64'24   QA76.73.P2
ISBN 0-13-806837-2
ISBN 0-13-806828-3 (pbk.)

© 1984 by Prentice-Hall International, Inc.

ISBN 0-13-806828-3 {PAPER}
ISBN 0-13-806837-2 {CASE}

PRENTICE-HALL INTERNATIONAL INC., London
PRENTICE-HALL OF AUSTRALIA PTY., LTD., Sydney
PRENTICE-HALL CANADA, INC., Toronto
PRENTICE-HALL OF INDIA PRIVATE LIMITED, New Delhi
PRENTICE-HALL OF JAPAN, INC., Tokyo
PRENTICE-HALL OF SOUTHEAST ASIA PTE., LTD., Singapore
PRENTICE-HALL INC., Englewood Cliffs, New Jersey
PRENTICE-HALL DO BRASIL LTDA., Rio de Janeiro
WHITEHALL BOOKS LIMITED, Wellington, New Zealand

Printed in the United States of America

10 9 8 7 6 5 4 3 2 1

Contents

Preface

The topics covered in this book are the structures, both in program and in data, that arise in substantial computer programs of a sequential nature—those which imply no concurrency in their execution. In practical terms, it provides an introduction to the classification and organisation of data structures, to their encapsulation as abstract data types, and to modular (sequential) programming in general.

The book begins by reviewing the objectives that are relevant to the construction of all computer programs. The conceptual tools and strategies that we must use to achieve these objectives are then considered. Subsequent chapters analyse the strengths and limitations of simple programming languages, such as Pascal, in supporting these conceptual strategies. From the limitations identified, the need for *modular programming* is established, together with a notation for expressing the modular program structures concerned. In this way Chapters 1 to 5 introduce a methodology for the design, implementation and testing of programs with a well-defined modular structure, and a notation for expressing that structure within the program text.

Chapter 6 then introduces the concept of *abstract data types,* using the concept of a program module to maintain a clear separation of the definition and use of an abstract type from the means chosen for its implementation. Within this general model, subsequent chapters introduce stacks, queues, lists, trees, graphs and tables as abstract data types. For each type a specification is developed, an external representation is defined, its use in practical programming context is illustrated, and major methods for its internal representation are described. The representations described are those suitable for use in primary stage only, but a final chapter outlines how these representations can be saved in, and retrieved from, secondary storage when necessary.

Throughout the book stepwise refinement is used as the means of presenting the design and implementation of programs and program modules, but in most major cases detailed listings of the final modules that result are also given. For modules that implement basic abstract data types in particular, these listings provide a valuable reference library of implementation techniques, or indeed of directly usable code, for many programming applications. The exercises given at the end of each chapter enhance this aspect, by suggesting modifications and applications of the listed modules as well as original design and implementation assignments.

The level of presentation is suitable for students (or other readers) with at least one year's experience in high level computer programming. Pascal is adopted as the initial programming notation, making the book ideal for students who have learnt to program in that language, but the review of Pascal's features given in Chapter 3 is sufficient to enable those familiar with other languages to follow the remainder of the text.

Extensions to Pascal are introduced to express modular program structure. The extensions are those of an existing programming language, Pascal Plus. This makes the book usable on a practical programming course in one of two ways:

* In conjunction with an implementation of Pascal Plus, the book offers a highly practical experience in the use of modular programming and abstract data types. To this end, Appendix 1 provides a concise working summary of the relevant features of Pascal Plus, and further information on the implementations available.

* Alternatively, the Pascal Plus features used may be regarded as a notation for the design of modular programs, to be translated into some other language at the implementation stage. In this context Chapter 9 relates the features of Pascal Plus to corresponding features in Ada, and Appendix 2 defines a general scheme for the translation of these features into standard Pascal.

By whatever means the book contents are translated into practical programming experience, we believe that it offers a sound introduction to data structures, to abstract data types, and to modular programming in general.

JIM WELSH, JOHN ELDER and DAVE BUSTARD
November, 1983

1

Goals in Programming

Computer programming is the major bottleneck in the successful exploitation of computers, and the widespread use of good programming methods is imperative if the problem is to be overcome.

This text is intended to illustrate the application of good programming techniques to a wide range of current programming problems, and to illustrate the programming language features required to support them, but before advocating any programming techniques it is important to establish the program qualities which 'good' techniques must realize.

Like the qualities sought in other areas, the desirable qualities of computer programs are determined ultimately by considerations of costs—the cost of program writing and the cost of program use. Obviously, programming methods must aim to minimize the aggregate of these costs, but the precise program qualities that help to realize this minimum are less obvious. Experience, often bitter experience, suggests that the most important program qualities are correctness, flexibility and efficiency. These are discussed in turn in the following sections.

CORRECTNESS

For some computer applications, by far the greatest *potential* cost comes from using a program which is incorrect. If a program controls a nuclear power station, a defense missile system, or a hospital life support system, the consequences of its failure are unthinkable. For other programs the consequences of residual errors may be less spectacular, but nevertheless, all such errors reduce the benefits of using the programs concerned, and so increase the aggregate net costs involved.

It is therefore an obvious objective in writing any computer program that the program should meet its intended purpose or specification correctly. For some programs the specification can be precisely stated, and for some of these it is possible to verify that the program meets its specification by formal analysis, or even to derive the required program from its specification by formal transformations. For most programs, however, the complexity of the program specification, or the inadequacy of formal techniques for the program verification or derivation, leaves the programmer to produce the required program by informal methods, and to 'demonstrate its correctness' by informal reasoning and/or testing. All too often, through inadequate understanding or care on the part of the programmer, the resultant program fails to meet some part of its specification.

A key factor in achieving program correctness is *simplicity*. By choosing the simplest algorithm or technique available, a programmer is more likely to see whether or not it meets the program specification, more likely to describe it correctly in the program, and more likely to detect any inadequacies or errors in the subsequent testing or verification process. In computer programming, as in other areas, unnecessary complexity serves no purpose whatsoever.

Some programs are, of course, inherently complex, and large programs are almost invariably so. For these the programmer must adopt a systematic approach that controls and limits the complexity dealt with at each stage. One such approach is outlined in Chapter 2 of this book, and illustrated throughout the subsequent chapters. It must be borne in mind that the objective of that approach is not simply to minimize the cost of writing programs, but to minimize the cost of writing *correct* programs. *In the end, these are the only programs worth writing.*

FLEXIBILITY

Because the cost of writing programs is high it is important to avoid all unnecessary writing or rewriting of programs, or parts of programs. Portability, adaptability, utility and clarity are all aspects of deliberate program flexibility that reduce overall programming costs.

Portability

When a program has been successfully developed for a given purpose in a given environment, using it for the same purpose in a different environment is an obvious adaptation, which ideally involves no reprogramming whatsoever. This portability depends on:

(a) writing the original program in a language common to both environments, and

(b) avoiding all unnecessary assumptions about the environment of its use.

The use of a high level language is usually assumed to meet both these requirements. However, in practice, significant variations occur between implementations of the same high level language on different computers, either through necessary machine dependencies in some of the language features or through poor implementation. To achieve a high degree of portability, a programmer must be aware of such variations and avoid them or provide for them in the program itself. A good programming language will identify possible variations in its definition and good implementations will provide options to detect the use of machine-dependent features in programs.

Adaptability

A computer program is usually written to fulfil a specific function in a specific environment. In practice, however, the required behavior of the program may change with changes in its environment, or as new uses emerge. Ideally, the cost of adapting a program to such changes should be less than the cost of constructing a completely new program. All too often, however, an attempt to make any substantial change to some part of an existing program results in such a cascade of consequential changes throughout the rest of the program that it is effectively rewritten, at a cost which may be greater than that of rewriting it from scratch. Program adaptation is successful only if it has been catered for, deliberately or accidentally, in the original construction of the program. Achieving deliberate adaptability involves:

(a) choosing a functional structure for the program which provides a clear separation of concerns, particularly those where change may be anticipated, and

(b) avoiding all unnecessary assumptions about the environment in which the program, or any of its component parts, operates.

In practice, of course, the programmer cannot hope to anticipate all the changes which may be required in the lifetime of a durable program, but the careful separation of concerns and avoidance of all unnecessary assumptions at each point go a long way to enable many unforeseen changes that arise.

Significant adaptability is a result of the design chosen for the program rather than the notation in which it is expressed. However, the programming language plays a significant role in supporting and reinforcing the design structure. As changes are made to an existing program, it is important that the language should protect the existing structure and reflect any significant structural changes that are introduced. The temptation to make a quick change to a program which alters its functional behavior without changing the corresponding structure of the program text all too often produces a program in which any further significant change is hazardous. A good language can, therefore, play a significant role in ensuring the on-going adaptability of a program throughout its lifetime, by reflecting and protecting its inherent structure.

Utility

Many programs with related purposes in some application area, and even programs with totally different purposes in different application areas, have a common functional requirement for some component part. For example, a similar sort routine may be needed in many different programs.

A good programmer should always consider the possibility of using some existing unit which is available in a library in his own environment, in some other environment, or simply in the programming literature, and a good programming environment should provide facilities which encourage him to do so. Conversely, when a new unit is written, the programmer should consider the possibility of its use in other programs. This general utility is achieved by:

(a)   a logical separation of concerns between the utility unit and the program that uses it, and

(b)   the avoidance of all unnecessary assumptions within the unit about the behavior of the using program.

Achieving this generality often adds little to the cost of writing the unit or the first program that uses it, and significantly reduces the cost of writing all subsequent programs that use it.

To encourage utility programming, the programming language and its implementation must help the programmer to incorporate existing units into new programs and to deposit new units in a library for future use in other programs. To this end, the language must provide an appropriate range of sub-program units that are suitable for library storage, together with a clear means of defining the relationship between such units and the program that uses them. The implementation must provide a simple means of assembling such units into an overall program, and must enforce all necessary consistency checks between the units and the program that uses them.

Clarity

Any form of program flexibility is effective only if it is apparent to those who may wish to use or change the program. Thus, program clarity is a prerequisite of program flexibility. Program clarity is achieved in much the same way as for any written text, such as an essay or book. It requires:

(a)   a logical division of the text into meaningful parts which reflect the distinction between the functions they describe, and their presentation in a logical sequence which reflects the relationships between them;

(b)   a careful choice of the language features used within each part to express its intended meaning as precisely as possible;

(c)   a further careful choice of the words used to denote the objects and concepts involved;

(d)   the inclusion of additional comments and preambles to clarify the main text when necessary;

(e)   an exploitation of text-layout devices, such as blank lines and indentation, to emphasize the relationship between the text's component parts.

Obviously, a good programming language must provide a range of features and notations that enable these requirements to be met. Within the limitations of the language involved, the programmer should be as assiduous in the use of these techniques for achieving clarity as the author of any text. In many cases the usefulness of a program is as much determined by the clarity of its text, as by the qualities of the algorithm which it describes.

EFFICIENCY

In the past the cost of executing a computer program was a dominant influence on its design, but as hardware costs have fallen relative to those of writing programs the importance of program 'efficiency' has also diminished. Nevertheless, program efficiency is a consideration which is vital for some programs and relevant for all.

The cost of executing a computer program is normally measured in terms of:

(a)   the *time* taken by the computer to carry out the sequence of operations involved;

(b)   the amount of computer *store* used in doing so.

In practice, the real time taken to execute the program is a combination of the time spent by the processor executing machine instructions and the time taken by input and output operations on peripheral or backing-store devices. For some programs the time spent on transfers far outweighs the processing time. For others the reverse is true and efficiency considerations may vary accordingly. For some programs efficiency of the overall program may be important, for others only the efficiency of particular parts may matter—for example the response time. In general, the meaning of 'efficiency' for a given program is a function of the program's purpose and of the environment in which it is to be used, and a good program specification will define limits on the various efficiency aspects of the program or its parts.

To achieve this efficiency the programmer must first choose an algorithm which is capable of meeting the performance requirements, since different algorithms for the same function may differ by orders of magnitude in their use of store or time. Secondly, care must be taken to avoid any unacceptable redundancy in encoding the algorithm as a computer program. Unfortunately, such efficiency considerations sometimes conflict with those of program correctness and flexibility discussed in previous sections. While simplicity and efficiency are by no means mutually exclusive, a more efficient algorithm is often more complex than its less efficient alternative, and hence more liable to programming error. Similarly, the most efficient encoding of an algorithm is usually achieved by the use of low-level machine-oriented programming, which detracts from program portability and again increases the likelihood of programming error.

Thus efficiency is a program quality which often must be balanced against those of correctness and flexibility. When a free choice exists it is always prudent to choose the most efficient algorithm or encoding available, and for some programs efficiency considerations may be the most important. As a general rule, however, the pursuit of correctness, flexibility and efficiency, in that order of priority, seems most likely to achieve the overall minimum cost in computer programming and computer usage.

SUMMARY

Correctness, flexibility and efficiency are vital objectives in the construction of significant computer programs. The main purpose of this book is to define and demonstrate a structured approach to programming that encourages both correctness and flexibility.

Within the program structures created, significant variations in efficiency may arise from the data representations and algorithms chosen. A second purpose of this book is to introduce a standard range of data structures and manipulation algorithms that arise in many computing applications. As such they are prime candidates for the flexible off-the-shelf program components to be created and exploited by our approach to programming.

Before addressing either topic, however, we review the basic tools of computer programming with which the reader should already be familiar. These are the method of stepwise refinement for program construction, and the features of a high-level programming language like Pascal.

2

Stepwise Refinement

SPECIFICATION, DESIGN AND CODING

In Chapter 1 we discussed desirable properties to be sought in writing a program, for which the existence of some 'specification' was assumed. In practice, however, the dividing line between program specifications and programs themselves is not always clear and not always relevant to the programming process.

In general, a program specification defines the effect that a program must produce, i.e. *what* it must do. In some cases the specification may be purely functional in form, giving no indication as to *how* the program should achieve the desired effect. For example, the simple specification:

> *Write a function to compute the square root of*
> *its real non-negative argument to 6 decimal places*

gives the programmer no indication of the algorithm that the function should use. However, if the specification reads:

> *Write a function to compute the square root of*
> *its real non-negative argument to 6 decimal*
> *places using the Newton–Raphson method*

the programmer, knowing the Newton–Raphson method, has an immediate indication of the algorithm to be used. A procedural specification of this sort, i.e. one that indicates *how* the program is to accomplish its task, can clearly be regarded as a first step in the design of the program itself. For some problems a procedural specification is the most natural or convenient way of defining the program solution that is required. When the program requirements are complex, the techniques needed to write a precise procedural specification are similar to those needed to write the program itself. For many programs a purely functional specification may be equally complex, and here, too, techniques to control complexity are required if a clear, precise specification is to be achieved.

Another distinction sometimes made is between program design and program coding. The former embraces the major decisions on data structures and algorithms that are taken without particular regard to the programming language or machine involved, while the latter is concerned solely with implementing the chosen design for a given language/machine pair. As we shall see, however, this distinction also disappears if particular design methods and sympathetic languages are used.

Thus the distinctions between program specification, program design and program coding have little impact on the basic techniques used to achieve them. In this book we concentrate on the design and coding of programs from assumed initial specifications which are informally stated. It should be noted, however, that the approach advocated in this chapter, and applied systematically thereafter, is relevant to all stages of the programming process, from initial program conception to final program code.

ABSTRACTION

Complexity, or rather our limited ability to cope with it, is the crux of the programming problem. The basic tool that we use to master complexity in any intellectual endeavour is *abstraction*. The role of abstraction in programming has been described lucidly by Hoare in *Structured Programming* and the summary given here is inspired by Hoare's description.

Abstraction is a decision to ignore those properties of objects which are not relevant in a particular situation at a particular time and to concentrate on those properties which are. To exploit this abstraction we require some representation or set of symbols for the abstracted properties, and a set of rules or procedures for manipulating these symbols in a way that reflects the effect of a corresponding manipulation of the objects themselves in the real world.

Consider Hoare's example of a computerized payroll system. This abstracts from a workforce of real employees (with physical characteristics that are irrelevant to payroll matters) to a set of employee numbers with associated tax codes, etc. The workforce is represented by a file of records, one record for each employee, with fields within each to represent the relevant data for that employee. The payroll process manipulates this representation to generate the necessary pay slips and update the employee file on each pay day, thus recording and controlling the payment of real money to the real employees required.

The abstraction from real-world employees to corresponding employee numbers typifies the vital first step in computerizing any real-world problem—that of reducing it to a well-defined system that is amenable to a computer solution. In practice, of course, most payroll systems are more complex than the simple outline given above, and, in general, a single abstraction from a real-world problem will not enable us to write down a solution to that problem in some available programming language, nor even to write down a complete program specification. To master such complexity our abstraction tool must be used repeatedly, in some systematic manner. One method that works well for a wide class of programming problems is *stepwise refinement*, which we now consider.

STEPWISE REFINEMENT

A First Example

As a first example of stepwise refinement consider a very simple and familiar process—the construction of an arithmetic expression. Suppose in a payroll program we require an expression for the net pay due to an employee. The mental process of devising the appropriate expression might be as shown in Fig. 2.1.

In practice the mental process of composing an expression on this scale may well be subconscious, but it clearly must follow the structural framework illustrated. This expression-composing process is typical of the programming process at all levels. While it is within our mental capacity to compose expressions of 5 to 10 terms without conscious effort, this is not so for expressions of 20 terms or more. For these we have to resort to some conscious structural breakdown before we can begin to write down the expression in its final format. The same is true of programming at other levels. We can conceive a program of 5 to 10 statements without formally pre-determining its structure, but we cannot do so for larger programs. In fact, this limit on our capacity to conceive of the necessary required program or expression at a single step is not peculiar to computer programming as such, but follows from a more general limit on the capacity of our human intellect to comprehend systems composed of multiple components. The same limit on the number of system components that the human mind can cope with has been observed in many different areas. As programmers we

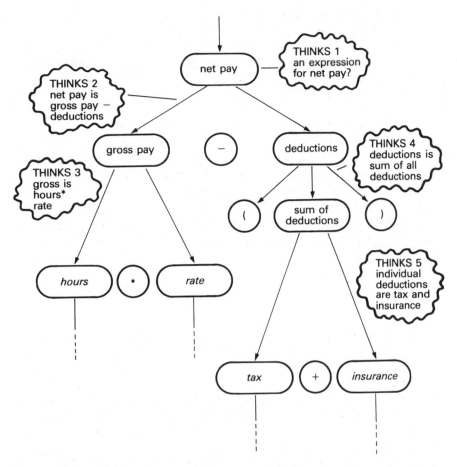

Figure 2.1   Composing an expression for net pay

are aware that such limits on our mental capacity exist, but too often we assume our particular limit to be of an order of magnitude greater than it really is. Stepwise refinement, by limiting the awareness required at each step, helps us to avoid this pitfall and so reduce the likelihood of programming errors.

A Second Example

As a second example, using a more convenient refinement notation, consider the design of an 'algorithm' for dealing with a flat wheel of a car.

Initially, we may express the algorithm as:

deal with flat wheel

where, for the moment, all details of how to deal with the flat wheel are ignored. Realizing, however, that the action required depends completely on whether the spare wheel is in a roadworthy condition or not, this initial statement may be broken down into

if *spare wheel is okay*
then *change the wheel*
else *call the nearest garage for help*

in which the refinement of *deal with flat wheel* is now expressed as a choice between two alternative actions.

We now concentrate on the refinement of *change the wheel*. The operation may be decomposed into a sequence of four simpler actions:

begin
   jack up the car;
   remove the flat wheel;
   fit the spare wheel;
   jack down the car
end

(We bracket the sequence of four actions by the words **begin** and **end** to indicate that they represent the decomposition of a single action). Ignoring further details of *jack up the car* we can express the removal of the flat wheel as a repetition of certain actions, i.e.

repeat
   remove a nut
until *all the nuts have been removed*

followed by removal of the wheel. Similarly, fitting the spare wheel involves a sequence of two actions—putting on the wheel, and then a repetition involving replacement of the nuts.

The stepwise refinement has now reached a stage where we may write down a fairly detailed algorithm, by fitting together the detailed actions according to the structure developed in the refinement, i.e.

```
if spare wheel is okay
then begin
        jack up the car;
        repeat
          remove a nut
        until all the nuts have been removed;
        take off the wheel;
        put on the spare wheel;
        repeat
          replace a nut
      , until all the nuts have been replaced;
        jack down the car
    end
else call the nearest garage for help
```

if, **repeat** and **begin,end** constructs reflect clearly both the composite action required, and the refinement that led us to it. This clear expression is further emphasized by the layout and indentation chosen for the text involved.

The General Case

These two examples show stepwise refinement in action in two familiar everyday contexts that reflect the essential characteristics of computer programming problems. At this point, it is worthwhile to attempt a more formal definition of the stepwise refinement method.

In stepwise refinement (of a computer program) we start with a highly abstract statement of the program in which all details of its requirements are ignored. By first concentrating on some dominant requirement, this initial abstract statement is then refined into a small number of (abstract) component parts which together meet that requirement. The decomposition is such that the contribution of each component to the whole is completely defined and understood, but the internal details of each component are not. Thus we have satisfied one requirement and reduced the initial problem to a number of simpler, less abstract sub-problems.

Now we proceed to refine each of the components of this first refinement in turn, i.e. in terms of some further, simpler components at a lower level of abstraction. This process of stepwise refinement of abstract actions continues until each abstract component may be directly expressed in terms of the programming language being used and all requirements of the program have been met. Hence we proceed from the initial abstract concept to the final concrete program text by steps, each progressing from a certain level of abstraction to a slightly lower level. The lowest level of abstraction is that supported by the programming language itself. At any given stage in the development of the program the complexity with which we are faced is restricted to the abstract action that we are trying to refine, and all the other parts of the program may effectively be ignored.

The effectiveness of stepwise refinement depends on this ability to ignore other parts of the program when refining a particular component, so reducing the complexity involved. Clearly an arbitrary division of a given component into sub-components need not ensure the necessary independence, so how is a useful division achieved? In the expression writing and wheel-changing examples the refinement chosen followed a natural precedence of concerns inherent in the problem itself. Perceiving this natural structure was not particularly difficult in these cases—clearly the details of how to change a wheel are relevant only if a roadworthy spare is available! Experience suggests that in most cases explicit structural independence is readily achieved by following some similar 'natural' structure suggested by the problem itself, the data involved, or the constraints that apply to its solution.

However, in many cases some implicit dependence between components remains, through the common data that they use, and/or the relationships assumed between data values. To minimize the complexity of his task the programmer must also minimize this implicit dependence between components, and must identify clearly such dependence that remains before proceeding with refinement of the components involved. The nature of such interdependencies and the techniques that may be required to handle them are illustrated by the next example.

A Further Example

To demonstrate the use of stepwise refinement on a more realistic programming problem we now consider a simple data processing application, the tabulation of examination marks for a class.

In a class of students, each student studies 5 subjects. The grades obtained by each student in each subject are input to a computer, as one line of text per student. Each line consists of the student's name, which is less than 30 characters long and terminated by a period, followed by five grade numbers in the range 0 to 10, separated by spaces, e.g.:

MARY SMITH. 7 7 10 6 4
HOWARD BLACKBURN. 4 7 5 4 5

A program is required to read this input and tabulate the students' overall performance in a table which shows each student's name followed by his overall total grade in a vertically aligned column.

For example, the above inputs might produce outputs:

> *MARY SMITH.*   34
> *HOWARD BLACKBURN.*   25

The initial concept of the program may be expressed quite simply as:

> *tabulate examination marks*

The program has an overall structure of a loop which is executed once for each input line:

> **while not** *eof*(*input*) **do**
>   *read and print data on one student*

The process *read and print data on one student* can be broken down into a sequence of simpler steps:

> **begin**
>   *read name and grades*;
>   *compute total grade*;
>   *print name and total*
> **end**

The step *read name and grades* can be further refined as:

> *read name*;
> *read grades*;
> *readln*

the final *readln* being included to leave the input properly aligned for the next student, if any. Before we can refine the steps *read name* or *read grades*, however, we must decide how the name and grades are to be held within the program. To do so we introduce two arrays, as follows:

> *name*   : **array** [1 . . 30] **of** *char*;
> *grades* : **array** [1 . . 5] **of** 0 . . 10;

With these the two steps quickly reduce to:

> {*read name*}
> *i* := 0;
> **repeat**
>   *i* := *i* +1;
>   *read* (*name*[*i*])
> **until** *name*[*i*] = ' . '
>
> {*read grades*}
> **for** *s* := 1 **to** 5 **do** *read* (*grades*[*s*])

assuming appropriate declarations of the variables *i* and *s*. The step *compute total grade* is also easily refined as:

> *total* := 0;
> **for** *s* := 1 **to** 5 **do**
>   *total* := *total* + *grades*[*s*]

Now consider the step *print name and total*. Like the step *read name and grades* this can clearly be refined as:

> *print name*;
> *print total*;
> *writeln*

again with the *writeln* being included to leave the output properly aligned for the next student. The steps *print name* and *print total* clearly must use the variables *name* and *total* whose values are assigned by the steps *read name* and *compute total grade*. A more interesting question is whether *print name* should also make use of the final value of the variable *i* which was originally introduced within *read name* to place the character read in the correct array position? Using it, *print name* can be expressed as a **for** statement, thus:

> **for** *j* := 1 **to** *i* **do** *write* (*name*[*j*])

but without it, a **repeat** loop that redetermines the length of the name is required:

> *i* := 0;
> **repeat**
>   *i* := *i* + 1;
>   *write* (*name*[*i*])
> **until** *name*[*i*] = ' . '

A further problem arises when we refine the step *print total*—because the number of characters printed for each name is variable, printing the total in a fixed column position also involves using the name length determined either by the step *read name* or by *print name*. Assuming the **repeat** loop version of *print name*, which leaves *i* equal to the number of name characters printed, we can print the value of *total* in an aligned column position by a statement:

> *write* (*total* : 40-*i*)

but in practice a clearer program may be obtained by extending the step *print name* to always print 30 characters, thus:

```
    i := 0;
    repeat
      i := i + 1;
      write (name[i])
    until name[i] = ' . ';
    if i < 30 then write (' ' : 30-i)
```

and then programming *print total* in the independent form:

```
    write (total : 10)
```

At various refinement steps we have introduced variables which denote data items whose values are manipulated by the actions involved, e.g. *name*, *grades*, etc. The final Pascal program may now be assembled from the various program fragments, together with suitable declarations of these variables. Listing 1 shows the program that results.

Listing 1

```
program studentgrades(input, output);

{ This program reads and tabulates student grades.
  Each input line consists of a student name of not
  more than 30 characters ending with a '.', followed
  by five grades in the range 0 to 10.
  The output consists of student names as input with
  an aligned column of grade totals                    }

var name: array [1..30] of char;
    grades: array [1..5] of 0..10;
    total: 0..50;
    i: 0..30;
    s: 1..5;

begin
  while not eof(input) do

    { read and print data on one student }
    begin

      { read name }
      i := 0;
      repeat
        i := i + 1;
        read(name[i])
      until name[i] = '.';
```

continued on page 18

Listing 1 *continued*

```
{ read grades }
for s := 1 to 5 do read(grades[s]);

readln;

{ compute total grade }
total := 0;
for s := 1 to 5 do total := total + grades[s];

{ print name }
i := 0;
repeat
  i := i + 1;
  write(name[i])
until name[i] = '.';
if i < 30 then write(' ': 30 - i);

{ print total }
write(total: 10);

writeln

    end
  end {studentgrades}.
```

The notations of Pascal allow the structure identified during the refinement process to be carried through explicitly into the final program while the various abstract actions themselves are shown as comments. This direct replacement of abstract actions by the code refined for them produces a final program as a structured but monolithic chunk of text. This works well enough for programs such as this example, where the final result fits on a single page of text, but for larger programs the direct replacement technique is less satisfactory.

PROCEDURES

When we design larger and more complex programs than our simple example, the stepwise refinement approach is of even greater value in controlling the complexity involved. However, the actions isolated in the early levels of the refinement process may themselves go through many further levels of refinement before developing into large and complex sequences of program text, each of which covers many lines, or even pages. In such cases, the sheer length of the text can make the structure of the program difficult to perceive. To overcome this problem we need a means of dividing the program text into units corresponding to the significant sub-problems identified in each refinement, and expressing the overall action of a level of refinement by a short sequence of text that refers to these units.

The procedure, or subroutine facility, provided by most programming languages allows exactly this to be done. We may define an action, or group of actions, in the form of a procedure to which we give a name. This procedure may then be invoked from another point in our program by means of a procedure call quoting its name.

The initial refinement of the examination marks program can now be retained as the statement part of the program by writing:

> **begin**
>> **while not** *eof(input)* **do**
>> **begin**
>>> *readnameandgrades*;
>>> *computetotalgrade*;
>>> *printnameandtotal*
>> **end**
> **end**

Here, *readnameandgrades*, *computetotalgrade* and *printnameandtotal* are now procedure *calls* and the procedures defining the required actions are declared elsewhere in the program.

The effect of this simple use of the procedure mechanism is to embed the underlying abstraction in the active program text itself, as a procedure call. Instead of a possibly complex sequence of statements, the program action at this point is expressed as a well-chosen procedure name, whose detailed definition is irrelevant to the surrounding program actions and is given elsewhere. Using procedures in this way at each level of its original stepwise refinement, the examination marks program may be rewritten as shown in Listing 2.

Listing 2

```
program studentgrades(input, output);

  { This program reads and tabulates student grades
    Each input line consists of a student name of not
    more than 30 characters ending with a '.', followed
    by five grades in the range 0 to 10.
    The output consists of student names as input with
    an aligned column of grade totals                    }

  var name: array [1..30] of char;
      grades: array [1..5] of 0..10;
      total: 0..50;
```

continued on page 20

Listing 2 *continued*

```
procedure readnameandgrades;

    procedure readname;
        var i: 0..30;
        begin
            i := 0;
            repeat
                i := i + 1;
                read(name[i])
            until name[i] = '.'
        end {readname};

    procedure readgrades;
        var s: 1..5;
        begin for s := 1 to 5 do read(grades[s]) end;

    begin
        readname;
        readgrades;
        readln
    end {readnameandgrades};

procedure computetotalgrade;
    var s: 1..5;
    begin
        total := 0;
        for s := 1 to 5 do total := total + grades[s]
    end {computetotalgrade};

procedure printnameandtotal;

    procedure printname;
        var i: 0..30;
        begin
            i := 0;
            repeat
                i := i + 1;
                write(name[i])
            until name[i] = '.';
            if i < 30 then write(' ': 30 - i)
        end {printname};

    procedure printtotal;
        begin write(total: 10) end;

    begin
        printname;
        printtotal;
        writeln
    end {printnameandtotal};
```

```
begin
  while not eof(input) do
    begin
      readnameandgrades;
      computetotalgrade;
      printnameandtotal
    end
end {studentgrades}.
```

In this revised program, the statement-part of the main program shows explicitly the overall structure conceived for the program—that of a loop whose body involves a sequence of three subsidiary actions—while the procedure declarations give the details of how each of these actions is to be carried out, using further procedures as required. In this example some of these actions are trivial and their expression as procedures may seem somewhat extravagant. However, the example shows clearly how, in a larger and more complex program, the significant levels of refinement of the program's actions may be expressed as short sequences of statements including procedure calls. This leaves the clarity of the original refinement levels unobscured by subsequent detail, and so helps a reader of the program to see the design decisions taken.

In Pascal the body of a procedure declaration (known as a block) may, in turn, include further procedure and variable declarations and the overall structure of a program is thus a set of blocks, some of which are nested within others to an arbitrary level of nesting. In the revised grades program the refinement of *readnameandgrades* led to the introduction of further procedures *readname* and *readgrades*, whose declarations are nested within *readnameandgrades*. When used in this way the nested hierarchy of blocks in the final program directly reflects the nested hierarchy of refinement levels involved in its creation.

The nested block structure of the revised program has also been used to associate the declaration of variables directly with the procedure in which they are used. For example, the variable i is now declared within the procedure *readname*. This local declaration emphasizes that the variable is used only in the internal details of implementing *readname*, and is quite independent of the variable of the same name used in procedure *printname*. The systematic use of such local declarations, whenever possible, is a means of minimizing the interdependence between refinement components, and of guarding against inadvertent interdependence through programming error. Some data, however, such as the variables *name*, *grades* and *total*, are necessarily shared by the program components represented as separate procedures and must be declared in the enclosing program block to enable and reflect this sharing and consequent interdependence.

The benefits and limitations of the block structure provided in Pascal will be discussed again in Chapter 4. In the meantime, we will freely use procedures and block structure to reflect the significant levels of refinement in the programs we develop and the association between data and actions that is involved.

PROGRAM REVISION

In the original refinement of the examination grades program we initially overlooked an interdependence between the name-printing and grade-printing actions and were forced to revise the component *printname* accordingly.

The change required in this case was easily made within the original refinement, but the example shows that stepwise refinement itself is no guarantee of instant programming success—it merely helps us to reduce the complexity involved at each stage, and so reduce the likelihood of errors.

However, when a mistake is made and subsequently detected, the structure imposed by stepwise refinement does help us in tracing the fault and eliminating it. To see this more closely, consider further refinement of the expression for net pay developed in Fig. 2.1. Under most taxation systems the tax component of the deductions is a function of the gross pay involved and perhaps a tax code for the employee concerned. To avoid duplicating the calculation of gross pay some reorganization of the overall calculation is required. Retracing our steps, we see that the flaw lies in the initial design decision (labelled *THINKS* 1) which assumed that a single expression for net pay would suffice. Revising this decision, to use a two-stage calculation of gross pay and then net pay, gives a new structure as in Fig. 2.2. Having made this change we must now reconsider all the subsequent decisions on gross pay and deductions as, in principle, any of these may be invalidated by the change in a superior refinement. In practice, however, the previous refinements of gross pay and deductions remain valid, and we arrive quickly at a revised calculation of the form:

$$gross\ pay := hours * rate;$$
$$net\ pay := gross\ pay - (tax(gross\ pay, code) + insurance)$$

More significantly, the isolation of the net pay calculation as an independent component of the original refinement chosen implies that these changes have no impact on the remainder of the surrounding program.

Thus the structure imposed by stepwise refinement delimits those parts of the program which may be affected by an alteration at any point and those parts that clearly are not, so reducing the dangers inherent in any program modification.

It is noteworthy that this property is equally true whether the program change is dictated by a flaw identified at a later stage of its refinement, or by

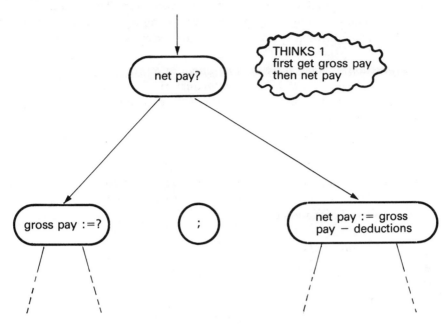

Figure 2.2   A revised calculation of net pay

an error detected during program testing, or by a subsequent adaptation of
the program to meet a changing specification. Thus the structural independence sought in stepwise refinement contributes to the program's flexibility
as well as its initial correctness. If the required change in an existing program
coincides with a particular component in its original refinement, and if the
implicit dependence between this component and the rest of the program is
clearly defined, then any change which leaves this interdependence unaltered should have no impact on the rest of the program. Foreseeing such
changes and choosing a suitable initial refinement structure for the program
is one more aspect of a good program design. However, even when such
foresight is not possible, the creation of a clear refinement structure, with
minimum and well-documented interdependence between its components,
is a significant aid to choosing and assessing the range of impact of changes
that are subsequently required.

LANGUAGE REINFORCEMENT

The examples of stepwise refinement used so far show how a programming
language may reinforce the useful structure developed in a program. Con-

sider first the original version of net pay expression. The structure for arithmetic expressions in many programming languages is similar to that defined by the following syntax (in Extended Backus–Naur form):

> *expression = [sign] term {adding-operator term}.*
> *term = factor {multiplying-operator factor}.*
> *factor = variable | unsigned-number | "("expression")".*
> *adding-operator = "+"|"−".*
> *multiplying-operator = "*"|"/".*
> *sign = "+"|"−".*

To demonstrate that a particular arithmetic expression conforms to such a syntax definition a syntax tree may be constructed. Figure 2.3 shows the syntax tree for the expression:

> *hours * rate − (tax + insurance)*

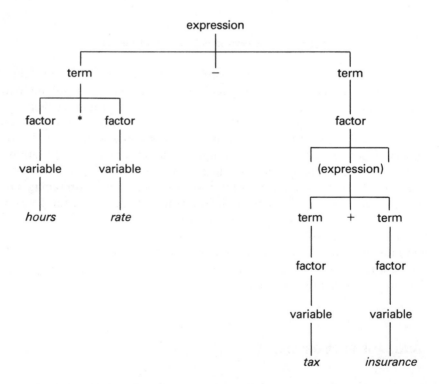

Figure 2.3   Syntax tree for arithmetic expression
*hours * rate − (tax + insurance)*

Comparison of this syntax tree with the 'construction tree' for the same expression in Fig. 2.1 shows how the expression's essential syntax reflects the step-by-step process of its realization. Since most programming languages incorporate this expression notation they are, by our definition, 'good' languages for expression writing. We find, however, a much greater variation in the quality of language features when we consider programming at other levels.

In the flat wheel example, we used three control constructs provided in Pascal, namely:

(a)   the compound statement, to describe a composite sequence of actions;

(b)   the **if** statement, to denote selection between two alternative actions;

(c)   the **repeat** statement for the construction of loops.

These three, together with the **case**, **while** and **for** statements that Pascal also provides, have the significant property that each defines a control structure with a single entry and single exit point. It is this property that makes them simple but powerful building blocks for more complex control structures, and ensures that the resultant structure remains comprehensible to our limited human intellect.

In contrast, some languages require the programmer to build these control structures using the **goto** statement and some accompanying conditional clause. In conjunction with an **if** statement the **goto** statement can be used to implement all the above control structures with exactly the same one-entry one-exit form. Unfortunately, it can also be used to create any number of other spaghetti-like structures, which are soon incomprehensible to their creators and to anyone who reads them.

Pascal's control constructs were also used to advantage in the examination grades program, but the second version of that program showed in addition how procedure calls can be used to embed the abstract intermediate levels of refinement in the active program text, and how the resultant block structure can also be used to limit interdependence between refinement components through access to shared data.

However, although it is useful and advantageous if the constructs we use in stepwise refinement are explicitly provided by our programming language, the principles of structured program design, as embodied in the stepwise refinement method, remain applicable whatever language is ultimately used to express the constructed program. The 'useful structure' evolved for the program will persist, at least implicitly, in the final program text. The original programmer can and should make this structure apparent by comments and supplementary documentation where necessary, and subsequent programmers should maintain not just the program but the documentation as well.

Throughout this book we use notations based on the language Pascal to illustrate the concepts we describe. The intention is not specifically to promote the use of Pascal (although we hope this may be the case) but to encourage the use of some structurally oriented programming language. In the final stage this language could be transcribed into whatever compilable 'coding' language is appropriate to the program or its environment. However, if this coding language does not support an adequate range of structuring concepts, the responsibility falls on the programmer to document the implicit structure, to ensure that it is correctly implemented in the final coded version of the program, and to maintain its consistency throughout any subsequent program modifications.

SUMMARY

Stepwise refinement is a fundamental tool in the solution of programming problems and is based on the systematic application of the most fundamental problem-solving tool of all, which is abstraction. Its objective is to control the complexity dealt with at any point in the programming process, and so increase the probability of a correct solution being chosen.

In principle, stepwise refinement is applicable regardless of the language or notation used to express the final program. As the scale of the programming problem increases, however, the successful application of stepwise refinement depends increasingly on the notation or language used to reinforce the abstractions chosen and to protect them from inadvertent misuse. If the programming language itself does not provide this protection an increasing burden falls on the programmer involved.

In the following chapter we review the features of the programming language Pascal, and in particular the way in which the range of abstractions embedded in Pascal support programming by stepwise refinement.

EXERCISES

2.1   Design a program to allow a person at a video terminal to play a series of tic-tac-toe (noughts and crosses) games with a computer. Use a simple strategy to determine the moves made by the computer in order to allow the user the occasional pleasure of a victory over the computer.

2.2   Design a program to find the first 1000 prime numbers, assuming 2 to be the first prime number.

2.3 The symbols of a certain computer programming language consist of the reserved words *BEGIN, END, IF, THEN, WHILE, VAR*, identifiers which are sequences of one or more letters, integer constants which are sequences of digits, operator symbols +, −, :=, and separators : and ;. Design a procedure which will obtain the next symbol from the text of a program and assign its value to a variable of an appropriate type.

3

The Abstractions in Pascal

In Chapter 2 we saw that the stepwise refinement of a program traces a series of levels of abstraction from an initial most-abstract level through to a final least-abstract level. The refinement terminates when the actions at the current level are directly expressible in the programming language in use. In this sense the programming language is the final concrete level to which we progress. In practice, programming languages themselves are abstractions of the actual machine facilities available. Thus, an integer variable as provided in Pascal is an abstraction of a location in the computer memory which is represented as a series of binary bits, or indeed of the underlying electronic signals used to represent those bits. Similarly, the integer operation + is an abstraction ultimately of an electronic circuit that carries out the binary addition process.

For any particular problem the ideal programming language is one that provides a single operation that solves that problem, thus eliminating the need to write a significant program for its solution. However, such a language feature would be useless in solving most other problems. A good general purpose programming language is one which provides a range of features that are useful in the solution of a wide range of programming problems. Programming languages stand or fall by the judicious combination of features that they provide.

In this chapter, we review the range of abstractions provided in the programming language Pascal. We shall see that the basic form of the features of Pascal supports and reinforces the stepwise refinement of programs, and that the range of features provided is a judicious balance of facilities for the description of data and for the description of the operations to be performed.

In general, there is a close correspondence between the structure of data and the structure of the processing that it requires. This correspondence is reflected in the features of Pascal, and we shall review them by considering the various features for the description of data in turn, at each stage noting the corresponding features or statements for describing actions as appropriate. We begin, therefore, by introducing the basic concept that underlies all of Pascal's data description facilities, that is the concept of type.

THE CONCEPT OF TYPE

Pascal, like many other programming languages, requires that every data item in a program must have an associated type, based on the following assumptions:

(a)   The type of a data item determines the range of values that it may take, and the range of operations that may be applied to it.

(b)   Each data item has a single type.

(c)   The type of each data item in the program can be deduced solely from its form or context, without any knowledge of the particular values that it may take during execution of the program.

(d)   Each operator in the language requires operands of specified types and produces a result of a specified type.

By providing a well-chosen range of available types together with appropriate operators, Pascal enables the programmer to describe data and its manipulation in terms natural to the data. By enforcing the above constraints the language protects the programmer from describing many illogical combinations of data and operators.

Any fixed range of data types, however well-chosen, would inevitably constrain the range of problems to which the programming language can be applied. A distinctive feature of Pascal is the ease with which the programmer may define new elementary data types appropriate to the problem in hand, and the ease with which new structured types may be defined as combinations of these elementary types. We begin by examining how Pascal provides for the definition of elementary or scalar data types, and for their manipulation.

SCALAR TYPES

The Type *Boolean*

If a data type defines the range of values that items of the type may take then the simplest useful data type is one that defines a range of two values. (Data types whose items can take only a single value are in general of limited practical use). Pascal provides one such two-valued type as the predefined type *Boolean*, whose values are denoted by the identifiers *true* and *false* and represent the logical truth values. The ability to combine such values by means of the operators **and**, **or** and **not**, and to assign the results to *Boolean* variables, provide a basic capability for logical or *Boolean* arithmetic. However, the chief importance of the type *Boolean* in Pascal lies in the key role that it plays in supporting the basic control structures of the language. Thus in Pascal's **if** statement:

> **if** *C* **then** *S*1 **else** *S*2

the controlling expression *C* yields a value *true* or *false* that determines which of the alternative actions *S*1 or *S*2 is to be executed. Similarly, in the repetitive control structures provided by the **while** and **repeat** statements:

> **while** *C* **do** *S*

> **repeat** *S*1 ; *S*2 ; . . . **until** *C*

the Boolean values produced by the controlling expression *C* in each case determine whether execution of the repetitive loop is to continue.

Boolean values may also be created by applying the relational operators such as:

> = <> > >= < <=

to operands of other types. The ability to use such operations as the controlling expressions in Pascal's **if**, **while** and **repeat** statements or to combine them by means of the Boolean operations **and**, **or** and **not** to give more complex controlling expressions is a significant contributing factor to the power and clarity of Pascal's control structures. Thus, statements such as:

> **repeat** *read* (*ch*) **until** *ch* <> ' '

> **while** *a*<>*b* **do**
>   **if** *a* >*b* **then** *a*:=*a*−*b*
>   **else** *b*:=*b*−*a*

are all examples of the role played by the type *Boolean* in Pascal programming and of the clarity that the corresponding relational and control operators extract from it.

Enumerations

Other types with two or more values may be defined in Pascal by enumerating the identifiers that denote those values. Thus, we can define types as follows:

$$sex \qquad = (male, female);$$

$$suit \qquad = (clubs, diamonds, hearts, spades);$$

$$rank \qquad = (two, three, four, five, six, seven, eight, nine, ten,$$
$$\qquad\qquad\quad jack, queen, king, ace);$$

$$dayofweek = (Sunday, Monday, Tuesday, Wednesday, Thursday,$$
$$\qquad\qquad\qquad Friday, Saturday);$$

For such types no intrinsic operators such as **and**, **or** or **not** are provided, but the standard operations of assignment and test of equality can be applied to the values of these types.

Just as the two-valued type *Boolean* provides a convenient basis for choosing between two alternatives, a type with n values is the basis for a n-way choice. In Pascal, such a choice is expressed by means of the **case** statement. Thus, if *d* is of type *dayofweek*, we can use the following **case** statement:

```
case d of
Sunday : hours := 0 ;
Monday, Tuesday,
Wednesday, Thursday : hours := hours + 8 ;
Friday : hours := hours + 6 ;
Saturday : if present then hours := hours + 3
end
```

The **case** construct reflects clearly and simply the choice between a range of alternatives according to the value of the controlling expression. Security against programming error or oversight is also provided by the automatic error trap that occurs if the **case** statement is executed with a value not listed among the labelled alternatives.

Ordered Types

For some scalar types a natural order exists between the individual values of
the type, but for other scalar types no corresponding natural order is appropriate. Thus, for example, the values of type *sex* have no natural inherent
order, nor have the values of type *suit*. However, the values of type *rank* and
of type *dayofweek* have a clear order which is that written down in the
definition, and moreover, it is useful to be able to exploit this order in
programs which manipulate the days of the week. To avoid introducing
distinction between unordered and ordered scalar types, Pascal adopts the
expedient of regarding the values of all enumerated scalar types as being
ordered, as determined by the order in which the identifiers denoting these
values are written down. Thus, with the types defined above we have:

Sunday < *Monday*

Tuesday > *Monday*

queen > *six*

male < *female*

though the final ordering should be of little significance in most contexts!

In such ordered types each value has a successor and a predecessor,
other than the last and the first values, respectively. In Pascal, the successor
or predecessor of a value of a scalar type may be obtained using the intrinsic
functions *succ* and *pred*. Thus, we have:

succ (*Sunday*) = *Monday*

pred (*Monday*) = *Sunday*

succ (*Monday*) = *Tuesday*

but *succ* (*Saturday*) and *pred* (*Sunday*) are undefined.

A natural extension of the *succ* and *pred* functions for ordered types is
the ability to iterate through a range of values in order. In Pascal, this is
provided by the **for** statement. Thus, we write:

for *d* := *Monday* **to** *Friday* **do**

to deal with each day of the week from *Monday* to *Friday*, in turn.

The Types *Integer* and *Char*

As well as the enumerated types, Pascal provides two predefined ordered types *integer* and *char*. The values of the type *integer* are denoted not by identifiers but by decimal integer numbers. As well as assignment and the relational operators that are available for all scalar types, integer values may be manipulated by means of special operators +, −, *, **div** and **mod**. These enable the full range of integer arithmetic operations to be programmed in Pascal, but the underlying properties of the values of type *integer* are still those of an ordered scalar type. Thus, the functions *succ*, and *pred*, the **case** statement and the **for** statement may all be applied to integer values with the expected results.

The values of the type *char* are the characters of a set determined by each implementation of Pascal, and are denoted by character literals thus *'A'*, *'7'*, *'*'*, etc.

For the values of type *char* the assignment, test of equality and **case** discrimination operators are defined as for other scalar types. The values of the type are ordered, but the exact ordering chosen is implementation dependent, and only a subset of relations are guaranteed over all implementations. Thus, the following are always true:

$$'A' < 'B'$$

$$'a' < 'b'$$

$$'0' < '1'$$

but the truth or falsity of relations such as:

$$'+' < '*'$$

$$'A' < '1'$$

will vary from one implementation to another. Similarly, the effect of the *succ* and *pred* functions and the **for** statement iteration is implementation dependent for character values, with predictable results guaranteed only for the decimal digit characters *'0'*, *'1'*, ... These machine-dependent properties of the values of type *char* reflect the corresponding variations in the character sets of the machines on which Pascal has to be implemented, and so allow a simple efficient implementation of the type *char* on all these machines. The guaranteed ordering relations for letters, digits and the guaranteed successor relationships for digits are the lowest common denominator of the character sets provided on current hardware.

The Type *Real*

Machine-dependent characteristics also affect the nature of the fourth pre-defined scalar type provided in Pascal, namely the type *real*. The values of this type are intended to be the approximate representations of real numbers provided by the floating-point hardware on most machines. With these representations the operations +, −, *, and / are easily provided and the ordering relations are also easily implemented. However, the precise set of real values that are exactly represented on any particular machine is not easily defined, and for this reason the *succ* and *pred* operations, **case** discrimination and the **for** iteration are all disallowed for real values in Pascal.

Subranges

The discrete ordered sequence property shared by all of Pascal's scalar types other than *real* also enables the provision of Pascal's final scalar type feature, the subrange. Thus we can declare variables as follows:

   index : 1..10 ;

   digit : '0'..'9' ;

   d   : *Monday..Friday* ;

A subrange type shares the values and the applicable operations of its parent or host type, that is *integer* in the case of 1..10, *char* in the case of '0'..'9' and *dayofweek* in the case of *Monday..Friday*. However, a variable declared to be of a subrange type is constrained to take values only within the range specified by that type and any occurrence of a value outside this range will be automatically detected as a programming error.

   In summary, the scalar types provided by Pascal have the following significant characteristics:

(a)   The type *Boolean* provides the essential concept of truth and falsity which is necessary to the conditional and repetitive control constructs of Pascal.

(b)   The predefined types *integer*, *real* and *char* enable the programming of integer, real and character manipulation within the hardware limitations of any particular implementation of the language.

(c)   The enumerated and subrange types provide a very precise and clear means of describing the nature of non-numeric and non-character data in a way that precludes the occurrence of many programming errors and aids the detection of errors.

(d) The uniform treatment adopted for the discrete ordered scalar types of Pascal other than *real* greatly simplifies their use and enables their correspondingly uniform manipulation by means of the **case** discrimination, relational operators and the **for** iteration. This uniformity is further exploited in the indexing of arrays and in the definition of the base types of sets, as described in the next section.

STRUCTURED TYPES

Scalar types describe the indivisible elementary values of which all data is composed. Structured types describe composite values that are built from these indivisible components. Such values may take a variety of forms or structures, with corresponding means of access to the individual components in each case. By providing a well-chosen range of structuring concepts and corresponding means of component access, Pascal enables the description and manipulation of complex data structures in a systematic manner.

In practice, there is a close analogy between the structuring concepts required for the description of data and the structuring concepts required in describing the actions of a program, that is between the structured types and the structured statements of Pascal. As one might expect, the structure of the processing applied to a data item often reflects the structure of the data itself, and we find, therefore, that the structured data types and structured statements of Pascal are used in a very regular pair-wise conjunction. In this section we examine the structured type concepts of Pascal in turn and illustrate the analogous structured statements used in processing such types. However, it must be remembered that these structured statements have an independently justifiable existence and are often used in contexts where no explicit corresponding data structure is involved.

Records

The simplest composite data item is one with two or more components which are perhaps distinct in nature and in type. In Pascal such composite items are described by record types. For example, given the types *suit* and *rank* defined earlier, we may define a type to represent a playing card as follows:

```
card = record
          s : suit ;
          r : rank
       end ;
```

Such a record type definition specifies the type of each component or field and introduces field identifiers to distinguish between them, in this case *s* and *r*. Variables of the record type may be manipulated as a whole, e.g., in an assignment:

> *card1* := *card2*

or they may be selectively manipulated by accessing the individual components:

> *card2 .r* := *ace*
>
> **if** *card1 .s* = *spades* **then** . . .

The data structure described by a record type is a simple juxtaposition of the values of its components and the processing that such a record value requires is often a corresponding juxtaposition of actions performed on the components in turn. In Pascal, such a composition of action is expressed using the compound statement, which encloses its component actions in **begin end** brackets.

> **begin**
>   *card1 .s* := *succ* (*card1 .s*) ;
>   *card1 .r* := *two*
> **end**

Just as a record type groups a number of component items together to form a composite value that may be manipulated as a whole, the compound statement groups together a number of component actions that may be regarded as a composite single action. Thus Pascal's record type and compound statement concepts realize analogous structuring concepts for data and for actions, and are often used in conjunction in the processing of such data.

When a record value is manipulated component by component, the resulting compound statement often contains several references to the fields of the same record value. Pascal's **with** statement simplifies the expression by taking the record variable outside the compound statement, e.g. the statement above can be rewritten as follows:

> **with** *card1* **do**
> **begin**
>   *s* := *succ*(*s*) ;
>   *r* := *two*
> **end**

Together, the compound statement and the **with** statement provide the necessary processing tools for the manipulation of composite data items of record form, and provide our first example of the analogous structures that exist in data and in the actions that are applied to that data.

Variant Records

Sometimes a data item takes two or more alternative forms during its lifetime, that is the nature and hence type of its component values may vary from one composite value to another. Potentially, such a data item is in conflict with the rules of type set out at the beginning of this chapter, but in practice such variations in form can be accommodated provided the form of a particular item can be determined at any moment and hence the manipulation of its corresponding component parts can be checked during execution of the program.

Consider for example the register of all cars in a country. Cars are distinguished either as local cars owned by residents of the country, or as foreign cars currently visiting the country. For local cars the data recorded is as follows:

```
localcar = record
             make : manufacturer ;
             regnumber : carnumber ;
             owner : person ;
             firstreg : date
          end ;
```

while for foreign cars the data recorded is:

```
foreigncar = record
               make : manufacturer ;
               regnumber : carnumber ;
               origin : country
            end ;
```

A data type covering both kinds of car may be regarded as the *union* of these two types. Such unions are catered for in Pascal by extension of the record concept to allow *variant parts*.

For example, the type *car* would be defined in Pascal as follows:

```
carkind = (local, foreign) ;
car = record
        make : manufacturer ;
        regnumber : carnumber ;
        case kind : carkind of
        local : (owner : person ;
                   firstreg : date) ;
        foreign : (origin : country)
      end ;
```

Manipulation of records with variant parts is expressed using the same notation as for simple records. For example, the tag field *kind* of a variable *c* of type *car* and the variant fields *owner*, etc. are denoted by *c.kind*, *c.owner*, etc.

However, reference to a variant field *c.owner* is logical only when *c* has the corresponding variant form, i.e. when *c.kind = local*. Use of the **case** statement with the normal **with** statement gives a natural expression of the selective processing involved and reduces the likelihood of error in this respect. For example:

```
with c do
begin
    . . .
    case kind of
    local : begin
                owner := . . .
                firstreg := . . .
            end ;
    foreign : origin := . . .
    end ;
    . . .
```

Thus, the form of a variant record is reflected in the form of the selective processing that it requires, and in this case the analogy is strongly emphasized by the similar **case** syntax chosen in Pascal for the description of each. Note, however, that no special notation is adopted for variant records whose tag field is of type *Boolean*, and there is no direct analogy to the **if then else** notation in the variant record syntax.

Arrays

The repetitive statements of Pascal describe a sequence of actions which are identical or similar in nature. The analogous data structure is one that consists of a number of component items identical in nature and type. In practice, such structures arise in a variety of practical programming contexts, and differ in the representations and in the component access mechanisms that are required. Some of these variants are provided for directly in the structured types of Pascal, but others have to be implemented by the programmer using lower level language features, as we shall see later. For the moment we concentrate on those that are provided directly in Pascal.

When the number of items of a repetitive structured type is predetermined and the individual items may be distinguished by a corresponding index value the composite data item may be thought of as an *array*, whose components are called *elements*. In Pascal, for example, we can define array types as follows:

array [*index type*] **of** *element type*

Array variables may be manipulated as a whole or by manipulating their individual elements as indexed variables. Thus, if we have an array declared as follows:

hours : **array** [*dayofweek*] **of** $0..24$;

its elements may be denoted individually as:

hours [*Sunday*], *hours* [*Monday*], . . .

The advantage of the array over corresponding record structures is that the index selecting a particular value may be computed dynamically so that an index variable of the form *hours* [*x*] may denote different elements of the array *hours* as the value of the index expression *x* varies during execution of the program. In conjunction with the **for** statement this gives a powerful means of manipulating the elements of the array in turn, a task required in many practical applications of arrays.

for *d* := *Monday* **to** *Friday* **do**
        hours[*d*] := *hours*[*d*] + 8

An array type describes a repetitive sequence of component values of identical type, where the number of components is predetermined, and where each component is identified by an index value of an ordered scalar index type. The **for** statement describes a repetitive sequence of identical actions whose number is also predetermined and associates with each a corresponding value in an ordered scalar range. Inevitably, the **for** statement is the natural tool for processing an array variable.

In Pascal, this correspondence between the structure of data and the structure of processing required also carries through to arrays of two or more dimensions. A two-dimensional array in Pascal is considered to be an array of one-dimensional arrays. Thus an array type of the form:

timesheet = **array** [*employeeno*, *dayofweek*] **of** $0..24$

is considered to be equivalent to:

timesheet = **array** [*employeeno*] **of**
                        array [*dayofweek*] **of** $0..24$

This nesting of the array construct is reflected in the corresponding means of processing two-dimensional arrays in Pascal and in other languages, namely by the use of nested **for** statements. Thus, if we have an array *t* of type *timesheet* it may be set to zero by the following Pascal code:

```
for e := 1 to 100 do
    for d := Sunday to Saturday do
        t[e,d] := 0
```

Nested **for** statements are a natural way of expressing the multiple repetition that such processing involves. In an analogous way Pascal's equivalence rules for multi-dimensional arrays emphasize that, while the single dimensional array is a fundamental structuring concept, any notation provided for multi-dimensional arrays is a mere shorthand for the facilities already available.

In drawing the analogy between record and array types and the structured statements used to process such data we have illustrated only the processing of the record and array elements in the sequence fixed by their declaration. It must be emphasized at this point, however, that the components of records and arrays can be accessed in any order, not just in sequence. This random access feature is an important quality of these structures, and is in marked contrast with the access permitted to other structures discussed later, such as files. In this sense our structural analogy is incomplete, and does not wholly reflect the full power of records and arrays. Nevertheless, it does serve to emphasize the relationship between the structure of data and its processing in many programs.

Files

We have seen that the array is the data analogue of the repetitive action sequence of predetermined length describable by a **for** statement. What then is the analog of the repetition expressed by the **while** or **repeat** statements? The characteristic of such repetition is that the answer to the question 'Is another iteration of the repetitive loop required?' is not determined until the preceding iteration is complete, and no predetermined bound on the number of iterations is in general available. In practice, analogous data structures arise in a wide variety of forms in different programming applications, but such structures are provided for explicitly in Pascal in one form only, namely the *file*.

When we define a file type such as:

```
carfile = file of car ;
```

no predetermined limit on the number of elements in the file is implied, and the existence of another component is determined only after the creation or examination of the preceding component. As we may expect, the natural means of creating or processing such a file is by use of **while** or **repeat** statements thus:

```
rewrite (cars) ;                    reset (cars) ;
while {more cars} do                while not eof (cars) do
begin                               begin
  cars ↑ := {next car}                {process cars ↑} ;
  put (cars)                          get (cars)
end                                 end
```

(The analogue of the distinction between a **while** loop and a **repeat** loop is between those files which have at least one element and those which may be empty, but this distinction serves little practical purpose in the description of files.)

In marked contrast to the **array** and **record** structures no random access is allowed to the components of file structures. Thus a particular component of a file can only be examined or altered after first examining or recreating each of the preceding components. Similarly, new components cannot be appended to the end of an existing file. A file value can be extended only by first copying its existing contents, its existing value, to a new file variable. These rigid constraints on the way in which the files may be accessed or updated do not follow directly from the structuring concepts on which they are based, but from the limitations of the media on which files are normally represented. Programming applications in which these constraints are not acceptable for the data structure involved force Pascal programmers to create new data structuring mechanisms for themselves. As we shall see, Pascal provides the basic facilities required to implement these new structures, but the proper abstraction of the new structures created requires features beyond those currently provided in the language.

Sets

So far, we have matched the record, variant record, array and file concepts of Pascal to corresponding control structures provided by the compound, conditional and repetitive statements of the language. Can we extend this analogy to include Pascal's other distinctive data structuring concept, namely the set type? Regrettably the answer seems to be 'no'.

Superficially the construct:

set of *base type*

is similar to Pascal's other type constructs in that it defines a new type in terms of a simpler component type. In this sense, the set type is structured. In practice, however, the limitations on how set types are used in Pascal make these significantly different from the array, record and file types.

(a)   The base type of a set is limited to a discrete scalar type. Thus, the **set of** construct cannot be used as an intermediate step in the refinement of a data structure, but inevitably occurs only at the final refinement level.

(b)   Set values may be manipulated as a whole and a wider range of operations are provided for this purpose than for other structured types. However, the elements of a set value are accessed and manipulated indirectly rather than directly, and the programmer does not normally think of each member element of a set value as an independently manipulated variable.

For both these reasons, sets in Pascal are more appropriately thought of as super-scalar types that enable a natural and powerful description of the data that occurs in many practical programming applications, rather than a general data structuring concept. No useful analogy can or should be drawn between the set type and the statements used for set manipulation.

Nevertheless, set types are a distinctive and important feature of Pascal's range of data types. By giving the ability to express the solution of problems in set terms they enable a simpler, clearer expression of many program features. Their application may range from the casual use of sets in expressing tests such as:

   if *operator* **in** $['+', '-', '*']$ **then** . . .

to significant combinatoric problems whose solution is expressed most naturally in set terms. The following case study includes a small but significant example of the power and convenience of sets.

A Case Study

At this stage it is useful to consider a case study of the use of Pascal's data structuring facilities, and the corresponding manipulation which the language statements enable.

Suppose a computer dating service records the following data on each of its clients: name and address, sex, age, and a range of interests chosen from arts, books, music, theatre, politics and sport. The total information accumulated by the service will be held as a file of records—one for each client. To describe this in Pascal, we first define an appropriate file type as follows:

   clientfile = **file of** *client* ;

With this definition a client file is a sequential file of undetermined length, normally held on backing store such as disk or tape, whose elements must be written or read in sequence. These restrictions are quite adequate for the computer dating service application.

Each element of a client file will consist of the data on one client, namely their identity, sex, age and interests. In Pascal this can be described by means of a record type defined as follows:

```
client = record
            identity : ...;
            sex : ...;
            age : ...;
            interests : ...;
         end ;
```

This expresses clearly the appropriate grouping of four fields with individual names as shown, but the nature, and hence type, of the fields we have still to determine. Each record may be manipulated as a whole, or as its individual field components denoted by the corresponding field names.

Now let us consider the nature of the individual fields in turn. Let us suppose that the identity, or name and address, of each client is held as a string of up to 60 characters. In Pascal, character strings are treated as packed arrays of characters. Thus, the identity field of our client record will be described as follows:

```
identity : packed array [1..60] of char ;
```

Defined in this way the identity field may be manipulated as a whole in a *write* statement, for example, or as its individual character elements.

Now consider the *sex* field of the client record. This field can take one of only two values, either male or female, and may be described by an appropriate enumerated type as follows:

```
sex : (male, female) ;
```

This definition makes clear the inherent nature of the *sex* field and precludes the assignment of any value other than *male* and *female* to it.

Now consider the *age* field. The age of a client may be recorded simply as an integer, but the values involved will lie in a very limited range. The age field of the client record can, therefore, be defined by a sub-range declaration as follows:

```
age : 16 .. 99 ;
```

The effect of this declaration for *age* is that the field may be manipulated by the usual operations allowed for integers in Pascal.

However, if any value outside the range of 16–99 is assigned to the field, then an error is automatically reported.

Now consider the final *interests* field. The individual topics in which a client may record an interest are easily described by a further enumerated type, defined as follows:

> *topics* = (*art, books, music, theatre, politics, sport*)

However, the interests of a particular client may be any combination of these elementary values, and may thus be described by means of a set type, as follows:

> *interests* : **set of** *topics*

This definition allows the representation of all of the possible combinations of interests that clients may record, and as we shall see, enables a convenient comparison of these interests.

We have now completed our description of the totality of data which the computer dating service holds on its clients, and we can collect these together as the following list of type definitions:

> **type** *topics* = (*art, books, music, theatre, politics, sport*) ;
>   *client* = **record**
>   *identity* : **packed array** [1 . . 60] **of** *char* ;
>   *sex* : (*male, female*) ;
>   *age* : 16 . . 99 ;
>   *interests* : **set of** *topics*
>   **end** ;
>   *clientfile* = **file of** *client* ;

As far as the Pascal program is concerned, the file of data on the computer dating service's clients is simply a variable of type *clientfile* declared as follows:

> **var** *clients* : *clientfile* ;

Suppose now a program is required which will read in the details of a new client for the dating service and then scan the existing client file to print out all clients found to be compatible in some way with the new client. As well as the client file itself this program will use two working variables to represent the new client and the current client extracted from the file, and its overall form will, therefore, be as follows:

```
program datingservice (input, clients, output) ;
   . . .
var clients : clientfile ;
    newclient, thisclient : client ;
begin
    . . . read data on newclient . . . ;
    reset (clients) ;
    repeat
       read (clients, thisclient) ;
       if compatible (thisclient, newclient)
       then writeln (thisclient.identity)
    until eof (clients)
end {datingservice}.
```

Here we see that the **repeat** statement gives a convenient expression of the repetitive processing required by the client file, assuming that it contains at least one client. Within the loop the client's records are manipulated as a whole in the compatibility test but access to the identity field allows a convenient expression of the printout of a compatible client's name and address.

Suppose now that the compatibility of two clients is defined as being of the opposite sex, with an age difference less than 10 years, and with at least one common interest. The compatibility test can then be defined as a function which takes two client records as its arguments and returns a *Boolean* value as a result. With the definition chosen for the type *client*, the function is easily defined as follows:

```
function compatible (c1, c2 : client) : Boolean ;
   begin
     compatible :=
        (c1.sex <> c2.sex) and
        (abs(c1.age − c2.age) < 10) and
        (c1.interests * c2.interests <> [])
   end {compatible} ;
```

Notice how the test to establish that the clients have at least one interest in common is achieved by taking the intersection of the corresponding interest sets and testing that this is not empty.

The type *client* describes the nature of the data recorded for one client and from this the Pascal system determines the representation used for this data within the computer's main memory and within the clients file on backing store. However, in Pascal such a definition does not determine any representation for the data on external legible media such as punch card input or line printer output. Because the identity field is a string of characters this can be printed directly on a line printer, but to input the information on a new client some conversion code is required to convert the external representation input to its internal client record form. Let us suppose, therefore, that the computer dating service collects and transcribes the data on a new client from some initial application form to a fixed record, on a punched card, say, with the following format:

Columns 1–60 .... name and address
Column 61 .... sex, punched as M or F
Columns 62 and 63 .... age, punched as two decimal digits
Columns 64–69 .... interests, where an X punched in the corresponding column denotes an interest in art, books, music, etc.

The process of reading such a card from the input file to obtain a new client record can then be expressed by a procedure as follows:

```
procedure readcard (var c : client) ;
  var i : 1 .. 60 ;
      ch : char ;
      t : topics ;
  begin
    with c do
    begin
      for i := 1 to 60 do read (identity[i]) ;
      read (ch) ; if ch = 'M' then sex := male else sex := female ;
      read (age) ;
      interests := [ ] ;
      for t := art to sport do
      begin
        read (ch) ;
        if ch = 'X' then interests := interests + [t]
      end
    end ;
    readln
  end {readname} ;
```

As we might expect, the overall action of reading in the data of a client record is a composition of the actions required to input data for the individual fields, and is expressed by a combination of the **with** and compound statements. For each field the code required to input the appropriate value reflects the inherent nature of that field.

We have now completed the refinement of the program to service a new client, and its final version is as shown in Listing 3.

Listing 3

```pascal
program datingservice(input, clients, output);

{ This program reads a new client's registration
  card from the standard input file, and outputs
  a list of compatible existing clients          }

type topics = (art, books, music, theatre, politics, sport);
     client = record
                  identity: packed array [1..60] of char;
                  sex: (male, female);
                  age: 16..99;
                  interests: set of topics
              end;
     clientfile = file of client;

var clients: clientfile;
    newclient, thisclient: client;
    t: topics;

procedure readcard(var c: client);
  var i: 1..60;
      ch: char;
      t: topics;
  begin
    with c do
      begin
        for i := 1 to 60 do read(identity[i]);
        read(ch);
        if ch = 'M'
        then sex := male
        else sex := female;
        read(age);
        interests := [];
        for t := art to sport do
          begin
            read(ch);
            if ch = 'X' then interests := interests + [t]
          end
      end;
    readln
  end {readcard};

function compatible(c1, c2: client): Boolean;
  begin
    compatible :=
      (c1.sex <> c2.sex) and (abs(c1.age - c2.age) < 10) and
      (c1.interests * c2.interests <> [])
  end {compatible};
```

continued on page 48

Listing 3 *continued*

```
begin
  readcard(newclient);
  reset(clients);
  while not eof(clients) do
    begin
      read(clients, thisclient);
      if compatible(thisclient, newclient)
      then writeln(thisclient.identity)
    end
end {datingservice}.
```

This simple example illustrates the essential qualities of the built-in abstractions provided by Pascal. These may be summarized as follows:

(a)   The provision of the user-defined enumerations, and subrange and set types, as well as the standard elementary types *integer*, *real*, *char* and *Boolean*, enables a significant increase both in program clarity and in security against programming error.

(b)   The array, record and file types provided for structuring data enable the systematic stepwise refinement of a data description in a way similar to that provided by the statements of Pascal for the description of programming actions.

(c)   The range of statements available is directly complementary to the range of data types, in that statements provide the actions and control structures for processing the data structures that the data types enable.

The net result is a judicious balance of language features that enable the description of data and its manipulation to be developed in a systematic manner. For those programs whose requirements map readily on to the abstractions supported by the language, the benefits are twofold:

(a)   A natural expression of the required program solution is enabled, whose clarity directly assists both the programmer who has to write the program and anyone who has to subsequently read, understand, or modify it.

(b)   The enforcement of appropriate restrictions for each abstraction by the programming language system excludes the possibility of many programming errors, and aids the detection of those that do occur.

SUMMARY

The features of Pascal are well suited to programming by stepwise refinement. Its control constructs encourage the refinement of composite actions as a well-formed hierarchy of component actions. Likewise, its data types encourage the refinement of data structures as well-formed hierarchies of atomic components. For those problems whose solutions decompose naturally into single hierarchic abstractions of data and associated manipulation Pascal is an ideal programming language.

As we shall see, however, not all programming problems have solutions based on a single hierarchy of abstractions. In the next chapter we illustrate these structural problems that arise, and explore a minimal extension to our programming notation that overcomes them.

EXERCISES

3.1 Modify the client dating program so that the procedure *readcard* validates the contents of the input data file, i.e., checks that each field of a new client description contains legal characters.

3.2 Implement in Pascal the tic-tac-toe (noughts and crosses) program designed in Exercise 2.1, using procedures and functions to maintain the abstraction at critical levels of the design, and enumerated and subrange types to describe the underlying data transparently and securely.

3.3 Implement in Pascal the prime number program designed in Exercise 2.2.

3.4 Implement in Pascal the procedure for recognizing language symbols designed in Exercise 2.3. Write a suitable program to test this procedure and output the results in a legible form.

4

Modular Programming

PROGRAM-DEFINED ABSTRACTIONS

The requirements of some programs do not map immediately on to the abstractions provided by Pascal. For these programs the programmer must realize the required abstractions in terms of the standard facilities provided by the language. This may involve the definition of a set of data types and variables to represent the features of the abstract concept, and a corresponding set of procedures and functions to implement the operations that can be applied to this representation. If the facilities of Pascal are used wisely this programmed realization of the abstraction may enable an expression of the final program solution which is as natural and clear as that enabled by a more sympathetic language. However, the enforcement of the appropriate restrictions on the use of the abstraction now become the programmer's responsibility rather than that of the programming language system, and thus the protection against programming error which is provided by the built-in abstractions of the language is no longer available.

We can illustrate this difference by exploring a typical use of the one remaining feature provided in Pascal for structuring data, namely the pointer type. Using pointers, a Pascal programmer can realize an appropriate representation of a wide variety of data structures not directly provided in the language itself. However, by doing so a significant loss of security against programming error may arise, as we see in the following specific example.

Consider a program which produces a sorted concordance of the words found in an input text and gives for each word a list of all the lines on which it occurs in the text. The overall form of the program to solve the problem can be as follows:

> *initialize input of text* ;
> *initialize list of words* ;
> **repeat**
>   *get word, and its line number from input text* ;
>   *record word and line number in list*
> **until** *end of text* ;
> *print words in list*

At this level we begin to identify two abstractions involved:

(a)   a stream of word, line number pairs which are extracted from the input text one by one, and

(b)   a list of the words extracted so far which will record all occurrences of each.

For the moment we will deliberately ignore the input stream abstraction and concentrate on the list of words. To achieve the required program effect the word list abstraction must allow operations to record a word, linenumber pair and to print the entire list contents in dictionary order, together with whatever initial action is required to start with an empty list. How do we meet these requirements in Pascal?

The number of words in the list is unpredictable and may vary widely from one use of the program to the next. For this reason the word list might be represented in Pascal as a chain of records connected by pointers defined as follows:

> *wordpointer* = ↑ *wordrecord* ;
> *wordrecord* = **record**
>   *spelling* : *wordspelling* ;
>   *occurrences* : . . . ;
>   *next* : *wordpointer*
>   **end** ;

Since the final list is to be printed in dictionary order, we assume that it is held in this order throughout. The complete word list is then represented as a single pointer variable which points to the first record in the list.

> *wordlist* : *wordpointer*

An empty list is trivially represented by the pointer value **nil**, so we have:

> **procedure** *initwords* (**var** *wordlist* : *wordpointer*) ;
>   **begin**
>   *wordlist* := **nil**
>   **end** {*initwords*} ;

The process of recording a word in the word list can be expressed as a procedure as follows:

> **procedure** *recordword (word : wordspelling ;*
> *line : linenumber ;*
> **var** *wordlist : wordpointer)* ;

The action required within this procedure is a standard example of updating an ordered list. Since the words are to be maintained in dictionary order, i.e. in ascending order of the spelling fields, the required action may be expressed as follows:

> *search list for first entry with spelling > word* ;
> **if** *none is found*
> **then** *create new word entry at end of list*
> **else if** *entryfound↑ .spelling = word*
>   **then** *wordentry := entryfound*
>   **else** *create new word entry before entry found* ;
> *add line to wordentry↑ .occurrences*

The pointer manipulation required to implement this is unimportant at this stage and will be detailed later. Note, however, that creating a new word entry involves initializing the *occurrences* field to represent the fact that no occurrences have been recorded so far:

> *new (wordentry)* ;
> **with** *wordentry↑* **do**
> **begin**
>   *spelling := word* ;
>   *initialize occurrences*
> **end** ;

Printing the ordered list of words and their occurrences is easily outlined as a procedure which deals with each entry in the chained list in turn, as follows:

> **procedure** *printwords (wordlist : wordpointer)* ;
>
>   **var** *nextword : wordpointer* ;
>
> **begin**
>   *nextword := wordlist* ;
>   **while** *nextword <>* **nil do**
>   **with** *nextword↑* **do**

```
        begin
          print spelling ;
          print occurrences ;
          nextword := next
        end
    end {printwords} ;
```

The three procedures *initwords*, *recordword* and *printwords* provide the only word list operations required by our concordance program, and as such they realize the abstraction of a word list introduced for this purpose. In implementing them, however, we have identified a further abstraction which is the list of occurrences associated with each word. This too must be implemented in some way.

The operations required on each list of occurrences are as follows:

(a)   initializing it to represent no occurrences,

(b)   adding a line number as a new occurrence, and

(c)   printing the complete list of occurrences in some suitable form.

In practice, the problem of representing a list of occurrences can be dealt with in a similar manner. Because the length of these lists may also vary considerably each list might be represented as a chain of records with pointers leading from the first to the last, and two auxiliary pointers that indicate the first and last records at all times. The second pointer is maintained because new occurrences are always appended to the end of an existing list. Such a list of occurrences is realized in Pascal by the following type definitions:

```
    listpointer = ↑linerecord ;
    linerecord = record
                    line : linenumber ;
                    nextline : listpointer
                 end ;
    listofoccurrences = record
                          first,last : listpointer
                        end ;
```

An empty list of occurrences is represented by two nil pointers, so the initialization of each *occurrences* field can be expressed using the following procedure:

```
    procedure initoccurrences (var list : listofoccurrences) ;
      begin
        list.first := nil ;
        list.last := nil
      end {initoccurrences} ;
```

The operation of adding a line number to an existing list of occurrences is then easily provided as a procedure with the following form:

> **procedure** *addoccurrence* (*newline* : *linenumber* ;
>   **var** *list* : *listofoccurrences*) ;

and the operation of printing out a list of occurrences can be provided by a procedure:

> **procedure** *printoccurrences* (*occurrences* : *listofoccurrences*) ;

When suitably implemented using the pointer facility of Pascal these three procedures provide the operations required by the concordance program for manipulating each list of occurrences involved. Together with the type definitions defining such a list they realize the abstraction of a list of occurrences which arose in solving the problem.

Consider now what happens when we bring these implementations together within an overall concordance program. Apart from any procedures needed for input of word, line pairs, the overall form of the Pascal program is as follows:

> **program** *concordance* (*input,output*) ;
>
>   **type** *wordspelling* = . . .
>   *linenumber* = . . .
>   *linepointer* = . . .
>   *linerecord* = . . .
>   *wordpointer* = . . .
>   *wordrecord* = . . .
>
>   **var** *word* : *wordspelling* ;
>   *line* : *linenumber* ;
>   *wordlist* : *wordpointer* ;
>
>   **procedure** *initoccurrences* . . .
>   **procedure** *addoccurrence* . . .
>   **procedure** *printoccurrences* . . .
>
>   **procedure** *initwords* . . .
>   **procedure** *recordword* . . .
>   **procedure** *printwords* . . .

```
begin
    initialize input of text ;
    initwords (wordlist) ;
    repeat
        get word,line from input text ;
        recordword (word,line,wordlist)
    until end of text ;
    printwords (wordlist)
end {concordance}.
```

The bulk of the final program is taken up with the implementation of the abstractions of a word list and of a list of occurrences. While introduction of these abstractions clearly benefited the derivation of the program, in its final form it has two significant disadvantages:

(a)   The rigid order that Pascal imposes on type, variable, and procedure declarations within the program results in the splitting of the corresponding type and procedure declarations for each abstraction in the final program text, so that the implementation of a given abstraction is fragmented throughout the overall program text with an inevitable loss of clarity. This fragmentation could be easily avoided by relaxing the rigid order of declaration imposed by Pascal so that associated groupings of types, variables and procedures can be juxtaposed in the program text, thus allowing all of the code associated with the implementation of a given abstraction to occur at a single point in the program text. However, even with this relaxed ordering the following, more serious, problem remains.

(b)   Although the main program does not and should not make any use of the way in which the abstraction of a word list is implemented, i.e. by using pointers, the corresponding pointer type definitions must appear in the main program block. This is the only way in Pascal that these definitions may be shared by the corresponding abstract operation procedures *recordword* and *printwords*. Similarly, although the abstraction of a list of occurrences is a secondary component of the word list abstraction itself, the type definitions supporting its implementation also have to appear in the main program block. The abstract operations *addoccurrence* and *printoccurrences* could each be hidden within the respective procedures *recordword* and *printwords*, but the type definitions that they share are again forced to appear in the main program. The presence of these type definitions in the main program block means that the main program body may inadvertently inspect and even alter the pointers involved in realizing the abstractions without violating any of the rules of Pascal. Thus, in contrast to the built-in abstractions of the language these program-defined abstractions are not protected from accidental misuse, since the program using them is not strictly confined to making calls on the procedure realizing the abstract operations.

These problems arise because the abstractions have to be implemented within the limited facilities of block structure and scope provided by Pascal. The fact that any definitions or declarations to be shared by two procedures must be located in some enclosing block means that the underlying implementation of an abstraction cannot be hidden from the user block, or from the code implementing other abstractions at the same level.

For large programs that involve many more than two independent abstractions the danger of such unwanted interactions is greatly increased, and diagnosing the nature of such errors when they occur is extremely difficult because the assumed independence of the abstractions involved is no longer guaranteed. If the systematic use of program-defined abstractions is to be an effective tool in the construction of large programs it is desirable, therefore, that the programming language supports the mutual security of such abstractions. In the following sections we explore the essential requirements of such a language and illustrate a modest extension to Pascal that meets them. The basic concept introduced is the *module*, which is available in a number of languages derived from Pascal, such as Concurrent Pascal, Modula, Pascal Plus and Ada. The style of program advocated here can be practiced with any of these languages. The essential feature that they provide is a tighter control over the scope and visibility of identifiers than that enabled by Pascal's block structure.

A LIST OF OCCURRENCES MODULE

Consider first the abstraction of a list of occurrences used in the concordance program. The only features of the abstraction required by the program using it are the type *listofoccurrences* itself together with the operations *initoccurrences*, *addoccurrence* and *printoccurrences*. All other details of the implementation of the list can and should be hidden and protected from the user program. What we require, therefore, is a construct that brings together all of the definitions and code involved in implementing the abstraction and hides from the using program all details except the identifiers *listofoccurrences*, *initoccurrences*, *addoccurrence* and *printoccurrences*. To do so we might envisage a new form of *module* block as follows:

```
module occurrences ;
    type linepointer = . . .
         linerecord = . . .
         *listofoccurrences = . . .
    procedure *initoccurrences (var list : listofoccurrences) ;
            . . .
    procedure *addoccurrence (newline : linenumber ;
                              var list : listofoccurrences) ;
            . . .
    procedure *printoccurrences (list : listofoccurrences) ;
            . . .
    begin
        . . .
    end {occurrences} ;
```

Like function and procedure blocks, such a module might appear in the head of any other block in our extended programming language. To fulfil its purpose, however, it has the following significant properties:

(a)   As with any Pascal block the identifiers declared within the module block are hidden from surrounding blocks. Thus, the identifiers *linepointer*, *linerecord*, etc., are unknown to the surrounding program.

(b)   However, those identifiers whose declarations are preceded by a star, in this case the identifiers *listofoccurrences*, *initoccurrences*, *addoccurrence*, and *printoccurrences*, may be referred to in the surrounding block as visible attributes of the module. To do so, we adopt the same notation as is used for record fields in Pascal—that is, in the surrounding block we may refer to the type:

$$occurrences.listofoccurrences$$

or to the procedure

$$occurrences.addoccurrence$$

Alternatively, using a **with** statement we may make several references thus:

```
with occurrences do
begin
    initoccurrences (    ) ;
        . . .
    addoccurrence (    ) ;
        . . .
    printoccurrences (    ) ;
end
```

(c)   For consistency with the form of other blocks we retain the compound
      statement that forms the final statement part of the module block. This
      statement can be used to carry out any initialization that is necessary in
      the module before any use is made of its starred attributes, but in this
      case no such initialization is required.

This module concept provides the essential requirements for protecting the
program-defined abstraction such as the *listofoccurrences* from misuse. It
makes available, as its *interface* to the using program, the type identifier that
represents the *listofoccurrences* abstraction itself, together with the procedure identifiers that denote the allowable operations on objects of the type.
It is now impossible for the user program to misuse a list of occurrences by
accessing the underlying pointer representation directly. In this way, we
have solved the security problem which the limitations of Pascal's simple
block structure had created.

A WORDLIST MODULE

Now we consider the wordlist abstraction required in the concordance
program. In principle, we can tackle the abstraction problem in exactly the
same way, that is we might produce a module with the following overall
form:

```
module words ;

   type wordpointer = . . .
        wordrecord = . . .
        *wordlist = wordpointer ;

   procedure *initwords (var list : wordlist) ;
      . . .
   procedure *recordword (word : wordspelling ;
                          line : linenumber ;
                          var list : wordlist) ;
      . . .
   procedure *printwords (list : wordlist) ;
      . . .
   begin
      . . .
   end {words} ;
```

However, in the case of the wordlist certain significant simplifications of its interface to the program using it are possible. In the concordance program, only one wordlist is required. Instead of having a declaration of the form:

>   *wordlist* : *words.wordlist*

in the main concordance program itself, we could, therefore, move the declaration of the pointer to the first word of the wordlist *module* inside the module. By doing so, a number of significant changes are then possible, as the following revised version shows:

```
module wordlist ;

   type
     wordpointer = . . .
     wordrecord = . . .

   var firstword : wordpointer ;

   procedure *recordword (word : wordspelling ;
                          line : linenumber)
     . . .
   procedure *printwords ;
     . . .
   begin
     firstword := nil
   end {wordlist} ;
```

The significant aspects of this version are as follows:

(a)   The pointer variable that indicated the first word of the wordlist is now declared within the module so that the representation of the wordlist is totally invisible to the using program. Only the necessary operations *recordword* and *printwords* are visible.

(b)   In coding the *recordword* and *printwords* operations it is now logical to omit the wordlist parameter from their parameter lists. By implication *any* call on one of these procedures operates on the wordlist represented by the pointer within the module.

(c)   The procedure for initialization of the wordlist has now been replaced by a non-empty body for the module itself. By definition this body will be executed before the user program can make any call on *recordword* or *printwords*. Thus, the initialization is guaranteed and is no longer the user's responsibility.

A MODULE FOR WORD INPUT

Already we have used our module concept in two significantly different ways. The *occurrences* module acts simply as a package of type and procedure definitions, some of which are hidden from the surrounding program text. The surrounding program used the module by declaring variables of a type defined within the module, and then manipulated these variables by calls on the corresponding procedures defined by the module. In the *wordlist* module, however, the data structure required was declared within the module itself, and only the applicable operations were defined as starred procedures. As far as the user program is concerned, the module itself is the data structure required.

In the case of the wordlist, none of the data involved was made visible to the user program, but in a module that creates a data structure this need not necessarily be so. As a further example of the modular approach let us now consider the part of the concordance program that we have not previously refined, namely, the extraction of words from the initial input text.

As far as the main program is concerned, there are two essential operations required for word input, one to obtain the spelling and line number of the next word in the text, the other to test whether the end of the input words has been reached. To provide these we might envisage a module as follows:

> **module** *wordinput* ;
>
> > **procedure** **getword* (**var** *word* : *wordspelling* ;
> >   **var** *line* : *linenumber*) ;
> >   . . .
> > **function** **endofwords* : *Boolean* ;
> >   . . .
> > **begin**
> >   . . .
> > **end** {*wordinput*} ;

To use this module, however, the main program is forced to declare variables to hold the current word and current line number and to call the procedure *getword* with these variables as parameters on each occasion. A more logical organization is to declare the variables that hold the current word and line as visible attributes of the word input module itself and to reduce the procedure *getword* simply to a request to update these variables with new values. This organization is now so reminiscent of the features of a sequential file in Pascal (in effect the module implements an abstract file of words) that we are led to go further and define the effect of the procedure *getword* as being *either* to update the word and line variables for the next word, *or* to set the end of words condition. Following the Pascal file protocol completely, the initial action of the module body will either make the first word available or set the end of words condition immediately should no words be found in the input file.

With these modifications the overall form of the *wordinput* module is now as follows:

```
module wordinput ;

    var *word : wordspelling ;
        *line : linenumber ;
        *endofwords : Boolean ;

    procedure *getword ;

        . . .
    begin {wordinput}
        endofwords := false ;
        line := 1 ;
        getword
    end {wordinput} ;
```

and the concordance program using the module now has the form of a standard file processing loop:

```
with wordinput do
    while not endofwords do
    begin
        wordlist.recordword (word.line) ;
        getword
    end ;
    wordlist.printwords
```

Note that the concordance program only inspects the values of the starred variables of the module, and does not alter them directly. As we see later, this is a desirable property of all such modules, which may be enforced by the programming language involved.

If we now assume that:

(a) the text input is via the standard input file;

(b) a word is any sequence of letters, and

(c) the tail letters of any word beyond a maximum word length may be ignored,

a simple implementation of a word input module with this interface can easily be derived, as will be seen later.

This simple version could easily be extended to:

(a)   generate a line numbered listing of the input text, and/or

(b)   replace upper-case letters by their lower-case equivalents in the word spellings made available,

without any alteration of the interface provided by the module.

Modular Refinement of Programs

This refinement of the *wordinput* module completes a modular version of our concordance program, whose overall form is as follows:

```
program concordance (input,output) ;

    type wordspelling = . . .
         linenumber = . . .

    module wordinput . . .
    module occurrences . . .
    module wordlist . . .

    begin {concordance}
       with wordinput do
         while not endofwords do
         begin
            wordlist.recordword (word,line) ;
            getword
         end ;
         wordlist.printwords
    end {concordance}.
```

We derived this modular form by imposing a modular structure on the existing code for the *wordlist* and *listofoccurrences* abstractions. Only in the case of the *wordinput* module did we first define its external characteristics and then refine the internal implementation of these. It should be noted, however, that this process of proceeding from the module specification to its implementation is applicable in all cases, i.e. the modular abstraction technique fits naturally within our stepwise refinement of programs. If we consider the above to be an early version in the stepwise refinement of our concordance program, it already implies that the *wordinput* module has an interface of the following form:

```
module wordinput ;

    var *word : wordspelling ;
        *line : linenumber ;
        *endofwords : Boolean ;

    procedure *getword ;
```

while the *wordlist* module has an interface of the following form:

```
module wordlist ;

    procedure *recordword . . . ;
    procedure *printwords ;
```

Having established these interfaces, each module can then be considered independently, and the code to implement the facilities that it provides can be developed by a further process of stepwise refinement. In refining the *wordlist* code, however, the further abstraction of a *listofoccurrences* will be encountered, at which stage the introduction of a further module with the following interface is appropriate:

```
module occurrences ;

    type *listofoccurrences = . . . ;

    procedure *initoccurrences . . . ;
    procedure *addoccurrence . . . ;
    procedure *printoccurrences . . . ;
```

Note, however, that since the *occurrences* module is used only in implementing the *wordlist* abstraction, the natural place to define it is in the head of the *wordlist* module and not in the main program as we showed it earlier.

```
module wordlist ;

    module occurrences . . . ;

    procedure *recordword ;
        . . .
```

This nested definition of the *occurrences* module reflects its role in the overall refinement of the concordance program.

A MODULE LIBRARY

This modular structure reinforces the significant levels of abstraction that are employed in refining the concordance program, and in doing so, divides the overall program text into a number of manageable units that can be developed or inspected in isolation. This sub-division of the program text is particularly beneficial where large programs are involved. However, if the texts of the various program modules are assembled as their natural definition points dictate, the sheer length of the overall program text obscures the modular structure involved, particularly when nested module definitions are used. To regain a concise representation of the overall module structure and to encourage the independent consideration of modules it is useful to adopt a further convention for representing modular programs, in which the definition of a module is replaced by a library reference indicating that the module text will be found in a corresponding library file. Thus, our concordance program might be represented as follows:

```
program concordance (input,output) ;

   type wordspelling = . . . ;
        linenumber = . . . ;

   module wordinput in library ;
   module wordlist in library ;

   begin {concordance}
      with wordinput do
         while not endofwords do
         begin
            wordlist.recordword (word,line) ;
            getword
         end ;
      wordlist.printwords
   end {concordance}.
```

With this representation, a reader of the program text who is not interested in the details of the *wordinput* or *wordlist* modules is not distracted by the bulky text involved. If he does wish to see the details, then he simply inspects the corresponding file in the module library. If a library module in turn contains a nested module definition, as in the case of *wordlist*, this again may be represented as a library reference to the appropriate separate library file. When the compilation of such a program is requested, the compiler simply incorporates the contents of the corresponding library file on encountering a reference to a library module. In this way, the compilation of the appropriately nested program text is achieved without requiring the program writer or its readers to deal with the text in this nested form.

This library mechanism encourages the development and use of a library of utility modules that are suitable for inclusion in a variety of programs in a given application area. Later, in Chapter 5, we will introduce an extension of this simple mechanism that enhances the versatility of such utility modules.

MODULAR TESTING

The division of a program into a set of disjoint modules with narrow well-defined interfaces between them, not only eases the problem of constructing and of understanding the program, but also helps in the task of demonstrating its correctness. In principle, so-called modular testing seeks to establish the correctness of each module in isolation before attempting any test of their combined behaviour in an overall program. In practice, this may be achieved by *isolated* modular testing, in which each module is completely tested using an artificial test harness constructed for the purpose, or by *incremental* modular testing, in which the modules are added one by one to the growing program framework, at each stage testing or re-testing the behaviour of the incremented program. In some cases, this incremental approach avoids the significant problems of providing an adequate test harness for each of the modules concerned. Consider as an example the modular concordance program developed in previous sections. The behaviour of the *wordinput* module can be tested in isolation by a trivial program of the following form:

```
program testwordinput (input,output) ;

    type wordspelling = . . . ;
        linenumber = . . . ;

    module wordinput in library ;

    begin {testwordinput}
       with wordinput do
       while not endofwords do
       begin
           writeln (line,word) ;
           getword
       end
    end {testwordinput}.
```

By running this program with a small but carefully chosen input data file, the adequacy of the word by word input facility provided by the module can be established.

Now consider the *occurrences* module. Its ability to record and print multiple lists of occurrences can be tested by a simple program that records the occurrences of individual characters in an input text.

```
program testoccurrences (input,output) ;

module occurrences in library ;

var line : integer ;
    c : char ;
    stars,pluses : occurrences.listofoccurrences ;

begin {testoccurrences}
  with occurrences do
  begin
    initoccurrences (stars) ;
    initoccurrences (pluses) ;
    line := 0 ;
    while not eof (input) do
    begin
      line := line + 1 ;
      while not eoln (input) do
      begin
        read (c) ;
        if c = '*'
        then addoccurrence (line,stars)
        else if c = '+'
            then addoccurrence (line,pluses)
      end ;
      readln
    end ;
    printoccurrences (stars) ;
    printoccurrences (pluses)
  end
end {testoccurrences}.
```

This test is actually more stringent than the concordance program requires in that, with suitable data, it will test the module's handling of an empty list, that is a list in which no occurrences have been recorded, something which cannot arise in the concordance program itself.

In testing each of the *wordinput* and *occurrences* modules, the necessary test harness was easily provided and, in conjunction with carefully chosen input data, an adequate test of the corresponding module could be achieved. A similar approach could be taken to test the *wordlist* module in isolation, but here two significant differences arise:

(a)   To test the *wordlist* module without the *occurrences* module proper, a dummy *occurrences* module would have to be provided. To establish that the *wordlist* was transmitting the proper linenumbers to this *occurrences* module in recording each occurrence, the dummy module would have to include logic almost as complex as that required in the *occurrences* module itself.

(b)   The test harness required to drive the *wordlist* module would not differ significantly from the main program of the final concordance program itself.

Thus, if the *wordinput* and *occurrences* modules have already been tested rigorously it is as effective, and a good deal more convenient, to use these in testing the *wordlist* module itself. This incremental approach to module testing is justifiable when:

(a)   The test harness required for isolated testing of the module is as complex, and hence as error prone, as the incremental program harness itself.

(b)   The modules are available for testing in an appropriate incremental order.

This second condition implies that the modules of a program are constructed or at least tested in an order appropriate for incremental testing. For large programs whose development may be split into a number of modules that are allocated to independent programmers or programming teams, such constraints on the timing of module development and testing may be inconvenient, and the development of substantial test harnesses for isolated module testing may be preferable in these cases.

SUMMARY

Substantial computer programs are based on a number of abstractions with limited interactions between them. The construction of such programs is eased, and their clarity is enhanced, if a corresponding separation is maintained between the 'modules' of program text that implement these abstractions. In addition, the modelling of programming error is further reduced if the permitted interaction between modules is defined and controlled by the programming notation used.

On this basis we have defined a minimal extension of Pascal for modular programming. We have seen that it provides an effective framework for the stepwise refinement of modular program designs, and for the systematic testing of program modules when they are constructed. In conjunction with a simple library mechanism, the module also provides the basic building block of 'utility programming', allowing programs to be assembled out of separately developed or existing general-purpose modules in an economic fashion.

In this chapter the modular notation used has been the minimum necessary to get across the essential concepts of modular programming. Chapter 5 introduces an actual programming language which extends these basic concepts slightly, to provide a powerful and more flexible language for programming in a modular style.

EXERCISES

4.1   Assuming that the base language supports only the file type **file of** *char* with operators *reset*, *get*, and *eof*, define the interface for a module that would recreate the range of facilities provided by Pascal's standard *input* file. What disadvantages has your module when compared with Pascal's standard *input* file? How might the interface be extended to allow users to handle input errors?

4.2   Redesign the tic-tac-toe (noughts and crosses) program of Exercise 2.1 so that it consists of modules which are abstractions of the computer, the player, and the tic-tac-toe grid.

4.3   Design a program which reads text, each line of which contains not more than 80 characters, from an input text file and outputs the text to another file as a sequence of lines containing not more than 60 characters. The input text consists of words (of not more than 16 letters), commas, semicolons, full stops and 'layout devices' such as blank lines and new paragraphs. Any non-blank line having three or more leading blanks is considered to be the start of a new paragraph.
  Your design should include the following:

  (a)   a word input module which administers the reading of the input file ;

  (b)   an output module which administers the formatted output stream ;

  (c)   a driver program which obtains items from the word input module and passes them to the output module.

5

Modular Programming in Pascal Plus

The modular version of the concordance program developed in Chapter 4 illustrates the essential features that a language must provide for modular programming, and demonstrates the benefits that result from using the modular approach. Similar features and similar benefits are provided by a number of current programming languages, such as Concurrent Pascal, Modula and Ada. In this chapter, we introduce the particular notation and the additional refinements on the basic module concept that are provided in the programming language Pascal Plus, which is the language used in the remainder of this book to demonstrate the programming methods and program structures discussed.

ENVELOPES

The basic modular construct provided in Pascal Plus is called the *envelope* for reasons that will become apparent if we consider the following example. In the *wordlist* module of the concordance program, we used the module body to express the initialization of the wordlist representation that must take place before any use of the procedures *recordword* and *printwords* is allowed. By doing so, we relieved the program using the *wordlist* module of the responsibility of carrying out or requesting this initialization. With the chosen implementation, which used a linked list of word records, the module thereafter builds up a list of dynamically allocated records which may be extended by calls on *recordword* and printed out by calls on *printwords*. However, no provision was made for disposing of the list of word records

69

when use of *wordlist* is complete. As a result, if the module is embedded in some block that is subject to repeated execution, each execution will fail to recover the storage used for the word records it has created, and a progressive dissipation of storage will result from the repeated executions.

To avoid this, some means of recovering the wordlist storage must be provided. From the viewpoint of flexibility, it is illogical to incorporate this in the procedure *printwords* itself since, in some cases, repeated printing of the same growing list of words may be required. Instead, we could provide an additional starred procedure *disposewords* in the *wordlist* module, as follows:

```
procedure *disposewords ;
  var nextword : wordpointer ;
  begin
    while firstword <> nil do
    begin
      nextword := firstword↑.next ;
      occurrences.disposeoccurrences (firstword↑.occurrences) ;
      dispose (firstword) ;
      firstword := nextword
    end
  end {disposewords} ;
```

with a similar procedure:

```
procedure *disposeoccurrences(list : listofoccurrences) ;
```

in the *occurrences* module. The user program could then call *disposewords* at the end of the wordlist's lifetime. In practice, however, it is more attractive to deal with the final disposal of the wordlist in the same way as we have dealt with its initialization, that is, by enforcing it within the definition of the *wordlist* module itself. In Pascal Plus a module is defined as an *envelope* module, whose body defines both an *initial* and a *final* action that respectively precede and follow the execution of the program or block using the module. In Pascal Plus, the wordlist would be defined as follows:

```
envelope module wordlist ;

  type . . .

  var . . .

  procedure *recordword . . .
  procedure *printwords . . .
  procedure disposewords . . .
```

```
    begin {wordlist}
      firstword := nil ;
      *** ;
      disposewords
    end {wordlist} ;
```

The *** symbol, which is called the *inner* statement, denotes the execution of the program or block in which the envelope module is embedded. Thus, if we include the *wordlist* module in some block *b* the sequence of events on entering block *b* is:

(a)   The statement *firstword* := **nil** of the *wordlist* module is executed.

(b)   The body of the block *b* is executed.

(c)   The final call to the procedure *disposewords* is executed to recover any storage allocated by the *wordlist* module.

In effect, the body of the *wordlist* module *envelops* the body of the block that uses it.

   If a module requires no final action to be enforced, then in Pascal Plus it is written with the inner statement as the final action of its body. Thus, the *wordinput* module would be expressed in Pascal Plus as follows:

envelope module *wordinput* ;

```
var *word : . . .
    *line : . . .
    *endofwords : . . .

procedure *getword . . .

begin {wordinput}
  endofwords := false ;
  line := 1 ;
  getword ;
  ***
end {wordinput} ;
```

If a module requires neither an initial nor a final action to precede or follow its use, as in the case of the *occurrences* module, its body consists solely of an inner statement, thus:

envelope module *occurrences* ;

```
type . . .

procedure . . .

begin
  ***
end {occurrences} ;
```

When two or more envelope modules are embedded in the same program block, the order of the resultant enveloping is determined by the order in which the envelope modules occur in the block. Each envelope module is defined to envelop either the next envelope module in the block or, if no further envelope modules exist, the body of the block itself. Thus, if our concordance program is defined as follows:

```
program concordance . . .
   envelope module wordinput . . .
   envelope module wordlist . . .
   begin
      {main concordance program}
   end.
```

The order of execution that results is as follows:

> *initialize wordinput module*
> *initialize wordlist module*
> *execute main program*
> *finalize wordlist module*
> *finalize wordinput module*

This order of enveloping is consistent with the normal scope rules of Pascal which imply that a later envelope module can make use of the facilities of a preceding module but not vice versa. With the order of enveloping chosen, the preceding module is initialized before any such use can occur, and is not finalized until any such use is complete.

MULTIPLE INSTANCES OF ENVELOPES

In implementing the list of occurrences abstraction we chose a module which defined a starred type *listofoccurrences*, each value of which was an ordered list of line numbers. Using this starred type, we were able to embed a list of occurrences in each word record of a wordlist and so to create, initialize, update and print out each list of occurrences as required.

In contrast, when we implemented the wordlist abstraction we chose a module that contained the wordlist data structure itself, together with its appropriate initialization, and exported only the necessary operations to record and print words. At the time, this seemed a logical simplification since the concordance program required only one wordlist in its implementation. In effect, the *wordlist* module was the wordlist required, whereas the *listofoccurrences* module only provided the means whereby lists of occurrences could be created.

Under suitable conditions, it is possible to retain the *wordlist* module approach, even when several instances of a wordlist are required. In Pascal Plus the word *module* may be omitted from the envelope definition, as follows:

```
envelope wordlist ;

    type . . .

    var firstword : . . .

    procedure *recordword . . .

    procedure *printwords . . .

    procedure disposewords . . .

    begin {wordlist}
      firstword := nil ;
      *** ;
      disposewords
    end {wordlist} ;
```

An envelope block of this form does not itself create any data, but instead defines an 'envelope type' or template of which multiple instances may subsequently be created. Suppose, for example, we wished to modify the concordance program to construct separate lists of the nouns, verbs and adjectives that it finds in the input text. We can define a wordlist envelope as above and then create three instances of it by an instance declaration of the form:

```
instance nouns, verbs, adjectives : wordlist ;
```

The effect of this declaration is to create three copies of the variable *firstword* defined by the envelope block, one for each of the instances declared, and to initialize each copy by a corresponding execution of the initial code defined by the envelope body. Thereafter, operations on a particular wordlist may be requested by calling the procedure *recordword* or *printwords* prefixed by the appropriate instance name. Thus, to add a word to the list of nouns we make a call:

```
nouns.recordword (word,line)
```

but to add a word to the list of verbs we make the call:

> *verbs.recordword (word,line)*

On completion of the block in which the instances are declared, the finalization code of the *wordlist* envelope will be executed for each instance to dispose of the corresponding chain of wordrecords.

The overall concordance program that discriminates between nouns, verbs and adjectives can now take the following form:

```
program concordance (input,output) ;
   . . .
   envelope module wordinput . . .

   envelope wordlist . . .

   instance nouns, verbs, adjectives : wordlist ;

   begin {concordance}
     with wordinput do
       while not endofwords do
       begin
         {. . . determine class of word . . .} ;
         case class of
           noun : nouns.recordword(word,line) ;
           verb : verbs.recordword(word,line) ;
           adjective : adjectives.recordword(word,line) ;
           other :
         end ;
         getword
       end ;
     page ; nouns.printwords ;
     page ; verbs.printwords ;
     page ; adjectives.printwords
   end {concordance}.
```

In some cases, such as this, it is more convenient to organize several instances of an envelope as an array and then to access the individual envelope elements by the normal array indexing notation. Assuming a scalar type as follows:

> *wordclass = (noun, verb, adjective, other) ;*

Pascal Plus allows an instance declaration of the following form:

instance *words* : **array** [*noun* .. *adjective*] **of** *wordlist* ;

in which case the body of the concordance program can be written as follows:

```
begin {concordance}
  with wordinput do
    while not endofwords do
    begin
      { . . . determine class . . .} ;
      if class <> other then words[class].recordword(word,line) ;
      getword
    end ;
  for c := noun to adjective do
  begin page ; words[c].printwords end
end {concordance}.
```

As far as enveloping order is concerned, the elements of an array of envelope instances are assumed to occur in the order of their index values, so that in the above case, the *wordlist* instances will be initialized in the order:

words[*noun*]
words[*verb*]
words[*adjective*]

and finalized in reverse order.

The envelope module introduced in the previous section is simply a shorthand for a particular case of the more general envelope concept. Defining an envelope module *m* with body *b* thus:

envelope module *m* ; *b* ;

is completely equivalent to the definition of an anonymous envelope type with body *b* followed by the declaration of a single instance *m* of this type as follows:

envelope ? ; *b* ;
instance *m* : ? ;

However, the ability to use the shorthand notation in contexts where the programmer does not necessarily think of the grouping of data and code involved as the only instance of an abstract type more than justifies its retention.

PARAMETERIZING ENVELOPES

The ability to define an abstract envelope and then use several instances of it within a given program or, indeed, to use instances of it in different programs, is a significant programming tool. In practice, however, minor variations in the detailed requirements of the various instances of an envelope may arise for various reasons. If such variations can be accommodated within a single envelope definition, then the power of the facility is significantly increased.

In practice, two levels of variation can be identified; one is the variation between the details of a library envelope that is to be incorporated and used in several different programs, the other is the variation in detail between different instances of the same envelope in the same program. Both levels of variation can be illustrated by considering a generalization of the *wordinput* module that was introduced for the concordance program.

Retrieval Parameters

As originally defined, the *wordinput* module assumed the existence of global type definitions for *wordspelling* and *linenumber* and a global constant definition for *wordlength*. In addition, the way these were used within the module assumed that *linenumber* was an integer subrange type including 1, that *wordlength* was a positive integer constant, and that *wordspelling* was a type of the form:

array [1 . .*wordlength*] **of** *char*

Within these constraints the coding of the module will function correctly for any variation of its global types and constants. As it stands, therefore, the module is suitable for inclusion in a library for use in a variety of programs that process words extracted from an input text. To do so, however, the program must define the global identifiers *wordspelling*, *wordlength* and *linenumber* in an appropriate way. In some cases, the use of these identifiers may be either inconvenient or impossible, depending on the existing identifier usage in the program. To overcome this problem, the retrieval mechanism in Pascal Plus is extended to allow the re-definition of the global identifiers assumed by the library block, in a way that does not disturb the use of identifiers in the surrounding program text. Thus, we may have a program in which the words that are extracted from an input text are represented by the values of the type:

wordchars = **packed array** [1 . .*n*] **of** *char* ;

and in which no explicit *linenumber* type exists. The *wordinput* module can be retrieved from the library, as follows:

> **envelope module** *wordinput* **in** *library*
>   (*where* **const** *wordlength* = *n* ;
>   **type** *linenumber* = 1 . .1000 ;
>   *wordspelling* = *wordchars* ;) ;

The constant and type definitions given within the *where* clause define the necessary non-local quantities for the library module without the use of these identifiers in the surrounding program itself.

In some cases, the name of the library module itself may be unacceptable in a user program, in which case the following alternative is permitted:

> **envelope module** *wordstream* = *wordinput* **in** *library* . . .

Thereafter, the identifier *wordstream* denotes the module within the program and the identifier *wordinput* may have any other significance that is required. It should be noted that the *where* clause in a library retrieval is not just a means of re-mapping the identifiers used to denote global quantities. Because the types and values associated with the identifiers may vary, it can be used to vary the nature of the data manipulated by the module from one retrieval to the next. Thus, if we have a library module procedure for sorting an array defined in the following form:

> **procedure** *sort* (**var** *a* : **array** [*i* . .*j*:*integer*] **of** *element*) ;

the procedure may be retrieved as a means of sorting arrays of integers as follows:

> **procedure** *integersort* = *sort* **in** *library*
>   (*where* **type** *element* = *integer* ;) ;

or as a means of sorting arrays of real numbers, as follows:

> **procedure** *realsort* = *sort* **in** *library*
>   (*where* **type** *element* = *real* ;) ;

In general, the library sorting procedure can be used in this way to provide a means of sorting arrays of any element type for which the operations used within the procedure are applicable. Typically, these will be assignment and the use of an ordering operation, such as <. For element types on which the < operator cannot be used, a more general library sort can be written which accepts an ordering function as an auxiliary parameter. The usual way of

accomplishing this in Pascal is to include the ordering function in the parameter list of the *sort* procedure, as follows:

procedure *generalsort* (**var** *a* : **array** [*i* . .*j*:*integer*] **of** *element* ;
                                 function *lessthan* (*e1*,*e2* : *element*) : *Boolean*) ;

In most applications, however, this is unnecessarily complicated in that the
lessthan function is fixed for the element type concerned and does not
change from one call of the procedure *generalsort* to the next. It is more
logical, therefore, to fix the particular *lessthan* function to be used when the
element type itself is fixed, i.e. at the point where the *generalsort* procedure
is retrieved from the library. To this end, our library mechanism allows the
global procedures and functions that are used in a library block to be
remapped by the *where* clause at its retrieval. Thus, if we have a program that
manipulates records of some type *datarecord* in which a function:

function *keyorder* (*d1*,*d2* : *datarecord*) : *Boolean* ;

has been defined, then we might retrieve a procedure from the library, as
follows:

procedure *datasort* = *generalsort* **in** *library*
          (*where* **type** *element* = *datarecord* ;
                 function *lessthan* = *keyorder* ;) ;

assuming that the library procedure has the following heading:

procedure *generalsort* (**var** *a* : **array** [*i* . .*j*:*integer*] **of** *element*) ;

and that it expresses its ordering decisions in terms of calls to a global
function *lessthan*.

For procedures and functions, the *where* clause facility is limited to a
remapping of names for existing procedures and functions. A procedure or
function declaration itself cannot appear in the *where* clause. In fact, the
ability to rename a procedure or function is useful in other contexts as well,
and Pascal Plus allows such renaming by declarations of the form:

procedure *newname* = *existing procedure name*

function *newname* = *existing function name*

at any point where a procedure or function might be declared. This facility is
particularly useful when a starred procedure or function of some existing
envelope has to be renamed as a starred procedure or function of an
enclosing envelope.

Instance Parameters

In the case of the *generalsort* procedure it was logical to identify the *lessthan* function at the point of retrieval, since the identity of the function was not to change at each use of the procedure; the same is true for the variations involved in a wide class of library envelopes. In some cases, however, variations do occur between individual instances of a single envelope in a single program. To illustrate this need, consider again the *wordinput* envelope. Suppose now we have a program that is required to read and compare in some way the sequences of words extracted from two or more input texts. To express this in our program, we might define an envelope *wordinput* that represents the facilities provided for any of the input texts and then create several instances, one for each of the texts concerned. The only variation between these instances is in the actual text file from which the sequence of words is extracted. Each instance will have a corresponding text file to read from. To provide for such variations, Pascal Plus allows an envelope definition to include a formal parameter list which is identical in form to those used for procedures and functions. In the case of the *wordinput* envelope the definition is now as follows:

> **envelope** *wordinput* (**var** *f* : *text*) ;
>   . . .
>   **procedure** **getword* ;
>   **begin**
>   {*extract next word from file f*}
>   **end** ;
>   **begin** {*wordinput*}
>   *reset* (*f*) ; . . .
>   *******
>   **end** {*wordinput*} ;

To create an instance of this envelope, we must supply a corresponding actual parameter list in the instance declaration. Thus, to create an instance *wordstream*1 that extracts its words from a text file *input*1, we use the following definition:

> **instance** *wordstream*1 : *wordinput* (*input*1) ;

The initialization sequence for this instance will reset the text file *input*1 and each subsequent call on the procedure *wordstream*1.*getword* will operate directly on the file *input*1 by the usual rules of parameter correspondence. When two instances of such an envelope are created in the same declaration, the separate parameter lists required are written, one after another, as

follows:

> **instance** *wordstream*1,*wordstream*2 : *wordinput* (*input*1),(*input*2) ;

Where an array of instances is created, the sequence of parameter lists for the elements of the array is enclosed in an additional set of brackets, thus:

> **instance** *words* : **array** [1 . .3] **of** *wordinput* [(*input*1),
> (*input*2),
> (*input*3)] ;

The same rules of parameter correspondence apply to the parameters of envelope instances as apply for the parameters of procedures and functions in Pascal.

Instances as Parameters

In addition to accepting actual parameters, instances of envelopes may themselves be passed as parameters to procedures, functions or instances of other envelopes. To do so, we use a formal parameter declaration such as the following:

> **procedure** *countwords* (**instance** *wordstream* : *wordinput*) ;

Within the procedure *countwords*, the formal parameter *wordstream* may be manipulated like any other instance of the envelope *wordinput*, but this manipulation will apply to the actual envelope instance supplied as parameter at this point of call.

Retrieving Envelopes as Modules

An envelope of which multiple instances can be created is inherently more flexible than a single instance envelope module. For this reason, flexibility dictates that library modules should be held as envelopes rather than envelope modules whenever possible. Thus, the wordlist abstraction is most flexible if stored in the envelope form, thus:

> **envelope** *wordlist* ;
>   . . .

To encourage this flexibility, but at the same time allow the economy of expression of the envelope module form for user programs, Pascal Plus allows a library envelope to be retrieved as an envelope module, thus:

envelope module *wordlist* **in** *library* . . .

In practice, of course, this can be done only for library envelopes without parameter lists.

THE CONCORDANCE PROGRAM IN PASCAL PLUS

To illustrate the use of Pascal Plus, and the way in which considered flexibility affects the form of library modules, we now re-express the modular concordance program developed in Chapter 4, as a Pascal Plus program using three library envelopes.

Consider first the *wordinput* module. To maximize its flexibility we store in the library an envelope with a text file parameter as shown in Listing 4. Note also the initial comment that makes clear the global definitions on which it depends and which must be satisfied at the point of retrieval, using a *where* clause if necessary.

Listing 4

```
envelope wordinput(var wordfile: text);

{ This envelope extracts words from the file wordfile   }
{ one by one, leaving the word spelling in the variable }
{ word and its line number in the variable line.        }
{ The first word if any is immediately available. There }
{ after procedure getword  gets the next word, setting  }
{ endofwords true when no further words are available    }
{                                                        }
{ assumes const wordlength = maximum stored word length; }
{        type wordspelling =                             }
{                packed array [1..wordlength] of char;   }
{                linenumber = 1..maximum line number;    }

var *word: wordspelling;
    *line: linenumber;
    *endofwords: Boolean;
    letters: set of char;

procedure *getword;
  var wordfound: Boolean;
```

Continued on page 82

Listing 4 – *continued*

```pascal
  procedure findword;
    begin
      while not (eof(wordfile) or wordfound) do
        begin
          while not (eoln(wordfile) or (wordfile^ in letters)) do
            get(wordfile);
          if eoln(wordfile)
          then begin
                 line := line + 1;
                 get(wordfile)
               end
          else wordfound := true
        end
    end {findword};

  procedure copyword;
    var i: 0..wordlength;
    begin
      i := 0;
      repeat
        if i < wordlength
        then begin
               i := i + 1;
               word[i] := wordfile^
             end;
        get(wordfile)
      until not (wordfile^ in letters);
      while i < wordlength do
        begin
          i := i + 1;
          word[i] := ' '
        end
    end {copyword};

  begin
    wordfound := false;
    findword;
    if wordfound
    then copyword
    else endofwords := true
  end {getword};

begin
  reset(wordfile);
  letters := ['a'..'z', 'A'..'Z'];
  endofwords := false;
  line := 1;
  getword;
  ***
end {wordinput};
```

Test 4 shows an isolated module test for the *wordinput* envelope, as suggested in Chapter 4, using the paragraph you are now reading as input.

Test 4

```
program testwordinput(input, output);

{ a simple test for the wordinput envelope }

const wordlength = 20;

type wordspelling = packed array [1..wordlength] of char;
     linenumber = 1..9999;

envelope wordinput in library;

instance words: wordinput(input);

begin
  with words do
    while not endofwords do
      begin
        writeln(output, line, ' ', word);
        getword
      end
end {testwordinput}.
```

```
          1   Test
          1   shows
          1   an
          1   isolated
          1   module
          1   test
          1   for
          1   the
          1   wordinput
          1   envelope
          1   as
          2   suggested
          2   in
          2   Chapter
          2   using
          2   the
          2   paragraph
          2   you
          2   are
          2   now
          2   reading
          2   as
          2   input
```

Now consider the list of *occurrences* module. This is shown as a Pascal Plus
library module in Listing 5.

Listing 5

```
envelope module occurrences;

{ This module enables the creation and printout of    }
{ lists of occurrences, i.e. line numbers.            }
{                                                      }
{ assumes const linemax = maximum output line length; }
{               indent  = left margin for printing a  }
{                         list of occurrences;        }
{          type linenumber = integer (or subrange of) }

type linepointer = ^linerecord;
     linerecord = record
                      line: linenumber;
                      nextline: linepointer
                  end;
      *listofoccurrences = record first, last: linepointer end;

procedure *initoccurrences(var list: listofoccurrences);
  begin
    list.first := nil;
    list.last := nil
  end {initoccurrences};

procedure *addoccurrence(newline: linenumber;
                         var list: listofoccurrences);
  var occurrence: linepointer;
  begin
    new(occurrence);
    with occurrence^ do
      begin
        line := newline;
        nextline := nil
      end;
    with list do
      begin
        if first = nil
        then first := occurrence
        else last^.nextline := occurrence;
        last := occurrence
      end
  end {addoccurrence};

procedure *printoccurrences(list: listofoccurrences;
                            var printfile: text);
  var spaceleftonline: 0..linemax;
      nextoccurrence: linepointer;
```

```
    begin
      write(printfile, ' ': indent);
      spaceleftonline := linemax - indent;
      nextoccurrence := list.first;
      while nextoccurrence <> nil do
        begin
          if spaceleftonline < 6
          then begin
                 writeln(printfile);
                 write(printfile, ' ': indent);
                 spaceleftonline := linemax - indent
               end;
          write(printfile, nextoccurrence^.line: 6);
          spaceleftonline := spaceleftonline - 6;
          nextoccurrence := nextoccurrence^.nextline
        end;
      writeln(printfile)
    end {printoccurrences};

  procedure *disposeoccurrences(list: listofoccurrences);
    var thisoccurrence, nextoccurrence: linepointer;
    begin
      nextoccurrence := list.first;
      while nextoccurrence <> nil do
        begin
          thisoccurrence := nextoccurrence;
          nextoccurrence := thisoccurrence^.nextline;
          dispose(thisoccurrence)
        end
    end {disposeoccurrences};

begin
  ***
end {occurrences};
```

Note that the text file used to print a list of occurrences is now a parameter of
the *printoccurrences* procedure, which increases the module's flexibility. An
isolated module test for the occurrence module, as suggested in Chapter 4, is
shown in Test 5.

Test 5

```
program testoccurrences(input, output);

  { a simple test for the occurrences module }

  const linemax = 60;
        indent = 6;
```

continued on page 86

Test 5 – *continued*

```
type linenumber = 0..9999;

envelope module occurrences in library;

var line: linenumber;
    c: char;
    stars, pluses: occurrences.listofoccurrences;

begin
  with occurrences do
    begin
      initoccurrences(stars);
      initoccurrences(pluses);
      line := 0;
      while not eof(input) do
        begin
          line := line + 1;
          write(output, line: 5, '   ');
          while not eoln(input) do
            begin
              read(input, c);
              write(output, c);
              if c = '*'
              then addoccurrence(line, stars)
              else if c = '+' then addoccurrence(line, pluses)
            end;
          readln(input);
          writeln(output)
        end;
      writeln;
      writeln(output, 'occurrences of stars:');
      printoccurrences(stars, output);
      writeln;
      writeln(output, 'occurrences of pluses:');
      printoccurrences(pluses, output);

    end
end {testoccurrences}.
```

```
    1   T+st 4 sh*ws an is*lat+d m*dul+ t+st f*r th+ w*rdinput
    2   +nv+l*p+, as sugg+st+d in Chapt+r 4, using th+ paragraph
    3   y*u ar+ n*w r+ading as input.

occurrences of stars:
          1       1       1       1       1       2       3       3

occurrences of pluses:
          1       1       1       1       1       2       2       2       2
          2       2       2       3       3
```

Finally, a library version of the wordlist envelope is shown in Listing 6.

Listing 6

```
envelope module wordlist;

  { This envelope creates and prints an ordered list of words }
  { each with an associated list of linenumber occurrences    }
  {                                                            }
  { assumes type wordspelling = any string type;              }
  {                linenumber = 1 .. some maximum;             }

  envelope module occurrences in library
    (where const linemax = 60;
                  indent = 6; );

  type wordpointer = ^wordrecord;
       wordrecord = record
                      spelling: wordspelling;
                      occurred: occurrences.listofoccurrences;
                      next: wordpointer
                    end;

  var firstword: wordpointer;

  procedure *recordword(word: wordspelling; line: linenumber);
    var nextword, previousword: wordpointer;
        positionfound: boolean;

    procedure insertword;

      { inserts new word between those pointed }
      { to by previousword and nextword        }

      var newword: wordpointer;
      begin
        new(newword);
        with newword^, occurrences do
          begin
            spelling := word;
            initoccurrences(occurred);
            addoccurrence(line, occurred);
            next := nextword
          end;
        if previousword = nil
        then firstword := newword
        else previousword^.next := newword
      end {insertword};
```

continued on page 88

Listing 6 – *continued*

```
begin
  nextword := firstword;
  previousword := nil;
  positionfound := false;
  while not positionfound and (nextword <> nil) do
    if nextword^.spelling >= word
    then positionfound := true
    else begin
            previousword := nextword;
            nextword := nextword^.next
         end;
  if positionfound
  then if nextword^.spelling = word
        then occurrences.addoccurrence(line, nextword^.occurred)
        else insertword {before nextword}
  else insertword {at end of list}
end {recordword};

procedure *printwords(var printfile: text);
  var nextword: wordpointer;
  begin
    nextword := firstword;
    while nextword <> nil do
      begin
        writeln(printfile, nextword^.spelling);
        occurrences.printoccurrences(nextword^.occurred, printfile);
        nextword := nextword^.next
      end
  end {printwords};

procedure disposewords;
  var nextword: wordpointer;
  begin
    while firstword <> nil do
      begin
        nextword := firstword^.next;
        occurrences.disposeoccurrences(firstword^.occurred);
        dispose(firstword);
        firstword := nextword
      end
  end {disposewords};

begin
  firstword := nil;
  ***;
  disposewords
end {wordlist};
```

Again, the textfile used to print a list of words is now a parameter of the procedure *printwords*. Although stored as an envelope, *wordlist* can be retrieved as an envelope module in those programs which require only one instance. Test 6 shows how this is done for the complete concordance program, together with the output produced from this paragraph as input.

Test 6

```
program concordance(input, output);

{ This program creates and prints a sorted concordance }
{ of all words in the text input,  each with a list of }
{ the line numbers at which it occurs.                  }

const wordlength = 20;

type wordspelling = packed array [1..wordlength] of char;
     linenumber = 1..maxint;

envelope module wordlist in library;

envelope wordinput in library;

instance words: wordinput(input);

begin
  with words do
    while not endofwords do
      begin
        wordlist.recordword(word, line);
        getword
      end;
    wordlist.printwords(output)
end {concordance}.
```

```
Again
          1
Although
          2
Test
          4
a
          1    1
an
          2    3
as
          2    3    5
be
          2
can
          2
```

continued on page 90

Test 6 – *continued*

```
complete
            4
concordance
            4
done
            4
envelope
            2       3
for
            4
            .
            .
            .
```

SUMMARY

The envelope construct provided in Pascal Plus is a powerful and flexible aid to modular programming. It meets the basic requirements for modularity which were identified in Chapter 4. In addition, however, its finalization feature, multiple instances of envelopes, and parameterization of envelopes both at library retrieval time and at instantiation all increase the power and flexibility of the envelopes that can be created. These features are useful in any modular programming context, but are particularly effective when the envelope is used to extend the data structuring capabilities of Pascal by defining *abstract data types*, which is the topic of our next chapter.

EXERCISES

5.1   The output from Test 6 shows several limitations of the modules from which the concordance program has been assembled:

(a)   Upper case letters at the start of sentences affect the recognition and ordering of words.

(b)   Printing the list of occurrences on a separate line from the word itself is unappealing and extravagant for short occurrence lists.

(c)   Fixed format printing of each line number within a list is extravagant for small line numbers.

(d) Multiple occurrences of the same word on a single line cause the line number to be printed a corresponding number of times in the list of occurrences, which may be unnecessary.

Devise modifications to the modules which overcome each of these deficiencies. Consider carefully whether the module interface needs to change before making changes within the modules themselves.

5.2   Implement the program design of Exercise 4.2 in Pascal Plus.

5.3   Implement the program design of Exercise 4.3 in Pascal Plus.

6

Abstract Data Types

A FIRST EXAMPLE: INTEGERSET

In Chapter 2, we saw that a systematic approach to program construction depends upon the use of abstraction. In particular, the stepwise refinement technique describes the required program in terms of intermediate abstract actions, thus reducing the complexity and detail that must be considered at any point. These abstract actions identified by the stepwise refinement determine 'what' is to be done at various points of the program, rather than 'how' it is actually carried out.

In Chapter 3, we saw that the same abstraction principle applies to the description of data, and that Pascal provides a range of data abstractions—ranging from scalar types such as integers, Booleans and enumerations to the structured types such as arrays, records, sets and files. Every data type consists of a set of values and a range of operators on these values. The programmer need not be aware of how the values are actually represented on the machine, since he is supplied with a range of representation independent operators with which to manipulate them. We may thus consider objects of a particular data type as having two characteristic sets of properties or attributes. The first set, which we might term the *specification attributes*, define the operations which one can perform on objects of the type. The second set, the *representation attributes*, determine how such objects are represented by a particular implementation. The programmer, when using such objects, is ideally unaware of the representation attributes (i.e. the details of the representation of the objects) and is concerned only with manipulating them in terms of the specification attributes, i.e. the operators for the data type.

Hence, we define an *abstract data type* as a class of objects defined by means of a representation-independent specification. The specification will consist of a set of operators for creating such objects of the type, retrieving certain information from the objects, and updating the objects. For example the Pascal set abstraction provides:

(a)   a set construction operator for creating a set from its member values, e.g. [1 . .9,*x*]

(b)   a set membership operator, **if** *day* **in** [*Monday,Tuesday*] **then** . . .

(c)   operators for comparing sets, **if** *s* = [ ] **then** . . .

(d)   set arithmetic operators which can be used for combining or updating set values, e.g. *s* := *s* + [*x*]

The range of operators chosen is a language-design decision which in general involves a compromise between simplicity, flexibility and error security. For some problems the most convenient set operator may not be provided by Pascal, e.g. an operator to sequence through the member values of a set is one required in many problems. However, it is a characteristic of a good language design that such operations can be expressed in terms of the operators that are provided.

Whatever operators are provided, a basic language design principle is that the form of these operators in no way reflects how sets are actually represented on the machine. The operators specify only what is to be done—the implementation of the operators by the compiler determines how this is performed on the actual set representation chosen.

When we construct more complex data objects out of the basic data types provided by the language, we are really building higher-level data abstractions, which we represent using the lower-level data abstractions of the language. Once again, we prefer to manipulate these higher-level abstract objects without detailed knowledge of their representation, but in practice this representation and the implementation of the appropriate operations must be defined at some point in the program.

Consider for example a program which manipulates sets of integers where the members of a given set need not be distinct—hence the Pascal set abstraction is not appropriate for describing them. Irrespective of how these sets are represented we will need to perform basic operations such as clearing a set to the empty set, insertion and removal of members, and a test for membership. All of these operations may best be expressed in the form of procedures or functions whose specifications are independent of the representation chosen for the sets, e.g.:

     procedure *clear* (**var** *s* : *integerset*) ;

The programmer may thus use the operators specified without any knowledge of how the sets are actually represented. The implementation of the operators, i.e. the bodies of the specified procedures or functions, will reflect the representation involved, but their headings and calling sequence will not.

How can we best realize such an abstract data type in a high-level language? Since an abstract data type consists of a set of operators and also an implementation:

abstract data type = operators (visible to user)

+

implementation (hidden from user)

we would like a language construct that enables both sets of attributes to be encapsulated in the same program unit, such that the implementation details are invisible and inaccessible from the outside but the operators are accessible. These two requirements are satisfied by the module construct in general and by the Pascal Plus envelope construct in particular, which permits the combination of the definition of the chosen data representation and operators (in the form of procedures and functions) in the single program unit. The starring mechanism allows the designer of the abstract data type to select which operators he will make visible, while at the same time hiding the data structures that form the representation of the abstract objects described by the envelope. For instance, the following envelope definition specifies the abstract data type *integerset* with a minimum range of the possible operators:

```
envelope integerset ;

    . . . definition of representation . . .

procedure *clear ; . . .
procedure *insert (i : integer) ; . . .
procedure *remove (i : integer) ; . . .
function   *contains (i : integer) : Boolean ; . . .
function   *empty : Boolean ; . . .

begin {integerset}
  {initially the set is empty}
  ***

end {integerset} ;
```

Since the data representing the implementation of the abstract data type is unstarred it is invisible from outside the envelope, and the form of the starred operators is totally independent of the actual representation chosen. The body of the envelope also provides a default initialization of all *integerset* data objects to the empty set, and can provide any finalization required by the representation chosen.

USING INTEGERSET

To illustrate the use of our abstract data type *integerset* consider now a program which reads two positive integers and prints out a list of their common prime factors (in ascending order), followed by lists of the other prime factors of each. For example the input:

168   180

would produce the output:

> *Common prime factors of* 168 *and* 180 *are*   2 2 3
> *Other prime factors of* 168 *are* 2 7
> *Other prime factors of* 180 *are* 3 5

Since the prime factors of a number *n* may contain multiple occurrences of a given prime they cannot be held as a Pascal *set of integer*, but can be held as values of our abstract *integerset* type. Using two sets to hold the factors of the input numbers the required program may be defined as the following sequence of steps:

> *read* (*n*1,*n*2) ;
> *find prime factors f*1 *of n*1 ;
> *find prime factors f*2 *of n*2 ;
> *print and remove common factors in f*1, *f*2 ;
> *print other factors in f*1 ;
> *print other factors in f*2

The step to find the prime factors of either number can be expressed as a call to the following procedure, which uses a simple trial and error loop to find the factors required:

```
procedure findprimefactors (n : integer; instance f : integerset) ;
  var trial : integer ;
  begin
    f.clear ;
    trial := 2 ;
    while n <> 1 do
      if n mod trial = 0
      then begin
              f.insert (trial) ;
              n := n div trial
          end
      else trial := trail + 1
  end {findprimefactors} ;
```

The step to print and remove the common factors can be expressed as another trial loop:

```
procedure printandremovecommonfactors ;
   var trial,limit : integer ;
   begin
     write ( ' Common prime factors of ', n1, ' and ', n2, ' are ' ) ;
     trial := 2 ;
     if nl > n2 then limit := n2 else limit := n1 ;
     while trial <= limit do
        if f1.contains (trial) and f2.contains (trial)
           then begin
                   write (trial) ;
                   f1.remove (trial) ;
                   f2.remove (trial)
                end
           else trial := trial + 1 ;
     writeln
   end {printandremovecommonfactors} ;
```

The step to print the other factors remaining in either set can be expressed as an appropriate call to the following procedure:

```
procedure printotherfactors (n : integer ; instance f : integerset) ;
   var trial : integer ;
   begin
     write ( ' Other factors of ' , n , ' are ' ) ;
     trial := 2 ;
     while trial <= n do
        if f.contains (trial)
        then write (trial)
        else trial := trial + 1 ;
     writeln
   end {printotherfactors} ;
```

The overall form of the required program, assuming the envelope *integerset* is available in library form, is then as shown:

```
program factors (input,output) ;

envelope integerset in library ;

var n1,n2 : integer ;

instance f1,f2 : integerset ;
```

```
procedure findprimefactors . . . ;

procedure printandremovecommonfactors . . . ;

procedure printotherfactors . . . ;

begin {factors}
    read (n1,n2) ;
    findprimefactors (n1,f1) ;
    findprimefactors (n2,f2) ;
    printandremovecommonfactors ;
    printotherfactors (n1,f1) ;
    printotherfactors (n2,f2)
end {factors}.
```

The important feature of this solution is that its logical function depends only on the defined properties of the *integerset* abstraction, and is independent of how the abstraction is implemented.

IMPLEMENTING INTEGERSET

The use of the abstract type *integerset* in programs such as the prime factors program is independent of its implementation, provided this implementation meets the requirements of the abstract type specification. To reinforce this point, we will now consider several alternative implementations of the abstract type *integerset*, all of which would enable execution of the prime factors program.

Our first implementation will maintain a list of the member values of a set as a chain of records. Such a chain is enabled by the following pointer type declarations:

```
type memberpointer = ↑memberrecord ;
     memberrecord = record
                         value : integer ;
                         next : memberpointer
                    end ;

var firstmember : memberpointer ;
```

Since the order in which the member values of the set are held is unimportant we will choose to build the chain in the most convenient way possible, which is to add each new member at the head of the chain. With this decision the *insert* operator is easily programmed as follows:

```
procedure *insert (i : integer) ;
  var newmember : memberpointer ;
  begin
    new (newmember) ;
    with newmember↑ do
    begin
      value := i ;
      next := firstmember
    end ;
    firstmember := newmember
  end {insert} ;
```

The *remove* operator must search the chain of members for an occurrence of the value to be removed, and if one is found remove it from the chain. To carry out the removal, however, the pointer to the preceding member record, if any, is required, so the removal procedure has the following more complicated form:

```
procedure *remove (i : integer) ;
  var thismember,previousmember : memberpointer ;
      valuefound : Boolean ;
  begin
    thismember := firstmember ; previousmember := nil ;
    valuefound := false ;
    while not valuefound and (thismember <> nil) do
      if thismember↑.value = i
      then valuefound := true
      else
      begin
        previousmember := thismember ;
        thismember := thismember↑.next
      end ;
    if valuefound then
    begin
      if previousmember = nil
      then firstmember := thismember↑.next
      else previousmember↑.next := thismember↑.next ;
      dispose (thismember)
    end
  end {remove} ;
```

The function *contains* must also search the chain of members, but needs no pointer to the preceding member record at each stage, so the following simpler code suffices:

```
function *contains (i : integer) : Boolean ;
  var thismember : memberpointer ;
      valuefound : Boolean ;
  begin
    thismember := firstmember ; valuefound := false ;
    while not valuefound and (thismember <> nil) do
      if thismember↑.value = i
      then valuefound := true
      else thismember := thismember↑.next ;
    contains := valuefound
  end {contains} ;
```

The function *empty* simply tests whether the *firstmember* pointer equals **nil**, but the operator *clear* must dispose of the records representing any existing members of the set as well as re-setting *firstmember* to **nil**. Its implementation therefore is as follows:

```
procedure *clear ;
  var nextmember : memberpointer ;
  begin
    while firstmember <> nil do
    begin
      nextmember := firstmember↑.next ;
      dispose (firstmember) ;
      firstmember := nextmember
    end
  end {clear} ;
```

The initialization code within the body of the *integerset* envelope ensures that the set is initially empty by the simpler operation:

```
firstmember := nil
```

With this initialization, an initial call to *clear* by the user program is unnecessary, but if carried out will have no adverse effect. To recover any storage used by residual members of the set at the end of its lifetime the finalization code in the envelope body should make a final call to the procedure *clear*. Thus the overall form of the *integerset* implementation using a chained representation of the members involved is as shown in Listing 7.

Listing 7

```
envelope integerset;

{ This envelope maintains an initially empty multiset  }
{ of integers, with operators clear, insert and remove, }
{ and predicates contains and empty                     }

type memberpointer = ^memberrecord;
     memberrecord = record
                        value: integer;
                        next: memberpointer
                    end;


var firstmember: memberpointer;

procedure *clear;
  var nextmember: memberpointer;
  begin
    while firstmember <> nil do
      begin
        nextmember := firstmember^.next;
        dispose(firstmember);
        firstmember := nextmember
      end
  end {clear};

procedure *insert(i: integer);
  var newmember: memberpointer;
  begin
    new(newmember);
    with newmember^ do
      begin
        value := i;
        next := firstmember
      end;
    firstmember := newmember
  end {insert};

procedure *remove(i: integer);
  var thismember, previousmember: memberpointer;
      valuefound: Boolean;
  begin
    thismember := firstmember;
    previousmember := nil;
    valuefound := false;
    while not valuefound and (thismember <> nil) do
      if thismember^.value = i
      then valuefound := true
      else begin
             previousmember := thismember;
             thismember := thismember^.next
           end;
```

```
       if valuefound
       then begin
               if previousmember = nil
               then firstmember := thismember^.next
               else previousmember^.next := thismember^.next;
               dispose(thismember)
            end
   end {remove};


function *contains(i: integer): Boolean;
   var thismember: memberpointer;
       valuefound: Boolean;
   begin
     thismember := firstmember;
     valuefound := false;
     while not valuefound and (thismember <> nil) do
       if thismember^.value = i
       then valuefound := true
       else thismember := thismember^.next;
     contains := valuefound
   end {contains};


function *empty: Boolean;
   begin empty := (firstmember = nil) end;


begin
   firstmember := nil;
   ###;
   clear
end {integerset};
```

This implementation of *integerset* is typical of chained representations for a variety of abstract data types, in the following ways:

(a) The amount of storage used is proportional to the actual number of components that exist in the data structure at any time, and no preliminary assumptions about the number of such components are required.

(b) Storage of the pointers themselves imposes an overhead on the amount of storage used. Since the storage required for each pointer is comparable to the storage required for an integer, this overhead is significant in the case of the *integerset*. For other structures involving more significant data items, the pointer storage overhead may be much less significant.

(c) Insertion of a new component or removal of an existing component on a chained list is achieved without any movement of other components on the list.

(d)   Access to individual components can only be gained by following appropriate chains of pointers. In the case of the chained list such as that used for *integerset* this enforces the linear search technique within the procedure *remove* and function *contains* and means that the time taken for a *remove* or *contains* operation on average is proportional to *n*, the number of components in the set at that time.

By way of contrast, consider now two alternative implementations of the abstract data type *integerset* using an array to hold the member values. Such an implementation is possible if a reasonable upperbound *max*, say, can be placed on the number of members contained by the set at any time. The set can·be represented by an integer array with *max* elements, together with a size variable indicating the number of members actually in the array at any time, thus:

> **var** *member* : **array** [1 . .*max*] **of** *integer* ;

In our first version of an array representation the member values will be held in the most convenient order for insertion, which is to add each member to the end of the existing set of members, i.e. using the next available element of the array. The logic is otherwise similar to that used for chained representation, except that removing a member involves moving the latest members stored back to fill the gap created by the removal. The complete implementation using an array in this way is shown in Listing 8.

Listing 8

```
envelope integerset;

{ This envelope maintains an initially empty multiset   }
{ of integers, with operators clear, insert and remove, }
{ and predicates contains and empty                     }
{                                                        }
{ assumes const max = maximum number of members;        }

var member: array [1..max] of integer;
    size: 0..max;

procedure *clear;
  begin size := 0 end;

procedure locate(i: integer; var position: integer);

  { finds position of first element = i in the array member, }
  { if one is present; otherwise position = size+1           }
```

```
  var valuefound: Boolean;
  begin
    position := 1;
    valuefound := false;
    while (position <= size) and not valuefound do
      if member[position] = i
      then valuefound := true
      else position := position + 1
  end {locate};

procedure *insert(i: integer);
  begin
    if size < max
    then begin
          size := size + 1;
          member[size] := i
        end
  end {insert};

procedure *remove(i: integer);
  var position: integer;
      next: 1..max;
  begin
    locate(i, position);
    if position <= size
    then begin
          size := size - 1;
          for next := position to size do
            member[next] := member[next + 1]
        end
  end {remove};

function *contains(i: integer): Boolean;
  var position: integer;
  begin
    locate(i, position);
    contains := (position <= size)
  end {contains};

function *empty: Boolean;
  begin empty := (size = 0) end;

begin
  size := 0;
  ***
end {integerset};
```

With the member values held in the arbitrary order determined by insertion and removal, this implementation is again forced to use a linear search through the members to implement the *remove* and *contains* operators. With an array representation, however, this is not necessarily so. We can instead choose to hold the members within the array in ascending value order. Doing so makes the *insert* operator more complex since it must now determine the correct position for insertion, but the advantage gained is that the *insert*, *remove* and *contains* operators can all determine the possible position of a member value more efficiently, by use of the *binary split search* technique.

In essence, the *binary split search* involves splitting the array area to be searched in half by comparing the value sought with the value held mid-way through the area. If the value sought is less than this mid-point value, then further searching can be limited to the array area preceding this mid-point (since the values are in ascending order), whereas if the value sought is greater than the mid-point value, searching can be limited to the array area beyond the mid-point value. By repeatedly applying this splitting technique, the area of search is quickly reduced to zero or one element which, in effect, means that the required position has been determined. In detail, this *binary split search* technique can be introduced to the *integerset* implementation by using the following procedure to locate a value *i* during the insertion, deletion or containment operations:

```
procedure locate (i : integer ; var position : integer) ;
   var top,bottom,midway : integer ;
   begin
     bottom := 1 ; top := size ;
     while bottom <= top do
     begin
       midway := (bottom + top) div 2 ;
       if member [midway] < i
       then bottom := midway + 1
       else top := midway − 1
     end ;
     position := bottom
   end {locate} ;
```

On completion of a call to procedure *locate*, the variable parameter *position* gives the position of the first member in the array with the value greater than or equal to *i*, if such a member exists, otherwise it gives the first free position in the array, i.e. (*size* + 1).

Since the *binary split search* technique halves the area of search at each step, the number of comparisons required to locate the position of a value is given by $\log_2 size + 1$.

Listing 9 shows a complete version of an array representation of our *integerset* abstraction, using ordered member storage and the binary split search technique for the *insert, remove* and *contains* operators. Note that both insertion and deletion now involve moving all members beyond the point of insertion or deletion, to maintain contiguous ordered storage of member values as required. The advantage of doing so is that the time taken to carry out the search required by the *delete* or *contains* operators is now proportional to log n, where n is the number of members in the set, rather than to n itself, as is the case with the implementation given in Listings 7 and 8. For large values of n this difference may be significant.

Listing 9

```
envelope integerset;

  { This envelope maintains an initially empty multiset   }
  { of integers, with operators clear, insert and remove, }
  { and predicates contains and empty                     }
  {                                                        }
  { assumes const max = maximum number of members;        }

  var member: array [1..max] of integer;
      size: 0..max;

  procedure *clear;
    begin size := 0 end;

  procedure locate(i: integer; var position: integer);

    { finds position of first element = i in the array member, }
    { if one is present; otherwise position = size+1           }

    var top, bottom, midway: integer;
    begin
      bottom := 1;
      top := size;
      while bottom <= top do
        begin
          midway := (bottom + top) div 2;
          if member[midway] < i
          then bottom := midway + 1
          else top := midway - 1
        end;
      position := bottom
    end {locate};
```

continued on page 106

Listing 9 – *continued*

```
procedure *insert(i: integer);
  var requiredposition: integer;
      next: 1..max;
  begin
    if size < max
    then begin
            locate(i, requiredposition);
            for next := size downto requiredposition do
              member[next + 1] := member[next];
            member[requiredposition] := i;
            size := size + 1
         end
  end {insert};
procedure *remove(i: integer);
  var possibleposition: integer;
      next: 1..max;
  begin
    locate(i, possibleposition);
    if possibleposition <= size
    then if member[possibleposition] = i
         then begin
                 size := size - 1;
                 for next := possibleposition to size do
                   member[next] := member[next + 1]
              end
  end {remove};
function *contains(i: integer): Boolean;
  var possibleposition: integer;
  begin
    locate(i, possibleposition);
    if possibleposition <= size
    then contains := (member[possibleposition] = i)
    else contains := false
  end {contains};

function *empty: Boolean;
  begin empty := (size = 0) end;

begin
  size := 0;
  ***
end {integerset};
```

In summary, the characteristics of the array or contiguous representations considered for our *integerset* abstraction are as follows:

(a)   The storage used is proportional to some predetermined maximum number of components, not the actual number that arise in any particular use of the set.

(b)   There is no storage overhead in storing individual member values.

(c)   Array storage of ordered component values allows enhanced searching times by techniques such as the *binary split search*.

(d)   Insertion and deletion of an ordered list held in contiguous storage in general involves movement of existing components.

The different characteristics noted for the chained and contiguous representations of *integerset* are typical of the characteristics of such representations for a wide variety of data structures, and they may affect the choice of implementation chosen for a particular abstract data type in a particular application. However, the most important characteristic of the implementations we have examined is that none of them affect the outward specification and hence the use of the abstract data type involved. This separation of implementation and use is an important aid to the correctness of programs using the abstraction.

There is, in fact, one minor difference between the chained and array implementations given for *integerset*. The implementations using an array representation above assume that the surrounding program defines a constant *max* that determines the maximum number of members to be held in the set at any time. In contrast, the chained representation neither requires nor assumes any such limit. To use the array representation of *integerset* in a program manipulating sets of up to 1000 integers, an appropriate retrieval command would be as follows:

> **envelope** *integerset* **in** *library*
>   (*where* **const** *max* = 1000 ;) ;

When using the library envelope that provides the chained representation of *integerset* the *where* clause in the retrieval command would be unnecessary. Note, however, that its inclusion would have no detrimental effect, since the existence of a global constant identifier *max* is irrelevant to the implementation of the chained representation.

This minor difference emphasizes the point that the complete interface between an envelope such as *integerset* and the program that uses it comprises:

(a)   The outward interface specification defined by the envelope as the set of starred identifiers that occur within it, and

(b)   the inward interface specification assumed by the envelope, i.e. the non-local identifiers on whose definition it relies. Typically, this inward interface requirement is fulfilled by the *where* clause in a retrieval command together with those pre-defined identifiers such as *integer*, *real*, etc., whose definition is assumed by all programs and program components.

From now on we will use appropriate comments in the head of each abstraction envelope to emphasize the assumptions on which the envelope relies.

GENERALIZING THE INTEGERSET ABSTRACT TYPE

The implementations of the *integerset* envelope that we have considered implement an abstract type whose values are *multisets* of *integers*. In doing so, the implementations assume the following:

(a)   that the global identifier *integer* denotes the type of the set members involved;

(b)   that the operators := , <, and = can be applied to operands of the type *integer*.

Apart from these, no other assumptions are made about the attributes of the type of the member values of the *multiset* involved, and the logic used in either implementation will work equally well for any member type that meets the above requirements. Thus, by replacing appropriate occurrences of the identifier *integer* in the implementations given for *integerset* by a more general identifier *basetype* we obtain a library envelope called *multiset*, say, which implements the *multiset* concept for any *basetype* that meets the above conditions. The interface provided by the envelope would now be defined as follows:

> **envelope** *multiset* ;
>
> > {*assumes*
> >   **const** *max* = *maximum number of members in multiset* ;
> >   **type** *basetype* = *type of members, with*
> >   *applicable operators* := , <, =}
>
> > **procedure** *clear ;
>
> > **procedure** *insert (*i* : *basetype*) ;
>
> > **procedure** *remove (*i* : *basetype*) ;
>
> > **function** *contains (*i* : *basetype*) : *Boolean* ;
>
> > **function** *empty : *Boolean* ;
>
> > **begin** {*multiset*}
> > {*initially multiset is empty*}
> > ***
> > **end** {*multiset*} ;

This envelope could be retrieved to obtain an implementation of the *integerset* abstract type as before, as follows:

> **envelope** *integerset* = *multiset* **in** *library*
> (*where* **const** *max* = 1000 ;
>   **type** *basetype* = *integer* ;) ;

whereas to obtain an envelope that implements a *multiset* of not more than one hundred letters we could use the following retrieval command:

> **envelope** *letterset* = *multiset* **in** *library*
> (*where* **const** *max* = 100 ;
>   **type** *basetype* = *'A' ..'Z'* ;) ;

In Pascal, the types that conform to the requirements listed above for the *basetype* of our envelope *multiset* are the predefined types *integer*, *real*, and *char* together with any program-defined enumerated type, subrange or string type. The envelope *multiset* is immediately usable, therefore, for any of these *basetypes*.

In some applications, however, it may be logical to construct *multisets* with *basetypes* that do not meet those requirements, for example, *multisets* with member values of other more complex structured types. A more general *multiset* envelope that overcomes these limitations could be constructed by replacing all uses of the operators < and = on operands of type *basetype* by calls to functions *lessthan* and *equals*, each of which accepts two *basetype* values as parameters and returns an appropriate Boolean result. In effect, this alters the inward interface specification assumed by our *multiset* envelope to the existence of the named type *basetype* to which the operator := and the functions *lessthan* and *equals* are applicable, thus:

> **envelope** *multiset2* ;
>
> {*assumes*
>   **const** *max* = *maximum number of members in multiset* ;
>   **type** *basetype* = *type of members, with* := *applicable* ;
>   **function** *lessthan* (*b1,b2* : *basetype*) : *Boolean* ;
>   **function** *equal* (*b1,b2* : *basetype*) : *Boolean*}
>
> **procedure** **clear* ;
>   . . .
> **begin** . . . **end** {*multiset2*} ;

To use this more general abstraction to create and manipulate multisets of members of some type *T*, the user program must provide suitable functions for order and equality tests on values of type T, and supply these in an appropriate retrieval command, thus:

type $T = \ldots$;

function *equalT* ($t1,t2$: T) : *Boolean* ; . . .

function *lessT* ($t1,t2$: T) : *Boolean* ; . . .

envelope *Tset* = *multiset2* **in** *library*
   (*where* **const** *max* = . . . ;
            type *basetype* = T ;
            function *lessthan* = *lessT* ;
            function *equal* = *equalT* ;) ;

In this general form, the envelope *multiset2* may be used with a *basetype* that is any Pascal type, other than a *file* type. As such, it provides a very general facility for the use of *multisets* in Pascal programs.

DEALING WITH ERRORS

One benefit of using the data types provided in a language like Pascal is that illogical operations on values of a type are excluded. In some cases, this is achieved simply by limiting the operators available for certain types, for example, the operators + and − may be used on values of type *integer* but not on values of type *char*. In other cases, however, the illogical operations depend on the particular values of the objects involved; thus, while a division of one integer by another using the **div** operator is provided in Pascal, division by the value 0 is an error and will be detected if it occurs during the execution of a Pascal program. A third class of errors arises not from the properties of the types themselves, but from limitations that the implementation imposes upon them, for example, the type *integer* in principle imposes no limits on the range of values involved. In practice, however, implementations must impose such limits so that performing an operation which produces an integer value beyond the maximum permitted by a particular implementation gives rise to an error known as *overflow*. The detection at compile-time or at run-time of each class of error is an important benefit derived from the use of languages such as Pascal.

In general, a similar range of errors is possible for abstract data types. Consider again the *integerset* example: its specification limits the range of operators applicable to those provided as starred procedures and functions and so excludes the application of any other illogical operators at compile-time. In some cases, however, the available operators should not be applied to particular values of the abstract type. Thus, it is an error to attempt to insert a new member value in a set that already contains *max* members, and doing so should be detected as a run-time error. It is important that the implementation of an abstract data type pays as much attention to the detection of error situations as the implementation of a programming language pays to run-time errors, such as division by zero or integer overflow. In practice, there are several ways in which the implementor of an abstract data type may try to do so, and in this section we consider the various possibilities.

Two general strategies exist for handling run-time error situations. One is to treat all such errors as *fatal errors* that terminate the execution of the program concerned. This is the normal approach taken to run-time errors in Pascal. The other strategy is to treat such error situations as *exceptions* that the user program may detect and react to in some appropriate way. This approach is not illustrated by the handling of any run-time errors in Pascal systems but it has always been available in low-level programming systems such as assembly languages, where, for example, explicit instructions to test the overflow register of the machine are provided. The facility is now also provided by the exception handling mechanism in Ada, which is deliberately designed to provide a uniform approach to the programmed handling of both system-detected and program-detected error situations.

Consider first, the implementation of the fatal error approach to run-time errors detectable within abstract data types. In some cases, no explicit action is required at all as the abstract error leads directly to a corresponding language-defined error in the execution of its implementation. For example, if we program *insert* in the array implementations of *multiset* without any regard to the possibility that the array may already be full, as in Listings 8 and 9, an *array subscript error* will occur if insertion in a full multiset is attempted, and will be reported as such by the underlying Pascal system. Thus, the program error is detected but the diagnostic message provided by the language implementation is not meaningful in terms of the abstract *multiset* type. A better solution, therefore, is to include explicit code in the implementation of *insert* to detect and report the error in terms of a meaningful message for the abstract *multiset* type, as follows:

```
procedure *insert (i : basetype) ;
  begin
    if size = max
    then error ('multiset overflow on insertion')
    else begin
          . . . {insert i as before} . . .
        end
  end {insert} ;
```

where the procedure *error* is assumed to print or display the message provided as parameter and then terminate execution of the program in some way enabled by the underlying language system. The existence of such a procedure *error* will be assumed in handling all fatal errors detected in all subsequent abstract data type implementations in this text.

Enabling abstract data type errors to be handled by the user program is clumsy in Pascal. It can be done by adding an extra parameter to each operator procedure or function within which an error may be detected, whose purpose is simply to indicate to the calling program whether or not such an error has occurred. For example, the procedure *insert* for the array representation of our *multiset* abstract type might be extended as follows:

```
procedure *insert (i : basetype ;
                          var overflow : Boolean) ;
   begin
      if size = max
      then overflow := true
      else begin
             overflow := false ;
             . . . {insert i as before} . . .
           end
   end {insert} ;
```

The calling program must now supply a second Boolean parameter to receive this error indication, even in those cases when no error can possibly occur. A slightly less clumsy alternative is to replace individual error monitoring parameters by a single visible error flag for the envelope as a whole, whose value is reset when an error is detected:

```
envelope multiset ;
   . . .
   var *error : ( *none,*overflow, . . .) ;
   . . .
   procedure *insert (i : basetype) ;
      begin
         if size = max
         then error := overflow
         else . . .
      end ;

   begin {multiset}
      size := 0 ; error := none ;
      ***
   end {multiset} ;
```

No matter how the errors are indicated by the abstraction, immediate handling of such errors by the user program complicates the program logic concerned. For example, each use of the *insert* operator in the user program may now have the following general form:

> *S.insert* (*x*, *error*) ;
> **if** *error*
> **then** . . . {*take remedial action*} . . .
> **else** . . . {*continue normal processing*} . . .

It should be noted that with this approach the complexity of the user program code is no less than that required to avoid causing the error in the first place by making use of an appropriately defined abstract type facility. In the case of the *insert* operator this might be as follows:

> **if** *S.full*
> **then** {*take remedial action*}
> **else begin**
> > *S.insert* (*x*)
> > {*continue processing*}
> **end**

Thus the provision of a function *full*, to test whether a subsequent call to *insert* will cause a run-time error, creates no greater complexity either in the abstract *multiset* type or in the program that uses it than the facilities required to enable handling of the error after it has occurred.

In languages such as Ada that provide exception-handling facilities, the code required in the user program to handle errors detected within an implementation of an abstraction may be less clumsy. However, there is still a strong design argument for enabling the user program to avoid causing the error when this is possible, rather than dealing with it after it has occurred. In the remainder of this book, enabling the avoidance of run-time errors by the provision of appropriate facilities in the abstract data types considered will be the normal approach taken, together with the fatal error method for handling those errors that actually do occur.

STRUCTURE TRAVERSING OPERATORS

In writing the procedure *printotherfactors* for the prime factors program which we considered earlier we used the following loop to print out the members of the integerset f:

```
trial := 2 ;
while trial <= n do
  if f.contains (trial)
  then write (trial)
  else trial := trial + 1
```

The process of applying the same operation (in this case *write*) to each member of a set, or more generally to each component of a data structure with components of the same type, is required sufficiently often to justify its provision as a standard operator for the data structure concerned. In the case of the multiset abstraction we might extend the range of operators to include the following procedure:

procedure **traverse* (**procedure** $p(x : basetype)$) ;

whose effect is to apply its parametric procedure p to each member value of the multiset in turn.

With this additional operator the procedure *printotherfactors* can be rewritten as:

```
procedure printotherfactors (n : integer ; instance f : integerset) ;

  procedure printfactor (factor : integer) ;
    begin write (factor) end ;

  begin
    write ('Other factors of ', n, ' are') ;
    f.traverse (printfactor) ;
    writeln
  end {printotherfactors} ;
```

where the procedure *printfactor* is introduced only because Pascal does not allow predefined procedures such as *write* to be passed as parameters.

This introduction of a *traverse* operator has two advantages:

(a) the user program requirement is now directly expressible in terms of the abstraction provided, and

(b) the implementation of traversal can take advantage of the particular representation chosen for the abstraction.

How the latter is done depends on a more precise definition of the *traverse* operator. If we decide that the order in which member values are traversed is not pre-determined, then each implementation is free to carry out the traversal in whatever order suits the chosen representation. For the chained representation this would be as follows:

```
procedure *traverse (procedure p(x : basetype)) ;
  var thismember : memberpointer ;
  begin
    thismember := firstmember ;
    while thismember <> nil do
    begin
      p (thismember↑.value) ;
      thismember := thismember↑.next
    end
  end {traverse} ;
```

while for the array representations the most convenient code would be as follows:

```
procedure *traverse (procedure p(x : basetype)) ;
  var i : 1 . . max ;
  begin
    for i := 1 to size do p (member[i])
  end {traverse} ;
```

In the case of the chained representation shown in Listing 7 this would result in a traversal of the member values in the reverse order to that in which they were inserted in the multiset. For the un-ordered array representation (Listing 8) traversal would be in the same order as insertion, while for the ordered chained representation (Listing 9) traversal would be in ascending value order of member values.

If we were to stipulate ascending value order as part of the definition of the traverse operator, then the first two implementations would become significantly more complex. In effect, the most convenient way of enabling value order traversal is to maintain the members in value order throughout, as is already done in the third implementation. The general strategy for insertion, deletion and searching in a chained representation of ordered values has already been illustrated in the *wordlist* implementation given in Chapter 4.

Traversal operators are a convenient facility for many commonly occurring data structures, but in practice they must be defined and used with some care as they can give rise to programming errors which the implementation cannot always detect. To see this, consider now the procedure *printandremovecommonfactors* in the prime factors program, which used a trial and error loop to identify, print and remove the factors common to two sets, as

follows:

```
trial := . . . ;
limit := . . . ;
while trial <= limit do
    if f1.contains (trial) and f2.contains (trial)
    then begin
            write (trial) ;
            f1.remove (trial) ;
            f2.remove (trial)
        end
    else trial := trial + 1
```

If the *traverse* operator is available it is tempting to re-express this loop as:

```
f1.traverse (examinef2)
```

where the procedure *examinef2* tests whether the member found in *f*1 is also in *f*2, and if so prints and removes it from both, i.e.

```
procedure examinef2 (x : integer) ;
    begin
        if f2.contains (x) then
        begin
            write (x) ;
            f1.remove (x) ;
            f2.remove (x)
        end
    end {examinef2} ;
```

In practice, however, this solution would not work correctly with either implementation—because the *f*1.*remove*(*x*) operation alters the state of the multiset under traversal. In one case an attempt to access a field of a record already disposed of would occur, in the other the backward movement of member values during deletion would cause the immediately following member to be overlooked. In general, use of the traverse operator is valid only if the operation *p* applied to each member value leaves the overall multiset unaltered, which is not so in the case of the suggested code for *printandremovecommonfactors*.

Unfortunately, it is impossible for the implementation to enforce this rule on the use of *traverse*, and so the avoidance of such errors remains the user's reponsibility. Such unavoidable insecurity commonly arises when abstract operators take procedures as parameters and the actual procedures so called can alter the representation of the abstraction (by use of other operators). The fact that total security of the defined abstraction against misuse can no longer be guaranteed is a significant disadvantage which must be balanced against the convenience or efficiency provided by operators such as *traverse*. In subsequent chapters where the provision of traversal operators for a variety of data structures is illustrated, each case must be considered in the light of the security trade-off involved.

A FREQUENCY HISTOGRAM

To introduce the concept of an abstract data type, we have deliberately used a variation on the familiar set type provided in Pascal. By doing so, the analogy between abstract data types and those types provided directly within a programming language has been demonstrated. In practice, of course, abstract data types may take a wide variety of forms, some very different from the type concepts provided in any particular programming language. To illustrate this, consider the following alternative example.

   A frequency histogram is used to record the number of observations of the value of some variable falling in each of a number of intervals between two limiting values. For instance, given a set of examination marks for a class of students, a histogram might be constructed to record the number of students whose marks fall in each of the ten intervals 0..10, 11..20, ..., 91...100. Such a histogram is often represented graphically as shown in Fig. 6.1.

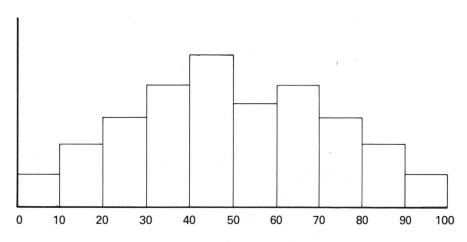

Figure 6.1 A graphical histogram display

Ignoring the implementation of such a histogram for the moment but considering it to be an abstract data object, what are the characteristic operations that might be performed in association with it? Three typical operations are:

- the recording, or tabulation, of a given observation;
- the display, in some standard form, of the contents of the histogram, either in graphical form (possibly as shown above) or as a sequence of printed values;
- a frequency function which returns a percentage indicating the relative frequency of the observations falling in a given interval.

Such a histogram may be provided as an abstract data type implemented by an envelope with the following interface:

envelope *histogram* ;

> *{assumes an integer constant numberofintervals, and real*
> *or integer constants lower, upper determining*
> *the range of values to be tabulated}*

type *interval* : $1 . . numberofintervals$;

procedure **tabulate* (*y* : *real*) ;

procedure **display* (**var** *f* : *text*) ;

function **relativefrequency* (*i* : *interval*) : *real* ;

begin
   {histogram is initially empty}
   ***
end *{histogram}* ;

Note that the value parameter of the function *relativefrequency* is specified as a subrange which is in turn determined by the constant *numberofintervals* supplied by the user program. Any actual parameter falling outside this range will automatically be flagged as an error by the Pascal system, with an appropriate message such as *value out of range*.

As an example of the use of the histogram, now consider the examination marks application. A file contains details of the examination marks for a class of students. Each record in the file consists of the name of the student together with an array containing the mark obtained by the student in each of five examination subjects, expressed as a percentage. A program is required which will calculate and display the number of students obtaining an average mark in each of the intervals $0 . . 10, 11 . . 20, . . . , 91 . . 100$.

Using the envelope specified above, the program might take the following form:

```
program exammarks (studentfile, output) ;

    const numberofintervals = 10 ;
        subjects = 5 ;

    envelope histogram in library
        (where const lower = 0 ; upper = 100 ;) ;

    instance marks : histogram ;

    var studentfile : file of record
                              name : packed array [1..15] of char ;
                              grade : array [1..subjects] of 0..100
                          end ;
        i : 1..subjects ;
        j : 1..numberofintervals ;
        total : 0..maxint ;

    begin {exammarks}
        reset (studentfile) ;
        while not eof(studentfile) do
        begin
            with studentfile ↑ do
            begin
                total := 0 ;
                for i := 1 to subjects do total := total + grade[i] ;
                marks.tabulate (total/subjects)
            end ;
            get (studentfile)
        end ;

        page ;
        writeln ( 'HISTOGRAM OF EXAMINATION MARKS ' ) ;
        writeln ;
        marks.display ;
        writeln ;

        writeln ('RELATIVE FREQUENCIES IN EACH INTERVAL' )
        writeln ;
        for j := 1 to numberofintervals do
            writeln (j : 3, trunc (marks.relativefrequency(j)) : 3, ' %')
    end {exammarks}.
```

Now consider the implementation of the *histogram* envelope. An array may be used to record the number of occurrences in each interval. The *tabulate* procedure then simply works out which interval its parameter belongs to and increments the corresponding element of the array by 1. The relative frequency function requires the maintenance of a count of the observations recorded in the histogram in order to work out the percentage lying within the interval specified as its parameter. Thus the *tabulate* and *relativefrequency* operators, and the corresponding initialization that they require, are easily programmed.

Most of the complexity in implementing the histogram envelope comes within the *display* operator. The simplest means of producing the 'graphical' output is to print a bar chart with the interval axis vertical. For example, assuming that the number of observations in each interval from the examination marks program are:

   8,10,12,15,18,20,18,6,6,1

then it might print the histogram in the form shown in Fig. 6.2.

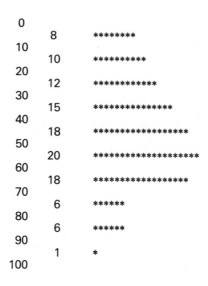

Figure 6.2   A horizontal histogram display

Careful coding is required to print the interval boundaries in the most appropriate format for the wide variety of scale and accuracy that may occur. Completion of the histogram envelope within the outline given above is left as an exercise.

SUMMARY

The examples in this chapter have served to introduce the concept of an abstract data type, and to demonstrate how a programmer may effectively extend the range of concepts provided in a general purpose language by defining such an abstract data type and implementing some suitable concrete representation of it.

The implementation of an abstract type can and should be separate or hidden from the program that uses it. In the case of the multiset example we have seen that several alternative implementations may be possible, with different characteristics in their performance and the storage they require. The two classes of representation illustrated—those based on contiguous storage as provided by Pascal arrays, and those based on chained storage as provided by Pascal's pointer mechanism—are typical of the choice available for the representation of many abstract data types.

We have also seen that with a suitable language facility, such data abstractions can be defined and implemented in a flexible general-purpose form for retrieval from a library. The savings in programmer effort and the increased reliability of programs that can be achieved by use of such standard tested library envelopes are obvious.

In the following chapters we look at various commonly required abstract data types not directly provided in languages such as Pascal, and also at their implementations. In each case, we illustrate how these data types can be implemented as envelopes suitable for inclusion in a library. Programs using these data abstractions can then retrieve them without concerning themselves in any way with their implementation.

EXERCISES

6.1 Modify the definition of the *histogram* envelope outlined in this chapter so that it accepts as a parameter a character string to be output as a heading before the histogram itself.

Complete an implementation of the *histogram* envelope you have defined.

Devise a test harness and suitable input data to test your *histogram* envelope systematically.

Use your *histogram* envelope in a program which reads a client file such as that defined for the computer dating service example in Chapter 3, and prints out separate histograms of the age distributions of male and female clients using 5 year age intervals.

6.2   The *Sieve of Eratosthenes* is a method of finding all the prime numbers in the range $2 . . N$. All the numbers in this range are initially put on the 'sieve' and the following actions repeated until the sieve is empty—

> select and remove the smallest number in the sieve (necessarily a prime)
> and then remove all multiples of that number from the sieve.

Write a program which uses the *integerset* abstract data type to find all the prime numbers up to some input value *N*. Why is this multiset form of integerset impractical when using the Sieve method to find large prime numbers?

6.3   An abstract data type is to be defined which provides the concept of a set of values of an ordered base type as defined in Pascal, i.e., as sets in which each element value can appear at most once. The required set operators include

> insertion and removal of values
> test of set membership
> test of set emptiness
> assignment of ranges of values to a set
> finding the number of elements present in a set
> finding the minimum value in a set.

Specify this type as an envelope suitable for inclusion in a library. Implement the envelope using a contiguous representation and use it to rewrite the Sieve of Eratosthenes program of the previous exercise.

6.4   The names of the teams in a league are held, one per line, in a text file. League tables are to be maintained for each of a number of such leagues as instances of an abstract data type with the following interface:

> **envelope** *leaguetable* (**var** *teamnamefile* : *text*) ;
>
> { *assumes* **const** *maxteams* = . . . *maximum number of teams in* }
> {   *any such league* . . .   }
> {   **const** *namelength* = . . . *maximum team name length* . . .}
> {   **type** *teamname* = **packed array** [1 . . *namelength*] **of** *char* }
>
>   **type** *leagueposition : 1 . . *maxteams* ;
>   *pointsrange = 0 . . *maxint* ;
>   *scorerange = 0 . . *maxint* ;

> **procedure** *recordresult (team1 : teamname ;
>   score1 : scorerange ;
>   team2 : teamname ;
>   score2 : scorerange) ;
>   { records result of a game }
>
> **procedure** *givedetailsof (team : teamname ;
>   **var** teamnameerror : Boolean ;
>   **var** position : leagueposition ;
>   **var** points : pointsrange) ;
>   { gives details of a particular team's league record }
>
> **procedure** *traverse (**procedure** p (team : teamname ;
>   position : leagueposition ;
>   points : pointsrange)) ;
>   { apply p to each team's record in order of league position }

Implement this envelope using a contiguous representation (and employing some appropriate scheme for the awarding of points to the teams involved in each result recorded). Use it to build a system which records league results, enables queries about league standings and team records to be answered, and prints out ordered league tables on demand.

7

Stacks and Queues

SEQUENCES AND THEIR SUBCLASSIFICATION

A *sequence* is an abstraction of a number of practical data structures such as strings, stacks, lists and queues. In abstract data terms a sequence may be defined as:

An arbitrary number of items of a given type in some significant order.

For example:

(a)   Character strings such as words and sentences may be thought of as values of a type which is a sequence of characters whose order is clearly significant. Although it may be possible to place an upper bound on the number of characters in a word, it is not possible to place a bound on the length of a sentence.

(b)   A collection of client records for the computer dating system described earlier might be held on, say, magnetic tape, thus forming a sequence of such records. The client records on this file might be held in alphabetical order.

(c)   A list of towns visited on a coach tour form a sequence in which the town names are held in the order in which they were visited, e.g. Amsterdam   Cologne   Heidelberg   Munich   Salzburg   Vienna Budapest.

Sequences occur in many forms in programming. Pascal itself provides two kinds of sequence—an array may be thought of as a fixed-length sequence of values of the same type, and a Pascal file is a sequence of variable length.

In general, a wide variety of basic operations may be applied to sequences. In particular, updating operations applied to sequences may add or
remove individual items at the beginning, at the end of, or at any point
within, the sequence. In practice sequences, and the implementations chosen for them, are usually classified according to the updating operations
applied.

An *input stream* is a sequence on which the only updating operation
allowed is the removal or *reading* of the first item and its assignment to some
variable. An *output stream* is a sequence for which the only permitted
operation is the appending or *writing* of a new value to the end of the
sequence. We have already met such sequences in Pascal as the standard
input and output streams (sequences of characters) represented as the
standard text files *input* and *output*, for which the procedures *read* and *write*
respectively are provided as operators. Input and output streams held on
external storage media are commonly known as *sequential files*, and Pascal's
file concept supports their manipulation.

A *stack* is a sequence for which the only permitted operations are those
of appending a new value to its end and removing the last item appended, i.e.
insertion and removal take place at the same end. The order of manipulation
of items within a stack is thus last-in, first-out or alternatively, first-in,
last-out. For this reason stacks are sometimes referred to as LIFO or FILO
data structures.

A *queue* is a sequence which permits only the operations of appending a
new value to the end and removing an item from the start of the sequence. In
this case items are processed on a first-in, first-out, or last-in, last-out
basis—hence the acronyms FIFO or LILO.

A *deque* (double ended queue) is a sequence which permits reading and
writing of items at both ends.

A *list* is a sequence which permits insertion and deletion of component
items at any point within the sequence, as determined by the requirements of
its application. Thus an ordered list is a sequence whose component data
items are held in a particular order determined by some property of the
items.

In the remainder of this chapter we concentrate on the definition,
implementation and use of stacks, queues and deques. In the following
chapter we consider lists in a similar manner.

DEFINING A STACK

A stack is a sequence in which all insertions and deletions take place at one
end of the sequence, usually referred to as the *top* of the stack. Hence, the
item most recently inserted in a stack is always the first to be removed.

An everyday example of a stack-like structure is a pile of plates in a kitchen cupboard. As plates are returned to the cupboard, they are placed on the top of the pile—whenever plates are required, they are taken from the top of the pile. If plates are taken and returned individually, then the last plate to be returned to the pile is always the first to be removed.

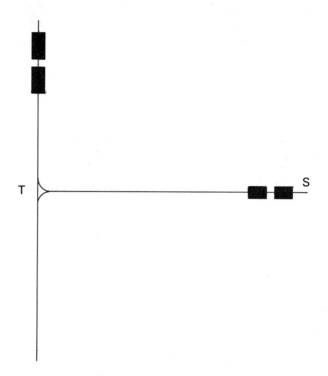

Figure 7.1   A railway siding

Another example is that of a railway siding, as illustrated in Fig. 7.1. As railway wagons enter the siding S they cannot leave again until any wagons that subsequently enter the siding have left. Thus, for instance, a siding may be used to reverse the order of a train of wagons or, in conjunction with a straight-ahead section T, to arbitrarily re-order the wagons of a train.

Stacks are of great importance in many computing applications. They are used in many problems that require looking ahead in a stream of information while remembering what has been scanned during the look-ahead. A common example is the computer evaluation of an arithmetic expression, such as:

$$3 * (5 - 2)$$

in which, for example, the value 3 and the operator * must be remembered until the sub-expression in parentheses has been evaluated.

The use of a stack is also fundamental to the implementation of recursive block-structured languages such as Pascal. Procedure calls and exits take place in a last-called first-exited fashion. To enable procedure calls to take place, return addresses are remembered by storing them in a stack—on entry to a procedure the return address (that of the instruction to be executed upon exit from the procedure) is added to a stack, and on exit from any procedure the address of the next instruction is obtained by removing an address from the stack. A stack is also used for holding the data items associated with the active procedures of a program. We shall examine this use of stacks in greater detail later in this chapter.

Figure 7.2 A conceptual stack

A stack is normally viewed as a vertical sequence of items, hence the use of the term *top*. In the stack shown in Fig. 7.2, the item most recently added to the stack, S4, is referred to as the *topmost* item while item S1 has been in the stack for the longest time.

Four operations associated with a stack may be identified immediately:

(a) the insertion of a new element X into a stack—this is usually described as *pushing* X onto the stack;

(b) the removal of the topmost element from a stack—this is usually described as *popping* a value off the stack;

(c) a test to determine whether a stack is *empty* or contains some elements—this is necessary to ensure that we do not try to pop a value from a stack which is currently empty;

(d) conversely, a stack may have a maximum size associated with it, and hence a test is required to ascertain whether it is possible to push a new value on to the stack, i.e. that the stack is not *full*.

These four operations may thus be defined as starred (externally accessible) procedures and functions of an envelope representing the abstract concept of a stack of items of some given type *itemtype*:

> **envelope** *stack* ;
>
>> {*assumes* **type** *itemtype for items in stack, with* := *applicable*}
>>
>> **function** *empty : *Boolean* ;
>>
>> **function** *full : *Boolean* ;
>>
>> **procedure** *push (*x* : *itemtype*) ;
>>   {*if stack is not full then x is added as the
>>   topmost item, otherwise an error occurs*}
>>
>> **procedure** *pop (**var** *x* : *itemtype*) ;
>>   {*if stack is not empty the topmost item is removed and
>>   assigned to x, otherwise an error occurs*}
>>
>> **begin**
>>   {*initially the stack is empty*}
>>   *******
>>
>> **end** {*stack*} ;

A SIMPLE USE OF STACKS

As an example of the use of this abstraction of a stack, consider a simple problem—that of reversing an input sequence of characters terminated by an asterisk '*'. Using the abstract data type defined above with *char* as the required item type, the following program will perform the task:

> **program** *reversecharacters* (*input,output*) ;
>
>> **envelope** *stack* **in** *library*
>>   (*where* **type** *itemtype* = *char*;) ;
>>
>> **instance** *S* : *stack* ;
>>
>> **var** *ch* : *char* ;
>>
>> **begin** {*reversecharacters*}
>>   **repeat**
>>   *read* (*ch*) ; *S.push* (*ch*)
>>   **until** *ch* = '*' ;
>>   **repeat**
>>   *S.pop* (*ch*) ; *write* (*ch*)
>>   **until** *S.empty*
>> **end** {*reversecharacters*}.

A solution to the same problem can be programmed using a recursive procedure, viz:

```
procedure reverseinput ;
  var ch : char ;
  begin
    read (ch) ;
    if ch <> '*' then reverseinput ;
    write (ch)
  end {reverseinput} ;
```

This illustrates a common property of many recursive procedures—that they may be programmed non-recursively as procedures which consist of one or more loops and which may make use of a stack to store the data items represented as local variables in the recursive procedure. This point is reinforced by a subsequent example later in this chapter.

CONTIGUOUS REPRESENTATION OF STACKS

If it is possible and convenient to place some upper bound *maxitems* on the maximum number of items that may be held at any time in a stack, then an array of *maxitems* elements may be used to hold the items of the stack, together with a variable whose value indicates the number of items currently in the stack, i.e. the length of the stack.

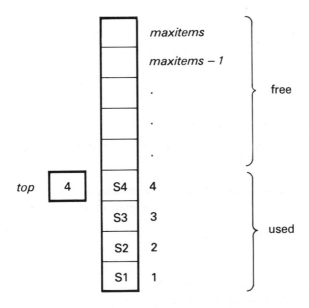

Figure 7.3 Contiguous representation of a stack

Insertions in the stack take place at element position $top+1$ (Fig. 7.3); deletions cause the value in element position top to be removed. Initially, the stack is empty and so top must be initialized to the value zero. Hence, if our stack contains elements of some type *itemtype*, then the data structure required to represent the stack is defined by:

```
var top : 0 . . maxitems ;
    items : array [1 . . maxitems] of itemtype ;
```

With this representation we may now define our four operators—*empty*, *full*, *push* and *pop*. The initialization action is simply to set the value of *top* to zero.

The full and empty operations are implemented as functions which examine the current value of *top* and return a Boolean result:

```
function *full : Boolean ;
  begin
    full := (top=maxitems)
  end {full} ;

function *empty : Boolean ;
  begin
    empty := (top=0)
  end {empty} ;
```

The *push* procedure inserts a given value x on top of the stack by incrementing *top* and assigning the value x to the element of the array *items* indexed by *top*, first checking that the stack is not already full:

```
procedure *push (x : itemtype) ;
  begin
    if top = maxitems
    then error ('stack overflow')
    else begin top := top+1 ; items[top] := x end
  end {push} ;
```

The *pop* operator assigns the topmost value in *items* to its variable parameter x and decrements *top*, but first checks for emptiness:

```
procedure *pop (var x : itemtype) ;
  begin
    if top = 0
    then error ('stack underflow')
    else begin x := items[top] ; top := top−1 end
  end {pop} ;
```

Listing 10

```
envelope stack;

{ This envelope implements a stack of up to maxitems items,     }
{ with operators push and pop, and predicates empty and full.  }
{                                                               }
{ assumes const maxitems = maximum number of items in stack;   }
{          type itemtype = any type with := applicable;         }

var top: 0..maxitems;
    items: array [1..maxitems] of itemtype;

function *empty: Boolean;
  begin empty := (top = 0) end;

function *full: Boolean;
  begin full := (top = maxitems) end;

procedure *push(x: itemtype);
  begin
    if top = maxitems
    then error('stack overflow')
    else begin
           top := top + 1;
           items[top] := x
         end
  end {push};

procedure *pop(var x: itemtype);
  begin
    if top = 0
    then error('stack underflow')
    else begin
           x := items[top];
           top := top - 1
         end
  end {pop};

begin
  top := 0;
  ***
end {stack};
```

Listing 10 shows a complete version of the stack envelope implemented using an array representation for the *stack* items.

Such an envelope could be held in source form in a library file and then retrieved from the library using a retrieval specification giving a suitable value for *maxitems* and supplying the type to be used as *itemtype*. Thus,

assuming the input sequence contains not more than one hundred characters, our character reversal program now needs to be modified so that the
retrieval specification takes the form:

> **envelope** *stack* **in** *library*
>   (*where* **const** *maxitems* = 100 ;
>   **type** *itemtype* = *char*;) ;

Once again, note that outside the envelope the implementation of a stack is
totally hidden from the user block, which is only aware of the abstract
operations that are provided by the envelope.

The obvious drawback of this contiguous representation is that the user
has to estimate an upper bound for the number of items in the stack. If this
estimate turns out to be too low, then stack overflow will occur during
execution of the program. On the other hand, if the estimate is too high, this
may result in poor storage utilization in a program using a number of such
stacks. A solution which overcomes this problem is the use of non-
contiguous or chained representations.

CHAINED REPRESENTATION OF STACKS

With this representation each item in the stack is stored in a dynamically
allocated record which is linked by a pointer to the record of the previous
item in the stack. A stack is thus represented by a pointer in the record for its

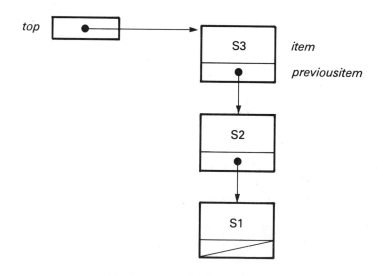

Figure 7.4   Chained representation of a stack

topmost item, as illustrated in Fig. 7.4. Since the last item in the stack has no predecessor, its *previousitem* pointer has the value **nil**. Note that the pointers link the records in the order in which they are removed from the stack.

Such a representation can be described in Pascal by means of pointer types, viz:

type *stackpointer* = ↑*stackrecord* ;
       stackrecord = **record**
                   item : *itemtype* ;
                   previousitem : *stackpointer*
             end ;

The stack is then represented simply as a pointer to its topmost item, i.e. as a value of type *stackpointer*:

var *top* : *stackpointer* ;

The initialization of the stack now consists of indicating that it is initially empty by setting the value of the pointer *top* to **nil**. .

The *empty* operator checks that the stack is not empty by testing to determine whether the stack is represented by the pointer value **nil**.

function **empty* : *Boolean* ;
   begin
     empty := (*top* = **nil**)
   end {*empty*} ;

Assuming that we cannot run out of dynamically allocated storage (and Pascal does not provide us with a means of checking for this possibility), the function *full* always returns the value *false*, and might be programmed as follows:

function **full* : *Boolean* ;
   begin
     full := *false*
   end {*full*} ;

However, it is more efficient to implement this as a starred constant of the envelope, i.e.

const **full* = *false* ;

This change is transparent from the outside since a call of a parameterless function of an envelope is syntactically equivalent to the use of a starred constant.

The operator *push* makes use of a local pointer variable *p* to create a new stackrecord for the item being inserted into the stack. This new record is then inserted at the front of the sequence of records pointed to by the top-of-stack pointer, viz:

```
procedure *push (x : itemtype) ;
  var p : stackpointer ;
  begin
    new (p) ;
    with p ↑ do
    begin item := x ; previousitem := top end ;
    top := p
  end {push} ;
```

and we do not have to concern ourselves with the possibility of stack overflow.

The *pop* operation returns the stackrecord of the popped item to free storage, after checking for stack underflow, thus:

```
procedure *pop (var x : itemtype) ;
  var p : stackpointer ;
  begin
    if top = nil
    then error ('stack underflow')
    else begin
         x := top↑.item ;
         p := top ; top := p↑.previousitem ;
         dispose (p)
      end
  end {pop} ;
```

One new problem now arises. When the use of the stack is complete, the storage occupied by any residual items that have not been popped off the stack should be recovered. This may be achieved by coding the finalization part of the envelope to dispose of any remaining stack records.

Our second version of the stack envelope, this time using a chained stack representation, is thus as shown in Listing 11.

Listing 11

```
envelope stack;

  { This envelope implements a stack of items of type itemtype, }
  { with operators push and pop, and predicates empty and full. }
  {                                                              }
  { assumes type itemtype = any type with := applicable;        }

  const *full = false;
```

```
type stackpointer = ^stackrecord;
     stackrecord = record
                       item: itemtype;
                       previousitem: stackpointer
                   end;

var top: stackpointer;

function *empty: Boolean;
  begin empty := (top = nil) end;

procedure *push(x: itemtype);
  var p: stackpointer;
  begin
    new(p);
    with p^ do
      begin
        item := x;
        previousitem := top
      end;
    top := p
  end {push};

procedure *pop(var x: itemtype);
  var p: stackpointer;
  begin
    if top = nil
    then error('stack underflow')
    else begin
           x := top^.item;
           p := top;
           top := p^.previousitem;
           dispose(p)
         end
  end {pop};

procedure finish;
  var p: stackpointer;
  begin
    while top <> nil do
      begin
        p := top;
        top := top^.previousitem;
        dispose(p)
      end
  end {finish};

begin
  top := nil;
  ***;
  finish
end {stack};
```

This version may now be used in the character reversal program in place of the previous envelope implemented using a contiguous representation. The library retrieval specification need not contain the constant specification for *maxitems* since *maxitems* is not used in this version. Outside the envelope this change in representation is invisible since the interface between the envelope and the rest of the program as defined by the starred constants, types, procedures and functions is unchanged.

BLOCKED REPRESENTATION OF STACKS

The disadvantage of chained representations of data structures is the extra storage that they use to hold the chaining pointers. Such overheads become particularly severe when the individual items of a stack are small and the number of items in the stack becomes large. For a stack in which the items are, say, integers, the storage overhead on some machines is as high as 100% (one word for the integer, one word for the chaining pointer). These overheads can be greatly reduced, and the flexibility of dynamic storage allocation and de-allocation retained, by *blocking*, which is a combination of the previous contiguous and chained representations.

Blocked representations involve chaining together groups of items rather than individual items. Fixed-length one-dimensional arrays, each sufficient to hold, say, ten to a hundred items of the stack are used, and these arrays are linked together by pointers to form a chain. As items are added to the stack and the first array eventually becomes full, a new array is allocated dynamically and chained to the previous array. As items are removed from the stack and an array becomes empty of any stack items, the storage block containing the array is then released to free storage. A blocked representation of a stack is illustrated in Fig. 7.5.

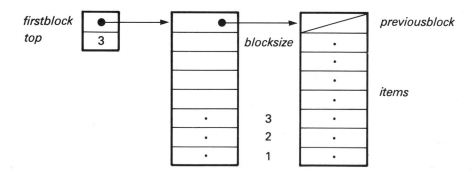

Figure 7.5   Blocked representation of a stack

Each individual block in the representation consists of an array and a chaining pointer, and so can be described by the following Pascal declarations:

```
const blocksize = . . . ;
type blockpointer = ↑blockrecord ;
     blockrecord = record
                          previousblock : blockpointer ;
                          items : array [1..blocksize] of itemtype
                   end ;
```

and the stack itself is then represented by two values. One is a pointer to the topmost block of the stack, and the other is the position of the topmost item in that particular block:

```
var firstblock : blockpointer ;
    top : 1..blocksize ;
```

The initialization consists of setting the *firstblock* pointer to **nil** and the *empty* operator is then a test of whether the *firstblock* pointer value is **nil**. The *full* operator is again implemented as the constant value *false*.

The *push* operator must test if the current block is full by checking if the value of *top* equals *blocksize* and, if it does, a new *blockrecord* must be acquired (note that if we also set the initial value of *top* to *blocksize*, the first call to *push* will automatically result in the first *blockrecord* being acquired). Likewise a *pop* operation which removes the only item remaining in a *blockrecord* must release that *blockrecord* to the free storage pool. The finalization of the envelope should release any blocks containing residual stack items.

The complete form of the *stack* envelope implemented using this blocked representation is given as Listing 12. Once again, this envelope may be substituted in the character reversal program in place of the two previous stack modules we have implemented, and the change in representation is invisible to the rest of the program.

Listing 12

```
envelope stack;

{ This envelope implements a stack of items of type itemtype, }
{ with operators push and pop, and predicates empty and full. }
{                                                              }
{ assumes type itemtype = any type with := applicable;        }
```

continued on page 138

Listing 12 continued

```
const blocksize = 256;
      *full = false;


type blockpointer = ^blockrecord;
     blockrecord = record
                         previousblock: blockpointer;
                         items: array [1..blocksize] of itemtype
                     end;


var firstblock: blockpointer;
    top: 1..blocksize;


function *empty: Boolean;
  begin empty := (firstblock = nil) end;


procedure *push(x: itemtype);
  var newblock: blockpointer;
  begin
    if top = blocksize
    then begin
           new(newblock);
           newblock^.previousblock := firstblock;
           firstblock := newblock;
           top := 1
         end
    else top := top + 1;
    firstblock^.items[top] := x
  end {push};


procedure *pop(var x: itemtype);
  var oldblock: blockpointer;
  begin
    if firstblock = nil
    then error('stack underflow')
    else begin
           x := firstblock^.items[top];
           if top = 1
           then begin
                  oldblock := firstblock;
                  firstblock := firstblock^.previousblock;
                  top := blocksize;
                  dispose(oldblock)
                end
           else top := top - 1
         end
  end {pop};
```

```
procedure finish;
  var oldblock: blockpointer;
  begin
    while firstblock <> nil do
      begin
        oldblock := firstblock;
        firstblock := firstblock^.previousblock;
        dispose(oldblock)
      end
  end {finish};

begin
  firstblock := nil;
  top := blocksize;
  ***;
  finish
end {stack};
```

STORAGE ORGANIZATION AND RECURSIVE BLOCK-STRUCTURED LANGUAGES

One important use of stacks in computing is for the run-time representation of data in programs compiled from languages such as Pascal and Ada, which support the use of recursive procedures. The rules of such languages determine the lifetime, or existence, of variables such that:

(a)   an instance of each variable declared within a block is created at entry to that block and destroyed on exit from it;

(b)   a distinct instance of each variable is created at each recursive re-entry to a recursive block.

Within these requirements the maximum economy of storage used during execution of a program can be achieved by a scheme of dynamic storage allocation based on the use of the available storage area as a stack, as follows:

(a)   the first locations of available storage are allocated to the global variables of the program, i.e. those declared in the outermost block;

(b)   thereafter, at entry to any given block, an area of storage is allocated in the next available locations, sufficient to accommodate:

   (i)   the required instances of all variables declared local to the block;

   (ii)   the representation of all parameters passed to the block (if it is a procedure or function);

(iii) some housekeeping information necessary for control of the stack and the program (e.g. the address of the instruction to be executed immediately upon exit from the block);

At any given moment, the total area of storage in use exists as a stack of such storage areas, one for each block instance currently in existence. The accessible instances of variables declared local to the block under execution at any time are always located in the topmost area on this stack and accessible instances of other non-local variables are in areas somewhere further down the stack.

(c)   At exit from a particular block the corresponding storage area is popped off the storage stack, thus becoming available for re-use at the next subsequent block entry.

The overall pattern of storage use is shown in Fig. 7.6.

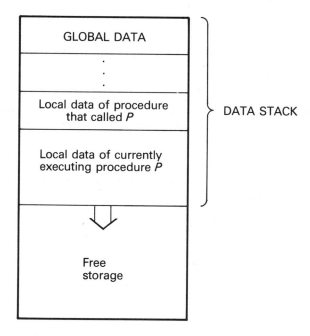

Figure 7.6   Storage organization for data in a block-structured language

Figure 7.7 illustrates a recursive nested block structure, together with snapshots of the stack usage pattern that it will generate at various points in its execution.

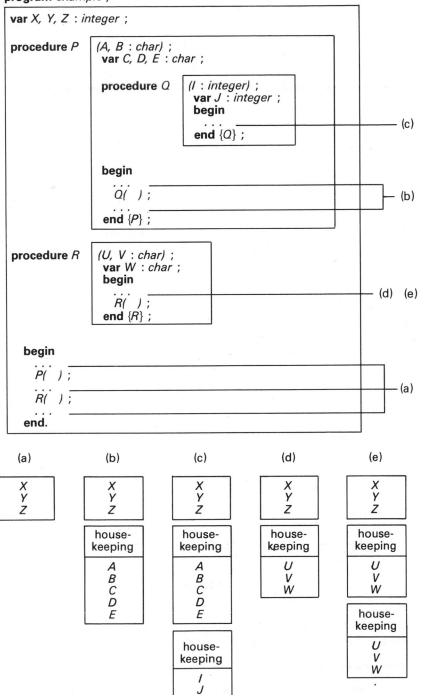

Figure 7.7 Storage snapshots for a Pascal program

Snapshots (a), (b), (c) show the pattern of storage use in the main program itself (a), in the procedure P (b), and in procedure Q called within P (c). Snapshot (d) shows the stack on entry to the call of R by the main program. Snapshot (e) shows the state of the stack on entry to the recursive call of R by R itself. Note that the storage used for variables local to procedures P and Q is available for re-use when R is entered. Also, recursive re-entries to R create a stack of identical areas for the distinct instances of the parameters and variables local to R.

An understanding of the run-time storage allocation scheme usage by programs written using recursive procedures can enable us to appreciate how a recursive program can be rewritten in the same language without recursion, or in a different language which does not provide recursion explicitly.

As an example, consider the well-known Towers of Hanoi problem. You are given three wooden poles (call them the left pole, middle pole and right pole). A stack of n disks of decreasing size (such that the disk of largest diameter is at the bottom) is held on the left pole which passes through a hole in the center of each disk. The initial layout of the pole and disks is illustrated in Fig. 7.8 for the case $n=5$.

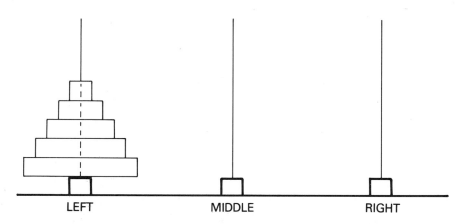

LEFT   MIDDLE   RIGHT

Figure 7.8   Towers of Hanoi, initial position

The problem is to move all the disks from the left pole to the right pole according to the following rules:

(a)   only one disk may be moved at a time;

(b)   a disk must never be placed on top of a smaller one;

(c)   at any time each of the disks must be on one of the three poles.

A recursive solution to this problem for a stack of x disks can be expressed as a call:

> $move$ $(x,$ $left,$ $middle,$ $right)$

of the following recursive procedure:

```
procedure move (n : integer ;
                source, auxiliary, destination : pole) ;
    begin
      if n = 1
      then move one disk from source to destination
      else begin
              move (n−1, source, destination, auxiliary) ;
              move one disk from source to destination ;
              move (n−1, auxiliary, source, destination)
            end
    end {move} ;
```

The parameter poles of the procedure are the source pole from which disks are to be moved, the destination pole to which the disks are to be moved, and the auxiliary pole which is to be used to hold disks during the intermediate moves.

How can we write this program without using a recursive procedure? One approach is to try to simulate the use of the recursion stack for holding parameters of the procedure. We can see that each recursive call leads to either a simple single disk move or else the call is replaced by three other sets of moves. Thus, the effect of the initial procedure call:

> $move$ $(x,$ $left,$ $middle,$ $right)$

can be obtained non-recursively in the following way:

The initial four parameters concerned are pushed, as a group, onto a stack created for the purpose. To simulate the effect of this (or any) call we pop the parameter group off the stack and examine the value of the n parameter. If its value is 1, then a single disk move is performed between the disks described by the first and third pole parameters. Otherwise, three new groups of parameters are pushed onto the stack, where the value of each group corresponds to the parameters of the corresponding recursive call. To obtain the correct order of simulated calls, these groups are pushed onto the stack in the reverse order to that in which the recursive calls appear within the move. The process continues by repeatedly popping the top set of parameters off the stack and interpreting their effect, as above, until the stack is empty. At that stage, all the recursive calls have been interpreted and so the sequence of moves required has been determined.

The non-recursive program thus takes the abstract form:

S.push (*n,source,auxiliary,destination*) ;
repeat
   S.pop (*x,s,a,d*) ; {*parameters of next move*}
   if *x*=1
   then *move a disk from s to d*
   else begin
         S.push (*x*−1*,a,s,d*) ; {*parameters of third sub-move*}
         S.push (1*,s,a,d*) ; {*parameters of second sub-move*}
         S.push (*x*−1*,s,d,a*) ; {*parameters of first sub-move*}
     end
until *S.empty*

However, this abstract program cannot be expressed directly in terms of our abstract *stack* envelope, as each stack operation involves four operands, three of type *pole* and one of type *integer*. One way of overcoming the problem is to introduce an interfacing envelope that uses the standard facility to push and pop composite items received from the user programs as four separate components. This can be done as follows:

envelope module *parameters* ;

   type *group* = **record**
              n : *integer* ;
              s,a,d : *pole*
        end ;

   envelope module *stack* **in** *library*
     (*where* **type** *itemtype* = *group;*) ;

   procedure **push* (*n* : *integer* ; *s,a,d* : *pole*) ;
     var *g* : *group* ;
     begin
       g.n :=*n* ; *g.s* :=*s* ;
       g.a :=*a* ; *g.d* :=*d* ;
       stack.push (*g*)
     end {*push*} ;

   procedure **pop* (**var** *n* : *integer* ; **var** *s,a,d* : *pole*) ;
     var *g* : *group* ;
     begin
       stack.pop (*g*) ;
       n :=*g.n* ; *s* :=*g.s* ;
       a :=*g.a* ; *d* :=*g.d*
     end {*pop*} ;

function **empty* = *stack.empty* ;

begin
  * * *
end {*parameters*} ;

With this module the abstract program can be readily expressed in Pascal Plus.

Not all recursive procedures require the use of a stack to simulate their effect without recursion; in some cases, a simple repetitive loop suffices. In general, however, the use of a stack to hold the parameters and local variables of pending or partially completed 'recursive' calls is the key to simulating the effect of recursive procedures in a non-recursive language.

DEFINING A QUEUE

A queue is a sequence in which all insertions take place at one end, the *rear*, and all removals are from the other end, the *front* (Fig. 7.9). In this case, the item of the sequence which has been in the queue for the longest time is always the next to be removed—hence a queue is described as a first-in–first-out (FIFO) or last-in–last-out (LILO) data structure.

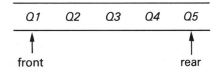

Figure 7.7   A conceptual queue

The concept of a queue is familiar in everyday life—queues of traffic waiting at lights and junctions, queues of people waiting at supermarket checkouts and bus stops, queues of names of people waiting to be called for treatment at a hospital. One joins a queue at the rear and, by the time the front of the queue has been reached, all the people or objects who joined it earlier have been dealt with.

Queues occur frequently in computing applications. An operating system for a large mainframe computer typically organizes the jobs waiting for particular resources of the system into one or more queues (where jobs with different characteristics, e.g. the amount of CPU time required, may enter different queues) and the jobs within each queue are serviced on a first-come, first-served basis.

The two main operations associated with a queue are the insertion and removal of items. The insertion operation adds a new item to the rear of a queue, provided that the queue is not already full. The removal operation takes out the item at the front of a queue, provided that such an item exists, i.e. the queue is not empty. Hence, we also need operators to enable us to determine when a queue is empty and when it is full, so that we know when it is safe to apply the removal and insertion operators.

We may now formulate an abstract specification of a queue of items of some type *itemtype*, in the form of an envelope providing a set of queue operators. In addition to the above operators, we define a *length* function to provide the number of items currently in a queue which is sometimes useful in determining how to service queues.

Our abstract specification is thus as follows:

> **envelope** *queue* ;
>
> > {*assumes* **type** *itemtype for items in queue with* := *applicable*}
> >
> > **function** **empty* : *Boolean* ;
> >
> > **function** **full* : *Boolean* ;
> >
> > **procedure** **append* (*x* : *itemtype*) ;
> >   {*if queue is not full then item x is appended*
> >   *to queue, otherwise an error occurs*}
> >
> > **procedure** **remove* (**var** *x* : *itemtype*) ;
> >   {*if queue is not empty the earliest appended*
> >   *item still in the queue is removed and assigned to x,*
> >   *otherwise an error occurs*}
> >
> > **function** **length* : *integer* ;
> >   {*returns number of items in queue i.e.*
> >   *number appended – number removed*}
> >
> > **begin**
> >   {*initially queue is empty*}
> >   * * *
> > **end** {*queue*} ;

The *empty* operator is not strictly necessary since the empty test may be expressed in terms of the *length* function, but we retain it for the clarity which it provides.

USING QUEUES

As an example of the application of our queue abstraction consider a program to monitor the movement of buses within a depot. As buses arrive at the depot shown in Fig. 7.10, they join a queue at an inspection point where each bus is checked. If some mechanical fault has arisen, the bus is sent to join another queue of buses at a service bay where a team of mechanics services each bus in turn. Also, at the inspection point, any dirty buses are sent to a cleaning point where another queue of buses is washed and cleaned in turn. After any necessary servicing and cleaning buses join a ready queue—each time a bus is required to make a journey it is taken from the front of the ready queue.

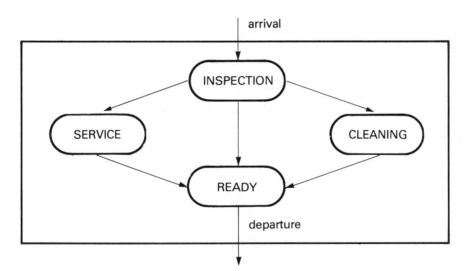

Figure 7.10   Bus movement through depot

Sensors at appropriate points send information about the movement of buses to a monitoring program. The arrival of a bus, internal movement of a bus within the depot, and departure of a bus on a journey, each cause a single message to be transmitted to the program. When a bus arrives at the inspection point a message *A* (for arrival) followed by the four-digit bus number is transmitted. When the inspection point decides what to do with the bus at the head of its waiting queue it sends one of three messages:

IC—sent to be cleaned
IS—sent to service bay
IR—sent to the ready queue

It is not necessary to indicate the number of the bus involved, since the control program will always be aware of which bus is currently at the head of any queue.

Each time a bus is cleaned, the single character message *C* is transmitted from the cleaning point and, likewise, completion of servicing causes the character *S* to be transmitted. Finally, to acquire a bus for the next journey the despatcher sends a message:

> *D route-number*

to the program, which replies with the number of the bus at the head of the ready queue, which is the bus to be used for the journey.

The monitor program makes use of four queues—the *inspection*, *wash*, *service* and *ready* queues—which are all objects of an abstract type *queue* introduced by retrieving the queue module with *itemtype* as the four-digit bus number type. The program then consists of an infinite loop which, according to the messages received, moves bus numbers between queues, and provides the numbers of buses for journeys, as required.

```
program busdepotcontrol (input,output) ;

   const eternity = false ;

   type busnumber = 0..9999 ;
        routenumber = 0..99 ;

   envelope queue in library
     (where type itemtype = busnumber;) ;

   instance inspection, wash, service, ready : queue ;

   var message : char ;
       bus : busnumber ;
       route : routenumber ;

   begin {busdepotcontrol}
     repeat
       read (message) ;
       case message of
         'A' : begin
                 read (bus) ; inspection.append (bus)
               end ;
```

```
'I'  : begin
           inspection.remove (bus) ;
           read (message) ;
           case message of
              'C' : wash.append (bus) ;
              'S'  : service.append (bus) ;
              'R' : ready.append (bus)
           end
       end ;
'C'  : begin
           wash.remove (bus) ; ready.append (bus)
       end ;
'S'  : begin
           service.remove (bus) ; ready.append (bus)
       end ;
'D'  : if ready.empty
       then writeln ( 'no buses available! ' )
       else begin
               ready.remove (bus) ; read (route) ;
               writeln ( 'bus ', bus:5, ' for route ', route:3)
            end
   end ;
   readln
 until eternity
end {busdepotcontrol}.
```

This program could be expanded to give a periodic print-out of the number of the buses waiting in each queue, to record the numbers of the buses currently in and out of the depot, or to maintain a service and usage history for each bus in the fleet. In practice, it should also be expanded to detect and report any inconsistencies in the data it receives.

CONTIGUOUS REPRESENTATION OF QUEUES

How can we represent a queue? As in the case of stacks, we shall consider three possible representations—contiguous, chained and blocked.

The contiguous representation, as in the case of a stack, uses an array of some fixed length *maxitems* to hold the items of the queue (Fig. 7.11). Two variables *front* and *rear* are required to indicate the limits of the queue.

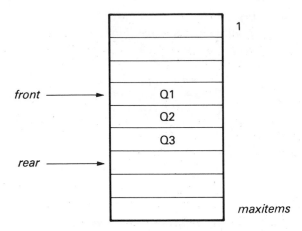

Figure 7.11   Contiguous representation of a queue

The variable *front* indicates the array element containing the first item of the queue and *rear* indicates the array element in which the next item to be added to the queue will be stored, i.e. it points to the array element immediately following the last item of the queue.

Hence, as items are added to and removed from the queue the values of *front* and *rear* increase, and the queue migrates down the array. What

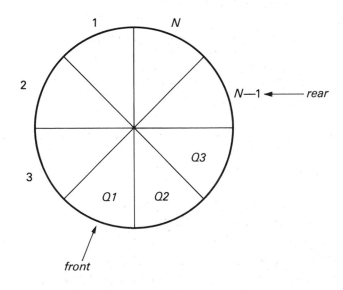

Figure 7.12   A conceptual cyclic buffer

happens when the rear of the queue reaches the end of the array? One solution is to allow the queue to 'wrap round' the end of the array and let the tail of the queue occupy any empty space at the start of the array as further items are added. The array may then be viewed as circular or cyclic (as in Fig. 7.12); this array representation is sometimes known as a *cyclic buffer*.

To initialize such a queue representation, *front* and *rear* are both assigned to value 1, denoting the empty queue. However, if the queue subsequently becomes full, *front* and *rear* will both have the same value (1 again if no removals have taken place). In order to distinguish between empty and full queues we need a third variable *length* to record the number of items currently in the queue. The cyclic buffer representation may thus be defined as:

> **var** *buffer* : **array** [1 . . *maxitems*] **of** *itemtype* ;
> *front, rear* : 1 . . *maxitems* ;
> *length* : 0 . . *maxitems* ;

The constant *maxitems* may be supplied by the user program. The initialization of a queue takes the form:

> *length* := 0 ; *front* := 1, *rear* := 1 ;

The *length* operation is implemented by allowing direct inspection of the *length* variable, i.e. by starring the declaration of *length*. The *empty* and *full* functions are then expressed simply in terms of the length of the queue, e.g.

> **function** **empty* : *Boolean* ;
> **begin**
>   *empty* := (*length* = 0)
> **end** {*empty*} ;

The *append* procedure (provided the queue is not full) places the new item in the buffer array element indicated by *rear* and increments both *length* and *rear* for the queue concerned. This latter increment operation may be expressed as:

> **if** *rear* = *maxitems* **then** *rear* := 1 **else** *rear* := *rear* + 1

or more concisely, in terms of the **mod** operator, as:

> *rear* := *rear* **mod** *maxitems* + 1

and the *append* procedure becomes:

```
procedure *append (x : itemtype) ;
   begin
     if length = maxitems
     then error ( 'queue overflow ' )
     else begin
              buffer [rear] :=x ;
              rear :=rear mod maxitems +1 ; length :=length +1
          end
   end {append} ;
```

Likewise, the *remove* procedure (provided the queue is not empty) takes an item from element *front* of the *buffer* array, and then increments *front* and decrements *length*.

Listing 13 shows the complete form of a queue envelope using the contiguous cyclic buffer representation.

Listing 13

```
envelope queue;

{ This envelope implements a queue of items of type itemtype }
{ with operators append, remove, and predicates empty, full  }
{                                                             }
{ assumes const maxitems = maximum number of items in queue; }
{          type itemtype = type of items in queue;           }

var buffer: array [1..maxitems] of itemtype;
    front, rear: 1..maxitems;
    length: 0..maxitems;

function *empty: Boolean;
  begin empty := (length = 0) end;

function *full: Boolean;
  begin full := (length = maxitems) end;

procedure *append(x: itemtype);
  begin
    if length = maxitems
    then error('queue overflow')
    else begin
            buffer[rear] := x;
            rear := rear mod maxitems + 1;
            length := length + 1
         end
  end {append};
```

```
procedure *remove(var x: itemtype);
  begin
    if length = 0
    then error('queue underflow')
    else begin
           x := buffer[front];
           front := front mod maxitems + 1;
           length := length - 1
         end
  end {remove};

begin
  length := 0;
  front := 1;
  rear := 1;
  ■■■
end {queue};
```

CHAINED REPRESENTATION OF QUEUES

As with stacks, queues may be represented using a chained representation in which records for the queue items are allocated dynamically and linked together by pointers. However, to allow the *remove* and *append* operations to be programmed, a queue is represented by *front* and *rear* pointers indicating the records for the first and last items of the queue. Each *item* record is linked to its successor in the queue by a pointer. The last *item* in the queue has no successor, hence its *nextitem* pointer has the value **nil**, as in Fig. 7.13. Again the pointers reflect the order in which items are *removed* from the queue.

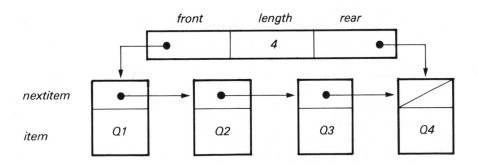

Figure 7.13   Chained representation of a queue

This representation is enabled by the following Pascal type definitions:

```
type queuepointer = ↑queuerecord ;
     queuerecord = record
                          nextitem : queuepointer ;
                          item : itemtype
                   end ;
```

The queue is then represented by three variables, the front and rear pointers, and the length variable:

```
var front, rear : queuepointer ;
    length : integer ;
```

The initialization of the queue sets *front* to **nil** and *length* to zero. The *length* function is again implemented by allowing direct inspection of the variable *length*. The *empty* function is again expressed in terms of *length*.

However, assuming that we cannot run out of dynamic storage space, the *full* function will always return the constant value *false* and so may be implemented by declaring *full* as a starred constant, i.e.

```
const *full = false ;
```

The *append* operator requires the creation of a new record variable which is added to the end of the chain of entries of the queue, i.e. as the successor of the record currently pointed to by the *rear* pointer (if such a record exists), as follows. Note the code needed to maintain both *front* and *rear* pointers in all cases.

```
procedure *append (x : itemtype) ;
   var p : queuepointer ;
   begin
     new(p) ;
     with p↑ do
        begin nextitem := nil ; item := x end ;
     if front = nil
     then front := p
     else rear↑.nextitem := p ;
     rear := p ;
     length := length + 1
   end {append} ;
```

The *remove* operator removes the item pointed to by *front* (provided the queue is not empty) and disposes of the record containing that item, as follows:

```
procedure *remove (var x : itemtype) ;
  var p : queuepointer ;
  begin
    if front = nil
    then error ( 'queue underflow ' )
    else begin
          p := front ; x := p↑.item ;
          front := front↑.nextitem ;
          dispose (p) ;
          length := length − 1
        end
  end {remove} ;
```

The finalization required for a chained queue is a traversal which disposes of the records for any items remaining in the queue. A complete envelope implementing the chained representation of a queue is given in Listing 14.

Listing 14

```
envelope queue;

  { This envelope implements a queue of items of type itemtype }
  { with operators append, remove, and predicates empty, full  }
  {                                                             }
  { assumes type itemtype = type of items in queue;            }

  const *full = false;

  type queuepointer = ^queuerecord;
       queuerecord = record
                       nextitem: queuepointer;
                       item: itemtype
                     end;

  var front, rear: queuepointer;
      length: integer;

  function *empty: Boolean;
    begin empty := (length = 0) end;

  procedure *append(x: itemtype);
    var p: queuepointer;
    begin
      new(p);
      with p^ do
        begin
          nextitem := nil;
          item := x
        end;
```

continued on page 156

Listing 14 continued

```
      if front = nil
      then front := p
      else rear^.nextitem := p;
      rear := p;
      length := length + 1
    end {append};

procedure *remove(var x: itemtype);
  var p: queuepointer;
  begin
    if front = nil
    then error('queue underflow')
    else begin
          p := front;
          x := p^.item;
          front := front^.nextitem;
          dispose(p);
          length := length - 1
        end
  end {remove};

procedure finish;
  var p: queuepointer;
  begin
    while front <> nil do
      begin
        p := front;
        front := front^.nextitem;
        dispose(p)
      end
  end {finish};

begin
  length := 0;
  front := nil;
  ***;
  finish
end {queue};
```

BLOCKED REPRESENTATION OF QUEUES

To reduce the overheads of the chaining pointers, a blocked queue representation may be used in which groups of queued items are chained together
rather than individual items. As for a stack, these groups are held in one-
dimensional arrays linked by pointers, where the arrays are dynamically

allocated and released. The *front* and *rear* variables now consist of two components: a pointer to the block holding the front or rear of the queue respectively, and an *offset* within that block of the actual frontmost or rearmost item, as in Fig. 7.14.

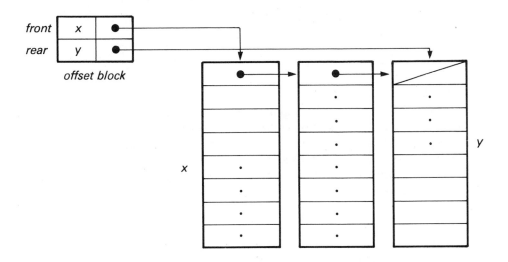

Figure 7.14 Blocked representation of a queue

This blocked queue representation may be defined in Pascal as:

const *blocksize* = . . . ;

type *blockpointer* = ↑*blockrecord* ;
    blockrecord = **record**
                 nextblock : *blockpointer* ;
                 items : **array** [1 . . *blocksize*] **of** *itemtype*
             end ;

var *front*, *rear* : **record**
              block : *blockpointer* ;
              offset : 1 . . *blocksize*
         end ;
      *length : *integer* ;

Completion of the blocked representation of queues is left as an exercise for the reader.

DEFINING A DEQUE

A double-ended queue is a sequence which permits addition and removal of items at either end. Such queues are often referred to by an abbreviated name, *deque*. Stacks and queues are in fact restricted forms of deques—a queue is a deque for which removal is restricted to the front end and insertion to the back end, while a stack is a deque in which removal and insertion are restricted to one end, the front.

Some card games make use of deques. Cards may be placed at either end of a row (either with faces exposed or hidden, depending upon the game) and players may remove a card from either end, but not from the middle of the row.

The extra operations required for a deque in addition to those for an ordinary queue are insertion at the front, and removal at the rear. Hence, we may extend the specification of a queue to that for a deque by renaming some of the queue operators (*remove* becomes *removefront* and *append* becomes *addrear*) and adding operators *removerear* and *addfront*, to give the following outline:

> **envelope** *deque* ;
>
>   **function** **length* : *integer* ;
>   **function** **empty* : *Boolean* ;
>   **function** **full* : *Boolean* ;
>
>   **procedure** **addfront* (*x* : *itemtype*) ;
>   **procedure** **addrear* (*x* : *itemtype*) ;
>   **procedure** **removefront* (**var** *x* : *itemtype*) ;
>   **procedure** **removerear* (**var** *x* : *itemtype*) ;
>
>   **begin**
>   {*initially deque is empty*}
>   *******
>   **end** {*deque*} ;

REPRESENTATION OF DEQUES

The contiguous representation of a deque is similar to that for a queue with the addition of the *removerear* and *addfront* procedures, both of which are straightforward to implement and left as an exercise for the reader.

Chained representations are more interesting because we are concerned with being able to remove items from the deque structure at either end. We noted for both stacks and queues that the direction of the pointers reflected the order in which items are removed, i.e. they lead away from the point of removal. In the case of deques the records must be chained in both directions to allow for removal from either end, as in Fig. 7.15.

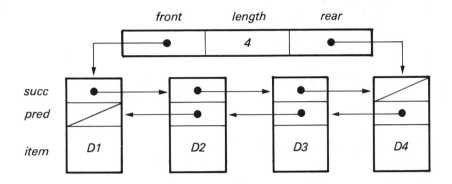

Figure 7.15   Chained representation of a deque

This representation is defined by the following type definitions:

type *dequepointer* = ↑*dequerecord* ;
    dequerecord = **record**
                  succ, pred : *dequepointer* ;
                  item : *itemtype*
        end ;

and the variable declarations:

var *front, rear* : *dequepointer* ;
    *length : *integer* ;

The *empty* and *full* operations are implemented as for queues, where *nextitem* is now denoted by the *succ* pointer field. The *removefront* operator now involves an additional resetting of the *pred* pointer to **nil** in the new frontmost item of the deque, viz:

procedure **removefront* (**var** *x* : *itemtype*) ;
    var *p* : *dequepointer* ;
    begin
      p := *front* ;
      if *p* = **nil**
      then *error* (*'queue underflow* ')

```
      else begin
          front := front↑.succ ;
          if front = nil
          then rear := nil
          else front↑.pred := nil ;
          dispose (p) ;
          length := length − 1
          end
      end {removefront} ;
```

Insertion at the front involves creation of a new record as before but also the resetting of the *pred* field in what was previously the frontmost item of the deque, viz:

```
      procedure *addfront (x : itemtype) ;
        var p : queuepointer ;
        begin
          new(p) ;
          with p↑ do
            begin item := x ; succ := front ; pred := nil end ;
          if front = nil
          then rear := p
          else front↑.pred := p ;
          front := p ;
          length := length + 1
        end {addfront} ;
```

Since this deque representation is symmetric, the insertion and removal operators on the rear of a deque are obtained directly from the above front-of-deque operators by interchanging the use of the *front* and *rear* pointers, and the *succ* and *pred* links. Completion of this doubly chained representation of a deque is again left as an example for the reader.

CASE STUDY : AN ENCODED MESSAGE SYSTEM

To illustrate the use of our stack, queue and deque abstractions in more substantial computer programs, we now consider the implementation of an encoded message system. In the system messages are held and transmitted as encoded character files. These encoded files can be generated and decoded only by using special programs which communicate directly with a terminal keyboard or screen. In Pascal terms, therefore, the system consists of two programs with headings as follows:

program *encode* (*input*, *EF*) ;

program *decode* (*EF*,*output*) ;

where the program parameter *EF* in each case is an encoded file held by the system.

Encoded messages are generated from the original message text according to the following algorithm:

(a)   all sequences of non-vowels in the messages are reversed;

(b)   the encoded message then consists of the first character of the sequence produced by (a), followed by the last character, then by the second character, then by the second last, and so on.

For example the message:

MAN EATS DOG.

is transformed by step (a) to:

MA NEAD STO.G

and then by step (b) to:

MGA. ONTESA D

Consider first the program *encode*. From the encoding algorithm itself it must have the overall form:

> **begin**
>   *reverse non-vowel subsequences of input to form a sequence D* ;
>   *recollate end characters of D to form EF*
> **end**

Since *EF* is produced by removing characters from both ends of *D*, and *D* can be produced by appending characters to its end, *D* has the essential characteristics of a deque of characters. We can thus declare *D* as an instance of our library deque envelope with *char* as *itemtype*:

> **envelope** *chardeque* = *deque* **in** *library*
>   (*where* **type** *itemtype* = *char*;) ;

> **instance** *D* : *chardeque* ;

The body of the *encode* program is then expressed as calls to two procedures *formD* and *formEF* which generate the deque D and the encoded file EF, from the input stream and from D, respectively.

```
program encode (input, EF) ;

    envelope chardeque = deque in library
      (where type itemtype = char;) ;

    instance D : chardeque ;

    var EF : file of char ;

    procedure formD :
      {D := character sequence from input stream
      with non-vowel subsequences reversed}

    procedure formEF ;
      {EF := alternating collation of head and
      tail characters from D}

    begin
      formD ;
      formEF ;
    end {encode}.
```

Consider first the procedure *formD*. This must read characters one by one from the input stream, at each step checking for end of input, and distinguishing between vowel and non-vowel characters. For this purpose the ideal characteristics of the input stream can be abstracted as an envelope with the following interface:

```
    envelope charstream (var f : text) ;

    var *endofstream : Boolean ;
        *nextchar : char ;
        *nextisvowel : Boolean ;

    procedure *getnextchar ; . . .

    begin
      {get first character, if any}
      ***
    end {charstream} ;
```

The initialization, and each subsequent call of *getnextchar*, will update the starred variables as required.

As we have already seen, reversing a non-vowel sequence can be accomplished by use of a stack of characters. This can be declared within the procedure *formD* by retrieving a library stack envelope with *char* as *itemtype*, thus:

> **envelope** *charstack* = **stack in** *library*
>   (*where* **type** *itemtype* = *char*;) ;

> **instance** *reversenvs* : *charstack* ;

With these decisions the procedure *formD* can be programmed as follows:

```
procedure formD ;
   {D := character sequence from input stream with
    non-vowel subsequences reversed}
   envelope charstream ; . . .
   envelope charstack = stack in library
      (where type itemtype = char;) ;
   instance reversenvs : charstack ;
            inputstream : charstream (input) ;
   var nonvowel : char ;
   begin
      with inputstream do
      while not endofstream do
      begin
         {copy a vowel sequence, if any, to D}
         while not endofstream and nextisvowel do
         begin D.addrear (nextchar) ; getnextchar end ;

         {reverse a non-vowel sequence, if any}
         while not endofstream and not nextisvowel do
         begin reversenvs.push (nextchar) ; getnextchar end ;

         {copy reversed sequence to D}
         while not reversenvs.empty do
         begin reversenvs.pop (nonvowel) ; D.addrear (nonvowel) end ;
      end
   end {formD} ;
```

In practice, the details of the *charstream* envelope are easily expressed in terms of Pascal's standard textfile facilities, as follows:

```
envelope charstream (var f : text) ;
{provides character by character access to textfile f,
 with discrimination between vowels and non-vowels}

var *endofstream : Boolean ;
    *nextchar : char ;
    *nextisvowel : Boolean ;

procedure *getnextchar ;
  begin
    if eof (f)
    then endofstream := true
    else begin
            read (f,nextchar) ;
            nextisvowel := nextchar in ['A', 'E', 'I', 'O', 'U',
                                        'a', 'e', 'i', 'o', 'u']
        end
  end {getnextchar} ;

begin
  endofstream := false ;
  getnextchar ;
  ***
end {charstream} ;
```

Now consider the second stage of the encoding process, to be carried out by the procedure *formEF*. In practice, this is easily expressed in terms of the deque operators applicable to *D* and Pascal's standard file operations.

```
procedure formEF ;
{EF := alternating collation of head and
 tail characters from D}
var nextchar : char ;
begin
  rewrite (EF) ;
  while not D.empty do
  begin
    D.removefront (nextchar) ; write (EF,nextchar) ;
    if not D.empty then
    begin D.removerear (nextchar) ; write (EF,nextchar) end
  end
end {formEF} ;
```

This in turn completes our development of the *encode* program.

The *decode* program in effect reverses the encoding algorithm, again in two steps. The reversal of the second step recreates the character sequence held as *D* in the encoding process. The reversal of the first step outputs this character sequence to the output stream, reversing non-vowel subsequences as it does so.

In practice, reforming the character sequence *D* involves reading alternate characters from *EF* to *D* and to a stack (which will reverse the order of the even characters), and then appending the reversed sequence from the stack to *D*. Thereafter, forming the final output involves copying characters one-by-one from *D* either directly to the output file, or to an auxiliary stack to reverse non-vowel subsequences. Thus, the required characteristics of *D* are those of a queue of characters, with an auxiliary reversal stack being used in each phase. With this realization we can finalize the global declarations of the *decode* program, as follows:

```
program decode (EF,output) ;

    envelope charqueue = queue in library
        (where type itemtype = char;) ;

    envelope charstack = stack in library
        (where type itemtype = char;) ;

    var EF : file of char ;

    instance D : charqueue ;

    procedure reformD ;
        {D := odd chars from EF + reversed (even chars from EF)}

    procedure formoutput ;
        {output := char sequence from D with
         non-vowel subsequences reversed}

    begin
        reformD ;
        formoutput
    end {decode}.
```

Here we have defined the *charstack* envelope in the main program, so that its definition is available to both procedures, but the stack instances used by *reformD* and *formoutput* are independent, and are therefore declared locally within each procedure.

The procedures themselves are now easily expressed as follows:

procedure *reformD* ;

   {*D* := *odd chars from EF* + *reversed* (*even chars from EF*)}

   instance *reversetail* : *charstack* ;
   var *headchar, tailchar* : *char* ;

   begin
      {*copy alternate characters from EF to D*
       and reversetail}
      reset (*EF*) ;
      while not *eof(EF)* **do**
      begin
         read (*EF,headchar*) ; *D.append* (*headchar*) ;
         if not *eof* (*EF*) **then**
         begin
            read (*EF,tailchar*) ;
            reversetail.push (*tailchar*)
         end
      end ;

      {*copy reversed tail characters to D*}
      while not *reversetail.empty* **do**
      begin
         reversetail.pop (*tailchar*) ;
         D.append (*tailchar*)
      end
   end {*reformD*} ;

procedure *formoutput* ;

   {*output* := *character sequence from D with*
    non-vowel subsequences reversed}

   envelope module *Dstream* ; . . .

   instance *reversenvs* : *charstack* ;
   var *nonvowel* : *char* ;

   begin
      with *Dstream* **do**
         while not *endofstream* **do**
         begin

```
        {copy vowel sequence, if any, to output}
        while not endofstream and nextisvowel do
        begin write (output,nextchar) ; getnextchar end ;

        {reverse nonvowel sequence, if any}
        while not endofstream and not nextisvowel do
        begin reversenvs.push (nextchar) ; getnextchar end ;

        {copy reversed non-vowels to output}
        while not reversenvs.empty do
        begin
            reversenvs.pop (nonvowel) ;
            write (output,nonvowel)
        end
    end
end {formoutput} ;
```

The module *Dstream* is identical in specification to the envelope *char-stream* used in program *encode*, except that it takes characters from the queue *D*, not from a text file. Its coding is, therefore, as follows:

```
envelope module Dstream ;

    {provides character by character access to
    the characters in queue D, with discrimination
    between vowels and non-vowels}

    var *endofstream : Boolean ;
        *nextchar : char ;
        *nextisvowel : Boolean ;

    procedure *getnextchar ;
        begin
            if D.empty
            then endofstream := true
            else begin
                    D.remove (nextchar) ;
                    nextisvowel := nextchar in ['A', 'E', 'I', 'O', 'U',
                                                'a', 'e', 'i', 'o', 'u']
                end
        end {getnextchar} ;

    begin
        endofstream := false ;
        getnextchar ;
        ***
    end {Dstream} ;
```

SUMMARY

Stacks, queues and deques are simple abstract data types within the general class of sequences, and are fundamental to many computing applications. The limited range of operators permitted for stacks, queues and deques, involving alteration of the sequence only at either end, makes their implementation particularly simple. With the straightforward implementations illustrated, the efficiency of the operators involved is independent of the sequence length. The only significant implementation choice is between the different storage overheads implied by the contiguous and chained representations, with the blocked representation offering an effective compromise between the two.

In contrast, we shall see in the next chapter that sequences with a more general range of operators create a more significant implementation challenge, with significant variations in the performance that results from the alternative strategies available.

EXERCISES

7.1   Complete the blocked representation of a queue outlined on page 157.

7.2   A *postfix* expression is one in which an operator is placed after the operand to which it refers instead of between the operands as in the more familiar *infix* notation, e.g.,

the infix expression $A+B*C$ becomes $ABC*+$ in postfix form, and $(A+B)*(C-D)$ becomes $AB+CD-*$

Write a program which reads from an input file an infix expression involving any of the four standard arithmetic operators, parentheses and single letter identifiers, and uses a stack to convert the expression to postfix form before outputting it to another file.

Write a second program which reads a postfix expression from one file, and reads from a second file a sequence of lines each containing a single letter identifier and its corresponding value of type *real*, and uses a stack to evaluate the expression.

7.3   Write a program to simulate a game of card patience played according to the following rules:

The player deals four cards, face upwards, in a row. If the four cards are of different suits then another four cards are dealt, as before, on top of the existing row. If two or more cards of the same suit are visible, then the highest ranking card of that suit (Ace counts high) is retained and the other(s) discarded, bringing a previously hidden card back into play. The discarding process is repeated until all suit duplicates have been removed. If one of the card piles becomes empty then any Ace on top of another pile may be moved into the empty position. When no more discards can be made, a further four cards are dealt on to the tops of the piles and the game continues in similar fashion until all the cards have been dealt. The game is successfully concluded if only the four aces remain at the end of the dealing. What extensions to the *stack* abstraction would simplify the programming of this game?

7.4 The Fibonacci numbers are defined by the recurrence relation
$$fibonacci_{n+1} = fibonacci_n + fibonacci_{n-1} \text{ for } n>0$$
and the first two numbers of the sequence are 0 and 1. Hence the Fibonacci numbers may be computed by the following recursive function:

```
function fibonacci (n : integer) ;
  begin
    if n=0 then fibonacci := 0 else
    if n=1 then fibonacci := 1 else
    fibonacci := fibonacci(n−1) + fibonacci(n−2)
  end
```

Rewrite this function in a non-recursive form which makes use of a stack. Is it possible to write it non-recursively without introducing a stack?

7.5 The bus depot control system implemented on page 148 is unsatisfactory in that incoming buses may be sent for servicing or for cleaning but not both. Modify the system to overcome this problem by adding a further inspection point message *IB* meaning 'send to be serviced and then to be cleaned'. (*Hint* : modify the existing implementation by extending the information on each bus in some or all of the queues).

7.6 Specify a queue traversal operator which applies some procedure *P* to each item in the queue, in the order in which the items joined the queue. Implement this operator in one of the versions of the *queue* envelope and use it to extend the bus depot control system so that it provides the user with an additional queue monitoring command *M* which causes the system to output details of the lengths of the various queues and the buses currently waiting in each queue.

7.7 Complete the doubly chained representation of a deque outlined on pages 159 and 160.

7.8 Simplify the definition of a deque to that of a queue in which items may be added at the front or rear, but removed only from the front. What corresponding simplification of the chained representation does this allow?

8

Lists

A *list* (sometimes called a *linear list*) is a sequence in which items may be inserted, deleted or inspected at any position. It is thus a more general kind of sequence than the stacks, queues and deques considered in Chapter 7, all of which are special cases of the list abstraction which we now define.

In practice, lists arise in many situations in everyday life. An example is the list of names of members of a club or society. These names are often held in some significant order, e.g. alphabetical order, which may enable more convenient usage of the list. From time to time names may be deleted from, or inserted in, the list at appropriate positions. This simple example demonstrates the essential characteristics that distinguish lists from stacks and queues, i.e. that insertion, deletion and manipulaton of items may take place at any point in the sequence of items involved, not just at its ends.

The classification of sequences into stacks, queues, lists, etc., is not always clear cut. In Chapter 7, we gave the itinerary of towns visited on a European tour, e.g.

Amsterdam, Cologne, Heidelberg, Munich, Salzburg, Vienna, Budapest,

as an example of a sequence. In practice such a sequence may play several roles depending on our approach to the tour involved.

If we are carrying out a tour with a pre-determined itinerary, such as that offered by a coach tour company, the itinerary acts as an input stream—the next town in the itinerary determines our next destination at each stage.

Alternatively, if we set off on a tour with no pre-determined itinerary, the sequence of towns visited may be thought of as an output stream—each decision on where to go next adds one more town to the itinerary of towns visited so far.

If, however, we think of planning a tour in advance, the itinerary under preparation behaves as a list as defined above, in that we may insert, delete, or replace towns at any point in that list during our decision making process.

This everyday example illustrates how data structures may play different roles at different stages of their existence—an itinerary behaves as a list during tour planning, but as an input stream as the tour is actually carried out. We had a similar example in the message encoding program considered at the end of Chapter 7. The intermediate structure D acted as an output stream for step 1 of the encoding algorithm, but as a deque for step 2.

The list abstraction which we now develop provides the essential characteristics commonly associated with lists, but may also be regarded as a general abstraction of sequential structures, which subsumes the abstractions of stacks and queues given in Chapter 7. As will be seen, these simpler abstractions are easily recreated from the list abstraction we define.

DEFINING A LIST ABSTRACTION

We now consider the range of operations appropriate for manipulation of a list of items of some type *itemtype*, say. At any stage the list is an ordered sequence of items $L1, L2, \ldots, Ln$ which we depict as shown in Fig. 8.1.

Figure 8.1   The list concept

Consider first the operations needed for inspecting the list. At any moment only one item of the list can be under inspection. A convenient way of visualizing this is to associate the concept of a *window* with each list. At any moment one item in the list may be in the window, and is the item under inspection. This we depict as in Fig. 8.2(a), where the third item $L3$ of our list is currently in the window. At some stages, however, for example after an unsuccessful search for a list item with some particular property, it is necessary to note the fact that no item is in the window. By convention, we depict this condition by positioning the window immediately beyond the last item in the list as in Fig. 8.2(b), and we define a function:

function **inlist* : *Boolean* ;

which returns the result *false* when the window is in this position, otherwise it returns *true*.

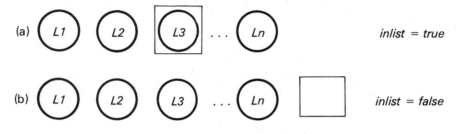

Figure 8.2   The window concept

The window associated with a list may be positioned by one of four operators:

procedure **locatefront* ;

which sets the window over the first item in the list, if one exists (if the list is empty *inlist* is false before and after).

procedure **locaterear* ;

which sets *inlist* false for any list.

procedure **next* ;

which advances the window to the next item in the list; if the item in the window is the last item of the list *inlist* becomes false; if *inlist* was already false an error occurs.

procedure **locate* (**function** *test* (*x* : *itemtype*) : *Boolean*) ;

which sets the window over the first item at or after the current position which satisfies the specified test; if no item satisfies the test *inlist* becomes false; if *inlist* was already false, *locate* has no effect.

The value of the item in the window of a list may be obtained by the operator:

procedure **contents* (**var** *x* : *itemtype*) ;

If *inlist* is false use of the operator *contents* causes an error.

Insertion and deletion of items in a list is also defined in terms of the window concept. Insertion is defined to take place immediately *preceding* the item in the window—if *inlist* is false the item is inserted as the last item in the list. Where should the window be positioned after a list insertion? For a sequence of insertions it is most convenient if the window remains over the existing item, so that each item inserted will follow the previously inserted items. In other cases, however, it is convenient if the window moves to the inserted item. For this reason two versions of the insert operator are provided:

procedure **precede* (*x* : *itemtype*) ;

procedure **precedeandmove* (*x* : *itemtype*) ;

Both insert the new item *x* immediately preceding the item currently in the window, or at the end of the list if *inlist* is false. In the first case, however, the item in the window remains unchanged as shown in Fig. 8.3(b), while in the second case, the inserted item *x* becomes the window item, as shown in Fig. 8.3(c).

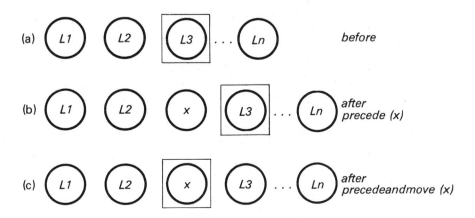

Figure 8.3 List insertion operators

Deleting the item currently in the window of a list is provided by the operator:

> **procedure** **delete* ;

On deletion the window moves to the item following the deleted item, if one exists, otherwise *inlist* becomes false. If *inlist* is false when a deletion is requested, an error occurs.

For convenience, an operator to replace the item currently in the window by a new item is also provided:

> **procedure** **replace* (*x* : *itemtype*) ;

The effect of *replace* is exactly equivalent to a *delete* followed by a *precedeandmove* operation.

As for stacks and queues it is convenient to provide functions *empty*, *full* and *length* for lists, with identical definitions. Note that for our window concept *empty=true* implies *inlist=false*. Initially, therefore, a list is empty, with *inlist* false.

For many applications of lists it is necessary to process each list item in turn in the order determined by their positions in the list. While such list traversal can be programmed in terms of the operators given above, it is convenient to provide an explicit traversal operator for this purpose:

> **procedure** **traverse* (**procedure** *p* (**var** *x* : *itemtype*)) ;

The operator *traverse* applies its parametric procedure *p* to each item in the list in turn, leaving the existing window position unaltered. Note however that, in general, successful use of the *traverse* operator implies the requirement discussed in Chapter 5, namely that each call of the actual procedure supplied for *p* leaves the list structure unaltered, i.e. that it makes no insertions or deletions in the list.

Our complete list abstraction, which is significantly more complex than those required for stacks and queues, is thus as follows:

> **envelope** *list* ;
>
> > {*assumes* **type** *itemtype* = *type of items in list*,
> >   *with* := *applicable*}
>
> **function** **length* : *integer* ;
>
> **function** **empty* : *Boolean* ;

function *full : *Boolean* ;

function *inlist : *Boolean* ;
  {*is window on item in list?*}

procedure *locatefront ;
  {*set window on first item in list, if any*}

procedure *locaterear ;
  {*set window at end of list*}

procedure *next ;
  {*if inlist then advance window else error*}

procedure *locate (**function** *test* (*x* : *itemtype*) : *Boolean*) ;
  {*set window on first item at or after current window position which
   satisfies test, if any, otherwise at end of list*}

procedure *content (**var** *x* : *itemtype*) ;
  {*if inlist then return value in window else error*}

procedure *replace (*x* : *itemtype*) ;
  {*if inlist then item in window := x else error*}

procedure *traverse (**procedure** *p* (**var** *x* : *itemtype*)) ;
  {*apply p to each item, in list order*}

procedure *precede (*x* : *itemtype*) ;
  {*insert x as new item immediately preceding window*}

procedure *precedeandmove (*x* : *itemtype*) ;
  {*insert x as new item immediately preceding window,
   and set window on x*}

procedure *delete ;
  {*if inlist then delete item in window and advance window
   else error*}

begin
  {*initially list is empty, inlist is false*}
  * * *
end {*list*} ;

THE CONCORDANCE PROGRAM REVISITED

To illustrate the use of this abstract list type, consider a simplified version of the concordance program developed in Chapter 4, which is required only to list the distinct words found in the input text together with the *number* of occurrences of each. Initially, we will accept the list printed in any order, but later we will arrange to print it in dictionary order, and also in order of frequency.

The overall form of the program will be as before:

```
program concordance (input,output) ;

    const wordlength = 16 ;
    type wordspelling = packed array [1 .. wordlength] of char ;

    envelope module wordinput ; . . .

    envelope module wordlist ; . . .

    begin
      with wordinput do
        while not endoftext do
        begin
          wordlist.recordword (word) ;
          getnextword
        end ;
        wordlist.printwords (output)
    end {concordance}.
```

We will assume the *wordinput* module as before, but we will now implement the *wordlist* using our abstract list envelope from the library to create a list of word records. The overall form of the *wordlist* module is thus as follows:

```
    envelope module wordlist ;

      type wordrecord = record
                           spelling : wordspelling ;
                           count : 1 .. maxint
                         end ;

      envelope module list in library
        (where type itemtype = wordrecord ;) ;

      procedure *recordword (word : wordspelling) ; . . .
```

```
procedure *printwords (var printfile : text) ; . . .

begin
  * * *
end {wordlist} ;
```

The procedure *recordword* searches the list to find if an entry for *word* already exists. It can now do so as follows:

```
with list do
begin
  locatefront ;
  locate (equals) ;
  . . .
```

where the Boolean function *equals* is declared local to *recordword*. This function returns the result *true* only if the value of the spelling field of its parameter wordrecord *w* is equal to *word*, viz:

```
function equals (w : wordrecord) : Boolean ;
  begin
    equals := (w.spelling = word)
  end {equals} ;
```

If an entry for *word* exists, the list window will be set to the entry; otherwise *inlist* will return *false*.

The subsequent updating operation is, therefore, programmed as follows:

```
if inlist
then increment count in entry found
else insert a new entry in the list
```

To increment an existing word count the entry found must be extracted from the list window, its count field incremented by 1, and the new record value used to replace the existing record in the window, thus:

```
contents (entry) ;
entry.count := entry.count + 1 ;
replace (entry)
```

An entry for a new word may be inserted by initializing a variable *entry* to the appropriate spelling and count, and then calling *precede*, thus:

```
entry.spelling := word ;
entry.count := 1 ;
precede (entry)
```

The final form of the *recordword* procedure is thus:

```
procedure *recordword (word : wordspelling) ;

    var entry : wordrecord ;

    function equals (w : wordrecord) : Boolean ;
      begin
        equals := (w.spelling = word)
      end {equals} ;

    begin {recordword}
      with list do
      begin
        locatefront ;
        locate (equals) ;
        if inlist
        then begin {update existing entry}
               contents (entry) ;
               entry. count := entry.count + 1 ;
               replace (entry)
             end
        else begin {insert a new entry}
               entry.spelling := word ;
               entry.count := 1 ;
               precede (entry)
             end
      end
    end {recordword} ;
```

The *printwords* procedure is implemented by a call of the *traverse* operator to execute a procedure *printword* (which outputs the spelling and frequency count stored in a given word record) for each word record in the list. *printwords* thus has the form:

```
procedure *printwords (var printfile : text) ;

    procedure printword (w : wordrecord) ;
      begin
        with w do writeln (printfile,spelling,count)
      end {printword} ;

    begin
      list.traverse (printword)
    end {printwords} ;
```

With the implementation chosen for *recordword* this will result in the words being printed in order of their first occurrence in the input text, which we will improve on later in the chapter. For the moment, we note the ease with which the *wordlist* manipulation, laboriously programmed using pointers in Chapter 4, can now be expressed in terms of our standard list abstraction.

REPRESENTATION OF LISTS

The significant differences between lists and the stacks and queues considered in Chapter 7 are as follows:

(a) Inspection of items at any point in the list is enabled by the window positioning and traversal operators. In many list applications repeated examination of list items to find items with particular properties is a dominant activity. The efficiency with which this searching can be carried out, using the *next* and *locate* operators, is a significant consideration in choosing a list representation.

(b) Insertion and deletion of items at any point in the list is allowed. For some list applications the dynamic insertion and deletion of items is a dominant activity, and the efficiency with which such changes can be carried out is a significant attribute of the representation chosen.

In the following sections we consider two possible representations for our list abstraction and, in particular, we examine their relative merits with respect to the specific requirements above.

A Contiguous List Representation

Like stacks and queues, a list can be represented using an array, or contiguous area of storage, if an acceptable upper limit on the number of items in the list can be determined. In addition to the array to hold the list items themselves, a list requires two indexing variables. One, called *length*, denotes the number of items currently in the array; the other, called the *window*, indexes the array element which is the current window item of the list, as shown in Fig. 8.4.

The Pascal declarations necessary to describe such a representation are as follows:

```
var items : array [1..maxitems] of itemtype ;
    length : 0..maxitems ;
    window : 1..maxint ;
```

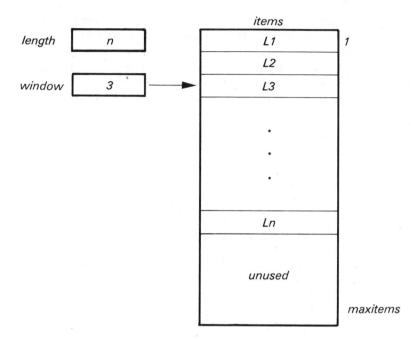

Figure 8.4   Contiguous representation of a list

The *inlist* condition is represented by a value of *window* not greater than *length*, the index of the last item in the array. With these conventions the complete implementation of the contiguous list representation, which follows as Listing 15, is easily programmed.

As for stacks and queues, the *empty* and *full* functions are implemented by examination of the *length* variable.

The window positioning operators *locatefront* and *locaterear* simply assign values 1 and *length* + 1 to *window*. The *next* operator increments the *window* variable, after checking for the *inlist* condition. The *locate* operator performs an ordered search through the elements of the *items* array, from the current window position onward, applying the parametric function *test* to each, until either a test result *true* is obtained, or all remaining items have been tested. By expressing the search loop in terms of the variable *window* itself the latter is left with the correct final value in either case, and the overhead per iteration is simply incrementing and testing this variable.

The operators *contents* and *replace* simply perform assignments between their parameters and the array element indexed by the variable *window*, after checking for the *inlist* condition. The *traverse* operator is a straightforward array-indexing for-statement over the significant length of the list.

With a contiguous representation the significant characteristic of the insertion and deletion operators is that movement of existing list items is required. Thus the *delete* operator deletes the window item by moving all following items back one position to occupy the gap left by the deleted item. By doing so, the existing value of the variable *window* automatically indexes the next item as required. The procedures *precede* and *precedeandmove* both create space for the item to be inserted by moving all following items forward one position. This leaves the variable *window* indexing the inserted item as required by *precedeandmove*, but for *precede*, *window* must be incremented to follow the window item moved.

envelope list;

Listing 15

```
{ This envelope maintains a linear list of items, with a   }
{ window for item manipulation. Operators provided are     }
{ locatefront, locaterear, locate, next for window movement, }
{ content and replace for manipulating the window item,    }
{ delete, precede and precedeandmove for altering the list. }
{ Predicates empty, full and inlist test the state of the  }
{ list and the window respectively.                        }
{                                                          }
{ assumes const maxitems = maximum number of items in list; }
{          type itemtype = any type with := applicable;    }
var *length: 0..maxitems;
    window: 1..maxint;
    items: array [1..maxitems] of itemtype;

function *empty: Boolean;
  begin empty := (length = 0) end;

function *full: Boolean;
  begin full := (length = maxitems) end;

function *inlist: Boolean;
  begin inlist := (window <= length) end;

procedure *locatefront;
  begin window := 1 end;

procedure *locaterear;
  begin window := length + 1 end;

procedure *next;
  begin
    if window > length
    then error('no window for next')
    else window := window + 1
  end {next};
```

continued on page 182

Listing 15 continued

```
procedure *locate(function test(x: itemtype): Boolean);
  var found: Boolean;
  begin
    found := false;
    while (window <= length) and not found do
      if test(items[window])
      then found := true
      else window := window + 1
  end {locate};



procedure *content(var x: itemtype);
  begin
    if window > length
    then error('no window for content')
    else x := items[window]
  end {content};



procedure *replace(x: itemtype);
  begin
    if window > length
    then error('no window for replace')
    else items[window] := x
  end {replace};



procedure *precedeandmove(x: itemtype);
  var i: 1..maxitems;
  begin
    if length = maxitems
    then error('list overflow')
    else begin
           length := length + 1;
           for i := length downto window + 1 do
             items[i] := items[i - 1];
           items[window] := x
         end
  end {precedeandmove};



procedure *precede(x: itemtype);
  begin
    precedeandmove(x);
    window := window + 1
  end {precede};
```

```
procedure *delete;
  var i: 1..maxitems;
  begin
    if window > length
    then error('no window for delete')
    else begin
         for i := window to length - 1 do
            items[i] := items[i + 1];
         length := length - 1
      end
  end {delete};

procedure *traverse(procedure p(var x: itemtype));
  var i: 1..maxitems;
  begin for i := 1 to length do p(items[i]) end;

begin
  length := 0;
  window := 1;
  ***
end {list};
```

In summary, therefore, the significant characteristics of the contiguous list representation, apart from the predetermined limit on the number of list items, are that the overheads involved in window movement, searching and traversal are minimal, but the overheads in insertion and deletion are significant because of the movement of existing items that is required.

A Chained List Representation

As with other sequences, the limitations of the contiguous representation, and in addition the need to move items around during insertion and deletion, can be avoided by using a chained representation. Like stacks and queues a list can be represented as a singly chained set of records, with pointers running from the first to last item. The list itself is represented by a single pointer to its first item, but to represent the window two additional pointers are needed. One of these points to the record for the item currently in the window, while the other points to its predecessor. The latter is necessary to allow the adjustment of pointers by the insertion or deletion operators. The singly chained representation of a list is thus as shown in Fig. 8.5.

An alternative approach, which simplifies the window representation, is to use double chaining of the item records, i.e. with each item record holding pointers to its successor and predecessor in the list. The window is then representable as a single pointer. A further refinement, which avoids the boundary problems of dealing with the first and last items in a list, is to connect the records as a *ring*, by introducing a dummy sentinel record

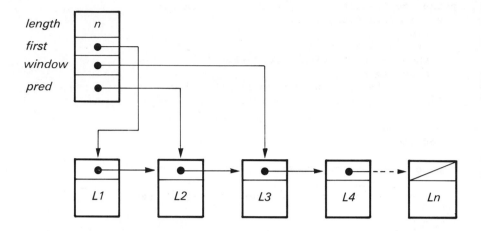

Figure 8.5   Singly chained list representation

linking the first and last items in both directions. The list is then accessed by a pointer to this sentinel, and by definition its first item is the successor of the sentinel, while the last item is the predecessor of the sentinel, as shown in Fig. 8.6.

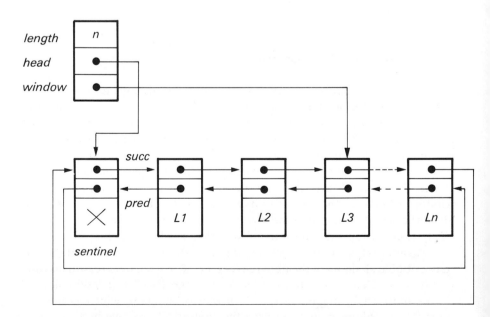

Figure 8.6   Doubly chained ring representation of lists

The declarations necessary to define this representation are:

type *listpointer* = ↑*listrecord* ;
　　listrecord = **record**
　　　　　　　value : *itemtype* ;
　　　　　　　succ, pred : *listpointer*
　　　　　　end ;

　var *length* : 0..*maxint* ;
　　head, window : *listpointer* ;

With the doubly chained ring representation an empty list is represented by a sentinel record whose *succ* and *pred* pointers point to itself. The *inlist* condition is false if the window pointer points to the sentinel record.

　　With these conventions the doubly chained ring representation of our list abstraction may be programmed as shown in Listing 16.

Listing 16

envelope list;

```
{ This envelope maintains a linear list of items, with a    }
{ window for item manipulation. Operators provided are      }
{ locatefront, locaterear, locate, next for window movement, }
{ content and replace for manipulating the window item,     }
{ delete, precede and precedeandmove for altering the list. }
{ Predicates empty, full and inlist test the state of the   }
{ list and the window respectively.                         }
{                                                            }
{ assumes type itemtype = any type with := applicable;      }

const *full = false;

type listpointer = ^listrecord;
     listrecord = record
                    value: itemtype;
                    succ, pred: listpointer
                  end;

var *length: 0..maxint;
    head, window: listpointer;

function *empty: Boolean;
  begin empty := (length = 0) end;

function *inlist: Boolean;
  begin inlist := (window <> head) end;

procedure *locatefront;
  begin window := head^.succ end;
```

continued on page 186

Listing 16 continued

```pascal
procedure *locaterear;
  begin window := head end;

procedure *next;
  begin
    if window = head
    then error('no window for next')
    else window := window^.succ
  end {next};

procedure *locate(function test(x: itemtype): Boolean);
  var found: Boolean;
  begin
    found := false;
    while (window <> head) and not found do
      if test(window^.value)
      then found := true
      else window := window^.succ
  end {locate};

procedure *content(var x: itemtype);
  begin
    if window = head
    then error('no window for content')
    else x := window^.value
  end {content};

procedure *replace(x: itemtype);
  begin
    if window = head
    then error('no window for replace')
    else window^.value := x
  end {replace};

procedure *precede(x: itemtype);
  var p: listpointer;
  begin
    new(p);
    with p^ do
      begin
        value := x;
        succ := window
      end;
    with window^ do
      begin
        p^.pred := pred;
        pred^.succ := p;
        pred := p
      end;
    length := length + 1
  end {precede};
```

```
procedure *precedeandmove(x: itemtype);
  begin
    precede(x);
    window := window^.pred
  end {precedeandmove};



procedure *delete;
  var oldwindow: listpointer;
  begin
    if window = head
    then error('no window for delete')
    else begin
            with window^ do
              begin
                pred^.succ := succ;
                succ^.pred := pred
              end;
            oldwindow := window;
            window := window^.succ;
            dispose(oldwindow);
            length := length - 1
         end
  end {delete};



procedure *traverse(procedure p(var x: itemtype));
  var next: listpointer;
  begin
    next := head^.succ;
    while next <> head do
      begin
        p(next^.value);
        next := next^.succ
      end
  end {traverse};



procedure finish;
  var this, next: listpointer;
  begin
    head^.pred^.succ := nil {to break circle};
    next := head;
    while next <> nil do
      begin
        this := next;
        next := this^.succ;
        dispose(this)
      end
  end {finish};
```

Continued on page 188

Listing 16 continued

```
begin
  length := 0;
  new(head);
  with head^ do
    begin
      succ := head;
      pred := head
    end;
  window := head;
  ###;
  finish
end {list};
```

The notable features of the code involved are as follows:

(a) Double chaining permits the window position to be represented by a single pointer, which in turn simplifies the code required for the *next* operator, and more particularly for each iteration of the search loop used by *locate*. This reduction in the overheads of window movement makes the doubly chained representation comparable in efficiency to the contiguous representation for repetitive list processing.

(b) The chained representation avoids the need to move existing items during insertion and deletion. In addition, the ring organization elimi- nates the need for special logic to deal with the boundary cases of inserting or deleting items at the start or end of the list.

Thus the doubly chained ring representation of a list avoids the insertion and deletion overheads associated with a contiguous representation, and achieves comparable efficiency for window movement, searching and trav- ersal.

The efficient window movement enabled by double chaining is of course achieved at the expense of storing two chaining pointers per list record rather than one, thus aggravating the inherent storage overhead of chained representations. For long lists of small items this aggravated storage overhead may be very significant indeed.

If the ring organization is retained, a singly chained representation of a list can be programmed which reduces the storage overhead, and is no more complex overall than the doubly chained representation. The significant difference, however, is that two pointer assignments rather than one are required in implementing the *next* operator, and in each iteration of the search loop used by *locate*. The time overhead for repetitive window move- ment created by this extra pointer assignment is the price paid for the saving in pointer storage achieved by adopting a singly chained representation.

CASE STUDY : A SIMPLE TEXT EDITOR

To illustrate the use of our general list abstraction, let us now consider the implementation of a simple text editor which enables text files to be edited from a video terminal. Each run of the editor program will read and display the contents of an existing textfile, and then allow its user to edit the contents using the following keyboard commands, each of which is terminated by the newline key appropriate to the terminal.

Mn : Moves the cursor forward n (> 0) characters in the text, or to the end of the text, whichever comes first. If n is omitted, a default value of 1 is assumed.

Fc : Find the next occurrence of character c, or the end of the text, whichever comes first, and leave the cursor there. If c is omitted, i.e. *F* is immediately followed by the newline key, the cursor moves to the end of the current line.

Dn : Delete the next n characters from the text, or the rest of the text if there are less than n characters remaining, and leave the cursor on the first character following those deleted. If n is omitted a default value of 1 is assumed.

Is : Insert the string of characters s immediately before the cursor. The string s may include newlines and is terminated by a special character *ESCAPE* which cannot itself be inserted in the text.

B : Move the cursor to the beginning of the displayed text.

E : Move the cursor to the end of the displayed text.

Q : Quit the edit without updating the textfile.

U : End the edit after updating the original textfile with the edited text.

The editor program must deal with three input/output streams: the keyboard input, the screen output and the text file to be edited. During editing it must also maintain a copy of the current text, together with a representation of the cursor position within it. For the range of edit commands specified, our list abstraction is a convenient means of doing so, with each list item being a character, and the list window representing the cursor position.

With these decisions the overall form of the editor program can now be written down, as follows:

```
program editor (keyboard, screen, textfile) ;

    var keyboard, screen, textfile : text ;
```

```
envelope charlist = list in library
  (where const max = ... ;
            type itemtype = char;) ;

instance textlist : charlist ;

begin {editor}
  read textfile and store as textlist ;
  repeat
    display current text ;
    obey next command
  until end of edit requested
end {editor}.
```

To maintain, and to allow the user to alter, the line structure of the initial text file the text list must include some explicit representation of the ends of line involved. This is done most conveniently by reserving a single character value, which we denote by the constant identifier *eol*, for this purpose. The actual value chosen will depend on the character set involved, but in general a suitable choice can be made without inconveniencing the user. With this decision the process of reading in the text file and storing it as the text list can be programmed as follows:

```
procedure readtext ;
  var ch : char ;
  begin
    reset (textfile) ;
    while not eof (textfile) do
    begin
      while not eoln (textfile) do
      begin
        read (textfile, ch) ;
        textlist.precede (ch)
      end ;
      textlist.precede (eol) ;
      readln (textfile)
    end
  end {readtext} ;
```

Our initial specification of the editor program did not define the initial position of the text cursor. Since it is to be represented directly by the window position of the list chosen to represent the text the above input procedure will automatically leave the cursor at the end of the text.

Displaying the current text on the screen requires careful consideration. For simplicity, we will treat the screen as a sequential text file that is completely rewritten each time the text is displayed. In practice such a simple approach may not be acceptable on efficiency grounds, but since the ways in which it might be improved are dependent on the video terminal and i/o system involved we will not consider it further here. Two other display problems remain to be tackled: one is the recreation of line structure in the displayed text, and the other is the display of the cursor position.

With explicit *eol* values stored in the text list, recreation of line structure is easily accomplished, but the cursor display deserves further consideration. A notable feature of our design decisions so far is that physical display of the cursor position is a problem local to the display procedure—for the remainder of the editor program the list window concept represents the cursor position, and its physical representation on the video screen is irrelevant. In practice, how the cursor position is displayed will also depend on the capabilities of the video terminal involved—it may be done by causing the appropriate text character to flash, to be displayed in reverse video, to be underlined, or simply to be preceded by a special cursor character. In most cases, whatever the display technique chosen, it will be implemented by outputting one or more additional characters, either visible or control, immediately before the text character at the cursor position. With our text list representation this can be achieved conveniently by:

(a)   temporary insertion of the necessary characters in the text list;

(b)   sequential output of the text list character by character to the screen, using the *traverse* operator;

(c)   removal of the temporary cursor characteristics inserted.

Using this approach the display of the current text can be programmed as follows:

```
procedure displaytext ;

   procedure insertcursor ; . . .

   procedure removecursor ; . . .

   procedure display (ch : char) ;
      begin
         if ch = eol
         then writeln (screen)
         else write (screen, ch)
      end {display} ;

   begin {displaytext}
      rewrite (screen) ;
      insertcursor ;
      textlist.traverse (display) ;
      removecursor
   end {displaytext} ;
```

The characters inserted and removed by the procedures *insertcursor* and *removecursor* will depend on the cursor display mechanism chosen, but in all cases, the procedures should be expressible using the list operators *precedeandmove* and *delete*.

Obeying each command input by the user involves obtaining a valid initial command letter and then selecting an appropriate command interpretation according to the letter involved. This leads directly to the following procedure:

```
procedure obeycommand ;
    var command : char ;
    begin
        readandvalidate (command) ;
        case command of
        'M' : obeymove ;
        'F' : obeyfind ;
        'D' : obeydelete ;
        'I' : obeyinsert ;
        'B' : textlist.locatefront ;
        'E' : textlist.locaterear ;
        'Q' : endofedit := true ;
        'U' : begin filetext ; endofedit := true end
        end
    end {obeycommand} ;
```

The *readandvalidate* procedure should obtain an initial valid command character in a 'user-friendly' manner, rejecting invalid characters with a helpful message until a valid character is input.

The *B* and *E* commands map directly onto corresponding *textlist* operators. The *Q* and *U* commands set a global flag *endofedit* to terminate the editor's command obeying loop, and the *filetext* procedure used by the *U* command rewrites the textfile from the current textlist contents, using the *traverse* operator in a similar way to the procedure *displaytext*.

The *M,F,D*, and *I* commands require more consideration, but again their effects are easily realized in terms of the list operators applicable to *textlist*, as the following procedures show:

```
procedure obeymove :
    var n,i : integer ;
    begin
        readoptional (n, 1) ;
        i := 0 ;
        while (i < n) and textlist.inlist do
        begin textlist.next ; i := i+1 end
    end {obeymove} ;
```

```
procedure obeyfind ;
  var target : char ;

  function matchtarget (ch : char) : Boolean ;
    begin matchtarget := (ch = target) end ;

  begin
    if eoln (keyboard)
    then target := eol
    else read (keyboard, target) ;
    textlist.locate (matchtarget)
  end {obeyfind} ;

procedure obeydelete ;
  var n,i : integer ;
  begin
    readoptional (n, 1) ;
    i := 0 ;
    while (i < n) and textlist.inlist do
    begin textlist.delete ; i := i+1 end
  end {obeydelete} ;

procedure obeyinsert ;
  var insertioncomplete : Boolean ;
      nextchar : char ;
  begin
    insertioncomplete := false ;
    repeat
      if eoln (keyboard)
      then begin
             textlist.precede (eol) ;
             readln (keyboard)
           end
      else begin
             read (keyboard, nextchar) ;
             if nextchar = escape
             then insertioncomplete := true
             else textlist.precede (nextchar)
           end
    until insertioncomplete
  end {obeyinsert} ;
```

The procedure *readoptional* used by *obeymove* and *obeydelete* has the form:

```
procedure readoptional (var n:integer ; default:integer) ;
```

and its effect is to read a valid integer from the keyboard and assign it to *n* if one is input, otherwise *n* is assigned the value *default*.

With these details resolved, we have now completed our development of the editor program, and the complete program that results is shown in Listing 17.

Listing 17

```
program editor(keyboard, screen, textfile, output);

{ a simple editor which updates the file textfile, }
{ in response to commands from the file keyboard,  }
{ while displaying the text so far on the screen,   }
{ which is treated as a rewritable textfile.        }
{                                                    }
{ The commands recognised are as follows:           }
{                                                    }
{    Mn    - move cursor forward n characters       }
{    Fc    - find next character 'c'                }
{    Dn    - delete n characters                    }
{    Is    - insert string s (terminated by ESC)    }
{    B     - move cursor back to beginning of text  }
{    E     - move cursor to end of text             }
{    Q     - quit without updating textfile         }
{    U     - quit after updating textfile           }

var keyboard, screen, textfile: text;
    eol, cursor, escape: char;
    endofedit: Boolean;

envelope charlist = list in library
  (where const maxitems = 10000;
         type itemtype = char; );

instance textlist: charlist;

procedure readtext;

  { reads contents of textfile into textlist }

  var ch: char;
  begin
    reset(textfile);
    while not eof(textfile) do
      begin
        while not eoln(textfile) do
          begin
            read(textfile, ch);
            textlist.precede(ch)
          end;
```

```
          textlist.precede(eol);
          readln(textfile)
        end
    end {readtext};

procedure filetext;

   { outputs contents of textlist to textfile }


     procedure filechar(var ch: char);
        begin
          if ch = eol
          then writeln(textfile)
          else write(textfile, ch)
        end {filechar};

     begin
        rewrite(textfile);
        textlist.traverse(filechar)
     end {filetext};

procedure displaytext;

   { outputs contents of textlist to screen, }
   { with cursor preceding window character. }


     procedure insertcursor;
        begin textlist.precedeandmove(cursor) end;

     procedure removecursor;
        begin textlist.delete end;

     procedure display(var ch: char);
        begin
          if ch = eol
          then writeln(screen)
          else write(screen, ch)
        end {display};

     begin
        rewrite(screen);
        insertcursor;
        textlist.traverse(display);
        removecursor
     end {displaytext};

procedure obeycommand;
     var command: char;
```

Continued on page 196

Listing 17 continued

```pascal
procedure readcommand;

   { obtains valid initial character for command }

   begin
     read(keyboard, command);
     while not (command in
                 ['M', 'F', 'D', 'I', 'B', 'E', 'Q', 'U']) do
       begin
         writeln(screen, 'invalid command character');
         read(keyboard, command)
       end
   end {readcommand};

procedure readoptional(var n: integer; default: integer);

   { reads integer n if input, otherwise n := default }

   begin
     while (keyboard^ = ' ') and not eoln(keyboard) do
       get(keyboard);
     if eoln(keyboard)
     then n := default
     else read(keyboard, n)
   end {readoptional};

procedure obeymove;
   var n, i: integer;
   begin
     readoptional(n, 1);
     i := 0;
     while (i < n) and textlist.inlist do
       begin
         textlist.next;
         i := i + 1
       end
   end {obeymove};

procedure obeyfind;
   var target: char;

   function matchtarget(ch: char): Boolean;
     begin matchtarget := (ch = target) end;

   begin
     if eoln(keyboard)
     then target := eol
     else read(keyboard, target);
     textlist.locate(matchtarget)
   end {obeyfind};
```

```
procedure obeydelete;
  var n, i: integer;
  begin
    readoptional(n, 1);
    i := 0;
    while (i < n) and textlist.inlist do
      begin
        textlist.delete;
        i := i + 1
      end
  end {obeydelete};

procedure obeyinsert;
  var insertioncomplete: Boolean;
      nextchar: char;
  begin
    insertioncomplete := false;
    repeat
      if eoln(keyboard)
      then begin
             textlist.precede(eol);
             readln(keyboard)
           end
      else begin
             read(keyboard, nextchar);
             if nextchar = escape
             then insertioncomplete := true
             else textlist.precede(nextchar)
           end
    until insertioncomplete
  end {obeyinsert};

begin
  readcommand;
  case command of
    'M' : obeymove;
    'F' : obeyfind;
    'D' : obeydelete;
    'I' : obeyinsert;
    'B' : textlist.locatefront;
    'E' : textlist.locaterear;
    'Q' : endofedit := true;
    'U' :
      begin
        filetext;
        endofedit := true
      end
  end;
  readln(keyboard)
end {obeycommand};
```

Continued on page 198

Listing 17 continued

```
begin
  eol := '*';
  cursor := '*';
  escape := '*';
  readtext;
  reset(keyboard);
  repeat
    displaytext;
    obeycommand
  until endofedit
end {editor}
```

     The notable feature of the editor program is the relative ease with which its features were expressed in terms of the generalized list abstraction previously introduced, with a consequent increase in clarity and reliability for the editor itself, assuming a reliable implementation of the list abstraction is already available. Some reservations must be noted about the adequacy of the methods used to re-display the modified text and cursor position on the screen after each user command has been executed. For some displays, or editing larger texts that require windowing or scrolling techniques, achieving efficient implementation via a single text list would involve alteration of the list abstraction itself. An alternative approach, however, is to adopt a more structured representation of the text based on the existing list abstraction, perhaps using several list instances each representing some convenient segment of the overall text involved. It is left to the reader to investigate the possibilities of such an approach.

SORTING LISTS

In general the order of the items in a list is determined by their insertion, according to the needs of the application. Thus, in the editor program, characters were inserted in the text list to reflect their positions in the text itself.

     In some cases, however, the items in a list may have an inherent natural order determined by the item values themselves, or indeed several such natural orders determined by different characteristics of the item values. Thus, for example, in the word list produced by the concordance program one natural order is the alphabetic or lexicographic order of the word spellings themselves. Another natural order is the order of descending frequency of occurrence, as determined by the *count* fields of the word records, perhaps with a secondary lexicographic ordering for words with the same frequency. In the concordance program it would be desirable to print the word list in either of these orders, rather than the arbitrary order determined by the first occurrence of each word. To achieve this, we need to rearrange or sort the items in our word list into the natural order required, a requirement which is typical of many list processing applications where items have an inherent natural order.

To cater for this requirement we therefore add a *sort* operator to the range of operators provided by our general list abstraction. This operator must be supplied with some means of determining whether two items are ordered, since the abstraction itself should not make assumptions about the nature, and hence natural ordering, of items of the list. To allow the different orders to be requested for the same list of items, the ordering function is supplied as an actual parameter to each call of the *sort* operator, which is specified as:

procedure **sort* (**function** *inorder* (*i*1, *i*2 : *itemtype*) : *Boolean*) ;

After a call of this procedure the items of the list will be in the order determined by the parametric function *inorder*, i.e., for any pair of adjacent items *a,b* occurring in the list *inorder* (*a,b*) will be true. We assume that *inorder* defines a transitive ordering, i.e. that

$$inorder(a, b) \text{ and } inorder(b, c) \quad \text{implies} \quad inorder(a, c).$$

To illustrate the use of this sort operator, let us consider how we might print the word list of our earlier concordance program in various orders. Firstly, let us print it in lexicographic order. We thus amend the *printwords* procedure to first sort the list by preceding the printing with a call of

list.sort (*lexorder*)

where *lexorder* is a local Boolean function which defines the ordering between two *wordrecord* values. Hence the *printwords* procedure becomes

```
procedure *printwords (var printfile : textfile) ;

   function lexorder (w1, w2 : wordrecord) : Boolean;
      begin
         lexorder := (w1.spelling <= w2.spelling)
      end ;

   procedure printword (w : wordrecord);
      begin
         writeln (printfile, w.spelling, w.count)
      end ;

   begin
      list.sort (lexorder);
      list.traverse (printword)
   end {printwords};
```

However, should we wish instead to print the words in descending order of frequency of occurrence, all that requires to be changed is the definition of the ordering function to reflect the new ordering required, viz:

```
procedure printwords (var printfile : textfile) ;

   function countorder (w1, w2 : wordrecord) : Boolean;
      begin
         countorder := (w1.count > w2.count) or
                       (w1.count = w2.count) and
                       (w1.spelling < w2.spelling)
      end {countorder} ;

   procedure printword (w : recordword);
      begin
         writeln (printfile, w.spelling, w.count)
      end {printword} ;

begin
   list.sort (countorder);
   list.traverse (printword)
end {printwords} ;
```

Implementing the Sort Operator

If a list is implemented using a contiguous array representation, then a wide variety of sorting techniques are available for implementation of the sort operator. We shall describe just two methods that are commonly used—the unsophisticated straight selection sort which illustrates the characteristics of major sorting methods, and a famous algorithm, Hoare's Quicksort—so-called because it is generally the fastest array sorting method. For a full review of array sorting techniques and a comparative analysis the reader is referred to the excellent treatment of the subject [Wirth, 1975].

Given an array A of n items the straight selection algorithm may be described as:

```
for i := 1 to n−1 do
begin
   find the least item of A[i], . . . , A[n] ;
   exchange A[i] and the least item
end
```

For example, the sorting of an array of 6 integer elements by the straight selection method proceeds as shown in Fig. 8.7.

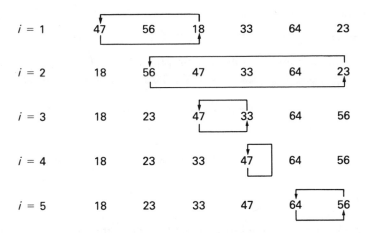

$i = 1$	47	56	18	33	64	23
$i = 2$	18	56	47	33	64	23
$i = 3$	18	23	47	33	64	56
$i = 4$	18	23	33	47	64	56
$i = 5$	18	23	33	47	64	56

Figure 8.7 Selection sort of 6 integers

The complete sort operator for our array representation of a list using straight selection is given below. By definition the window is not on any list item following a sort.

procedure *sort (**function** inorder (i1, i2 : itemtype) : Boolean) ;

 var firstunsorted, least, next : 1 . . max;
  leastvalue : itemtype;

begin
 for firstunsorted := 1 **to** length−1 **do**
 begin
  least := firstunsorted ;
  for next := firstunsorted +1 **to** length **do**
   if not inorder (items[least], items[next])
   then least := next;
  leastvalue := items[least];
  items[least] := items[firstunsorted];
  items[firstunsorted] := leastvalue
 end ;
 window := length +1
end {sort};

The performance of an *in situ* sorting algorithm, i.e. one that achieves its effect by re-arranging the items to be sorted within the storage originally occupied by them, is usually estimated by counting the number of ordering comparisons and the number of item exchanges involved. For the straight selection sort as given above, the number of comparisons involved in sorting a list of n items is

$$NC = (n - 1) + (n - 2) + \cdots + 2 + 1 = \tfrac{1}{2}n(n - 1)$$

The number of exchanges involved is simply

$$NE = n - 1$$

For large n, therefore, the comparisons will dominate the total effort involved in the sort, and the time taken will vary as n^2. This result is typical of simple sorting techniques, and improvement on this n^2 behavior is the goal of 'improved' sorting algorithms, the most famous of which we now consider.

Quicksort

Before developing the Quicksort algorithm we note that the stepwise refinement approach to problem solving can itself be considered as a recursive process, viz,

```
procedure solveproblem (p);
    begin
      if immediately soluble
      then write down solution
      else begin
            split p into n subproblems p[1], . . . , p[n];
            for i := 1 to n do solveproblem (p[i])
          end
    end {solveproblem};
```

The basis of stepwise refinement is that the complexity, the effort required, and potential for error in a solution all increase non-linearly with the problem size, and a divide-and-simplify strategy reduces each of these overall 'costs'.

The straight selection method illustrates that the costs of sorting items also increases non-linearly with n. Can we reduce the cost of sorting by a divide-and-simplify strategy similar to that of stepwise refinement?

We might conceive the following initial sorting strategy:

```
procedure sort (array A);
    begin
      if sorting is needed
      then begin
            split A into segments S1,S2;
            sort (S1);
            sort (S2)
          end
    end {sort};
```

For this procedure to meet its specification the segments $S1$ and $S2$ must be such that sorting each completes the sorting of A, i.e. all elements in $S1$ must already be ordered with respect to all elements $S2$, or

   inorder $(S1[i], S2[j])$ *for all valid i and j*

In a practical sorting algorithm we wish to avoid the use of additional storage and to minimize the movement of items, so the segments $S1$ and $S2$ must be held within A. With this in mind, we reformulate our solution as follows:

```
procedure sort (first, last : integer);
   begin
      if first < last
      then begin
               partition A[first . . last] into two segments;
               sort (first, lastoffirstsegment);
               sort (firstoflastsegment, last)
            end
   end {sort};
```

How can we carry out the partitioning operation?

Suppose we define our goal to be an initial segment of elements not greater than some partition value x, and a final segment of elements not less than x. We can define the partitioning process as one which begins with both segments initially empty and repeatedly extends each segment until they meet. Extension is trivial when the next element already fits that segment. When this is not so, the stopper values can be interchanged and the process continued:

```
x := some suitable value;
i := first; j := last;
repeat
   while inorder(A[i], x) do i := i+1;
   while inorder(x, A[j]) do j := j−1;
   if i <= j
   then begin
            interchange A[i] and A[j];
            i := i+1 ; j := j−1
         end
until i > j
```

How do we choose x? Ideally, we should like x to be the median value of those to be sorted so as to give two partitions equal in size. In practice, we settle for some arbitrary value chosen from those to be sorted, e.g.

$$x := A[(first + last) \textbf{ div } 2]$$

This arbitrary choice, however, means that the partition value x may be either the 'least' or the 'greatest' of those to be partitioned, in which case one or other of the while loops above will increase i beyond *last* or will decrease j below *first*. To avoid this the while loops can be rewritten to stop on an item value 'equal' to the partition value x and (unnecessarily) have it swapped into the other segment. In terms of the *inorder* function this is achieved by re-expressing the while loops as follows:

> **while not** *inorder* $(x, A[i])$ **do** $i := i+1$;
> **while not** *inorder* $(A[j], x)$ **do** $j := j-1$;

In practice the unnecessary item exchanges caused by this modification are significant only if the array being sorted contains large numbers of 'equal' items.

It should be noted that when the partition loop terminates the values of i and j are not necessarily adjacent, but if they are not, then the item values $A[j+1], A[j+2], \ldots, A[i-1]$ are all equal to the chosen partition value x and require no further consideration in the sort process. Thus, for the purpose of the recursive quicksort procedure outlined above, it is sufficient to take i as *firstoflastsegment* and j as *lastoffirstsegment* so that the procedure required to sort the array items of our contiguous list representation becomes:

```
procedure quicksort (first, last : integer);

    var i,j : integer;
        x,y : itemtype;

    begin
      if first < last
      then begin
              x := items[(first + last) div 2];
              i := first; j := last;
              repeat
                 while not inorder (x, items[i]) do i := i+1;
                 while not inorder (items[j], x) do j := j-1;
                 if i <= j
                 then begin
                         y := items[i]; items[i] := items[j];
                         items[j] := y;
                         i := i+1; j := j-1
                      end
```

```
            until i > j;
            quicksort (first, j);
            quicksort (i, last)
        end
end {quicksort};
```

The overall sort process as represented by the starred operator then contains *quicksort* as a local procedure and consists of an initial call of *quicksort* to sort the first *length* elements of the array, i.e.:

procedure **sort* (**function** *inorder* (*i1, i2 : itemtype*) : *Boolean*);

procedure *quicksort* (*first, last : integer*); . . . {*as above*}

```
begin
    quicksort (1, length);
    window := length +1
end {sort};
```

How does the performance of the Quicksort algorithm compare with the straight selection sort? In this case the analysis depends on how the arbitrary choice of the partition value x affects the subdivision of the sorting task. Consider two cases, one ideal, the other the worst that can occur.

First let us suppose that each arbitrary choice happens to produce the ideal value for x, i.e. one that splits the segment under consideration into two equal parts. In this case sorting proceeds through an equal number of recursion levels at all parts of the array. At each level every item in the array is compared with some partition value x, and, if we suppose a random disposition of items within each segment, on average half of these items need to be moved. Since each interchange 'corrects' the position of two items, we thus have that n comparisons and, on average, $n/4$ exchanges take place at each level of recursion.

How many levels of recursion actually arise? If we assume again that each partitioning operation produces two equal segments, then the number of recursive levels required to produce n segments of length 1 is $\log_2 n$, as shown in Fig. 8.8(a). Thus in this ideal case we have:

the number of comparisons $NC = n\log_2 n$, and
the average number of exchanges $NE = \tfrac{1}{4}n \log_2 n$

for the Quicksort algorithm.

Now consider the worst case that can arise. This is when the partition value x chosen for each segment is the 'least' or 'greatest' value in the segment, leading to its partitioning into two sub-segments, one containing a

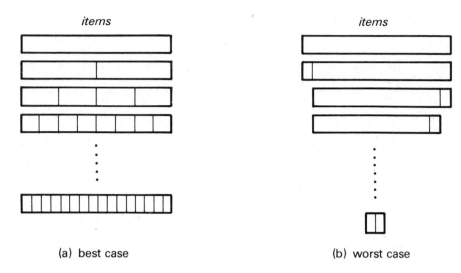

items   *items*

(a) best case   (b) worst case

Figure 8.8   Recursive levels of partitioning with Quicksort

single item, the other containing the rest. The recursive call to sort the single item segment terminates immediately and sorting continues via the recursive call to sort the rest. If this worst case choice of x occurs at every level, sorting will proceed through $n-1$ significant levels of recursion as shown in Fig. 8.8(b). At each level one exchange takes place, and the number of comparisons at successive levels is n, $n-1$, $n-2$, etc. Thus in this worst case the performance (and indeed the behavior) of the Quicksort algorithm is equivalent to that of the selection sort and will vary as n^2 for large n.

In practice, of course, neither of these extreme cases is likely to occur in an application of the Quicksort algorithm, and on average its performance will be somewhere between these extremes. In fact it can be shown by more complex analysis that the average performance of Quicksort lies significantly closer to the $n\log_2 n$ best case than the n^2 worst case, a property which makes Quicksort one of the most powerful array sorting algorithms available.

Sorting a Chained List

The sorting methods described for use with the array representation of lists have the common property that they achieve their objective by interchanging items within the available array storage. No extra storage is used to hold items during sorting. This is an important requirement in many sorting contexts.

In the case of chained representations the storage occupied by list items exists as a set of record storage areas linked by pointers. In principle, there is no reason why lists held in this way cannot be sorted by interchanging items within the existing chained storage, leaving the pointer connections between storage areas unaltered. Thus, the straight selection sort algorithm can be implemented for a single chained list representation, using pointers rather than array indices to express the inspection and item interchanges involved. With a double chained representation the Quicksort algorithm can also be implemented, though termination of the recursion and of the partitioning loop must be expressed in terms of segment lengths computed and passed through each level of recursion.

However, chained representations also make possible an alternative approach, which is to produce a sorted list by rearranging the pointers that connect the item records together, without any movement or copying of the items themselves. Given an unsorted chain of items, a sorted chain can be formed by detaching the items from the unsorted chain, one by one, and re-linking each into an appropriate position within an (initially empty)

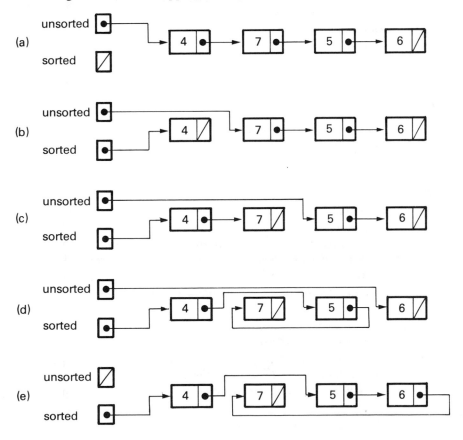

Figure 8.9 Insertion sort of chained list

sorted chain. The stages in sorting an unsorted chain of integer values is illustrated in Fig. 8.9.

Although two conceptual lists are involved in this sorting process, the list items occupy the same list records throughout and no copying or creation of extra records is required. Only the pointers connecting the records are changed. This *insertion sort* method is implemented for the doubly chained ring representation of a list as follows:

```
procedure *sort (function inorder (i1, i2 : itemtype) : Boolean);

    var oldlist, thisitem, possiblesucc : listpointer;
        positionfound : Boolean;

    begin
        {detach old list and reset head as empty list}
        oldlist := head ↑.succ;
        head↑.succ := head;
        head↑.pred := head;

        {insert items in new list one by one}
        while oldlist <> head do
        begin
            {detach next item from old list}
            thisitem := oldlist;
            oldlist := oldlist↑.succ;

            {find position in new list}
            possiblesucc := head↑.succ;
            positionfound := false;
            while possiblesucc <> head and not positionfound do
                if inorder (thisitem↑.value, possiblesucc↑.value)
                then positionfound := true
                else possiblesucc := possiblesucc↑.succ;

            {insert item in new list}
            thisitem↑.succ := possiblesucc;
            thisitem↑.pred := possiblesucc↑.pred;
            possiblesucc↑.pred↑.succ := thisitem;
            possiblesucc↑.pred := thisitem
        end;

        window := head
    end {sort};
```

Algorithms for sorting chained lists are characterized by the number of item comparisons NC and the number of item repositioning operations (by pointer rearrangement) NR that they involve. In the case of the insertion sort above, the average number of comparisons required to insert an item in the new list of length i is $i/2$, so the total number of comparisons on average in sorting a list of n items is:

$$NC = \tfrac{1}{2}(1+2+\cdots+(n-1)) = \tfrac{1}{4}n(n-1)$$

and the number of rearrangements is clearly

$$NR = n$$

Thus the number of comparisons on average is half that required by the selection sort, but still varies as n^2 for large n.

As with array sorting algorithms, improvements on this n^2 behavior can be obtained. The chained list analogue of the Quicksort algorithm recursively partitions each list into two sublists by comparison with some partition value, until n lists of length 1 are obtained, then concatenates these as the recursion unwinds to produce a single sorted list. With optimal partition values giving sublists of equal length at every level the number of comparisons NC and number of repositioning operations NR each vary as $n \log n$ for large n. With arbitrary partition values, say by using the first value on any list to partition the remainder, behavior somewhere between $n \log n$ and n^2 can again be obtained. It is left as an exercise to the reader to implement such a recursive sort for the doubly chained ring representation.

MAINTAINING SORTED LISTS

For some applications the ability to sort and resort a list (perhaps to different ordering criteria) is a necessity, and for these the *sort* operator of our list abstraction is essential. For other applications it may be equally valid to build and maintain the list in the required order, as was done in our original concordance program in Chapter 4. The principal advantage of building and maintaining an ordered list in this way is that the sort overhead is avoided and the insertion time for a new item is reduced (since, on average, only half the list need be searched to determine whether the value is already in the list, compared with the complete list search required in the case of an unordered list). However, note that subsequent searches for items already in a list are not faster since, for both ordered and unordered lists, half the list is searched on average.

In practice, ordered lists can be built and maintained using our existing list abstraction, often with very little additional programming effort. For example, we might wish to rewrite the concordance program so that it builds its word list in dictionary order. All that is required to achieve this modification is that the *test* function passed to the *locate* operator be modified so that the search of the list terminates as soon as an entry with the same or a greater spelling is located. If a new word is to be inserted into the list (i.e. the search terminates by finding an entry with a greater spelling), then the insertion must take place immediately in front of this entry to maintain the correct spelling. Hence, the only change required to the *recordword* procedure is to replace the local function *equals* by a new function *notless*, which is then passed in the call of the search procedure *locate*, i.e:

```
procedure *recordword (word : wordspelling);

   var entry : wordrecord;

   function notless (w : wordrecord) : Boolean;
      begin
        notless := (w.spelling >= word)
      end {notless};

   procedure insertword;
      var entry : wordrecord;
      begin
        with entry do
        begin spelling := word; count := 1 end;
        list.precede (entry)
      end {insertword};

   begin {recordword}
      with list do
      begin
        locatefront;
        locate (notless);
        if inlist
        then begin
             contents (entry);
             if entry.spelling = word
             then begin
                  entry.count := entry.count+1;
                  replace (entry)
                end
             else insertword {before entry found}
           end
        else insertword {at end of list}
      end
   end {recordword};
```

In this case the cost of building and maintaining the wordlist in word order is clearly no greater than before, and the substantial cost of sorting the list before printout is avoided. The same technique cannot be adopted, however, if printout in count order is required, since the final count values are not known when the list entries are created. In this case, sorting the list items when the final count values have been accumulated is the only way to obtain the required effect.

Thus, in general, building and maintaining a sorted list may be more economical if a single sorted order is required and if the item characteristics that determine that order are known when the items are first inserted. However, if more than one sorted order is required or if the item characteristics that determine the required order vary during the lifetime of the list, then sorting or resorting the list at the appropriate moment is the only means of achieving the required effect, and for a large list the sort algorithm chosen may have a significant impact on the overall efficiency of the program concerned.

AN ORDERED LIST ABSTRACTION

In the version of *recordword* which maintains an ordered list, two points deserve further consideration:

(a)   the required list ordering is achieved by careful choice of the *notless* function used as the parameter for the *locate* operator, and by the subsequent use of the *precede* operator;

(b)   the list entry for an existing word is updated by use of the *contents* and *replace* operators. In this case it is clear that the updating carried out alters only the *count* field, and not the *spelling* field from which the entry's position in the list was determined. In general, however, there is a danger that direct replacement of items in a previously ordered list may violate the ordering requirement. With our existing list abstraction it is the user's responsibility to ensure that this does not happen.

It is of course possible to respecify our list abstraction so that it is guaranteed to maintain each list in some predefined order, so relieving the user program of these responsibilities. The principal changes in specification required are as follows:

(a)   The ordering required for the items in any list must be specified and must remain fixed for the lifetime of that list. The most flexible way to do so is to have the ordering function supplied as a function parameter in each list instance declaration, by changing the envelope heading as follows:

        envelope *orderedlist* (**function** *inorder*(*i1*, *i2*: *itemtype*): *Boolean*);

Each list created as an instance of this envelope can then have a distinct ordering function. A simpler but less flexible alternative is that the envelope assumes a global definition of the function *inorder*, which may then be fixed in a *where* clause on retrieval of the list envelope from the library.

(b) The appropriate position for inserting a new item x in the list is determined by its value, and not by the existing window position. Thus it is logical to replace the operators *precede* and *precedeandmove* by a single operator

   procedure **insert (x:itemtype)*;

which positions the new item x in the list to maintain the required ordering. By convention we specify that *insert* leaves the list window on the inserted item.

(c) In the typical use of ordered lists, locating existing items involves searching for an item that is 'equal' to a specified item value. For this purpose the *locate* operator is either replaced or supplemented by an operator

   procedure **locatevalue (x:itemtype)*;

which searches the entire list for an item 'equal' to x and leaves the window on this item if one is found. What do we mean by item 'equality'? In practice equality can be defined in terms of the existing ordering function as follows: Two items x and y are 'equal' if *inorder(x,y)* **and** *inorder(y,x)* is true. This is consistent with normal convention, provided the *inorder* function does not define a strict ordering, i.e. provided *inorder(x,x)* for any item value x is true rather than false, an assumption we have already made in deriving the Quicksort algorithm.

(d) As the concordance program shows, it is still necessary to inspect and update the value of existing list items in an ordered list. In our general list abstraction this is enabled by the *contents* and *replace* operators. In an ordered list, however, we must ensure that alteration of an existing list item does not violate its ordering relationship with its neighbors. Thus if the *replace* operator is used to replace the window item w, with predecessor p and successor s, by item x it must ensure that the condition *inorder(p,x)* **and** *inorder(x,s)* is true. If x does not meet this condition the replacement must be accomplished by executing a *delete; insert(x)* sequence.

With these modifications to our list specification it is possible to modify the corresponding list implementations to support ordered lists. For the moment these modifications are left as an exercise for the reader. In the case of the array implementation, the ordered property of the list may be taken advantage of, by using the binary split search technique outlined in Chapter 6 to locate existing items and to position items being inserted. A correspondingly improved technique for pointer implementations will be discussed in Chapter 10.

Consider now the use of this ordered list abstraction in the concordance program. The list itself will be created within the *wordlist* module by the following declarations:

```
envelope orderedlist in library
    (where type itemtype = wordrecord;);

function wordorder(w1, w2: wordrecord): Boolean;
    begin wordorder := w1.spelling <= w2.spelling end;

instance list : orderedlist (wordorder);
```

The procedure *recordword* can then be defined as follows:

```
procedure *recordword (word:wordspelling) ;

    var entry : wordrecord ;

    begin
      with entry do
      begin spelling := word ; count := 1 end ;
      with list do
      begin
        locatevalue (entry) ;
        if inlist
        then begin
                contents (entry);
                entry.count := entry.count +1;
                replace (entry)
            end
        else insert (entry)
      end
    end {recordword} ;
```

Thus the ordered list abstraction further simplifies the *recordword* procedure of the concordance program, and relieves the programmer of any responsibility of ensuring that the word list remains ordered. Note, however, that when a new entry is inserted in the list its position is determined independently of the previous *locatevalue* operation, so that two 'searches' of the list structure will occur—one for the unsuccessful *locatevalue* operation, the other to determine the appropriate position for the resulting insertion.

These consequences of using the ordered list abstraction are typical of those involved in the use of higher level abstractions. The ordered list is a *higher level* abstraction than the general list abstraction defined previously. As such it simplifies the programming of those applications that need ordered lists, but in doing so reduces the programmer's control over how the required operations are implemented. Whether this loss of control is significant in efficiency terms will depend on how the search operations are implemented for the ordered list, and on the length of the ordered lists to be manipulated.

SUMMARY

In this chapter we have studied the list as our most general abstraction of a sequence, in which the user program determines the position of list items according to the needs of the application concerned. As such, it is a significantly more complex abstraction than the stacks and queues in Chapter 7.

Similar increases in complexity arise in the manipulations required by list applications, which are typified by the searching and sorting processes. The cost of such manipulations varies with the length of list concerned, a fact which must be borne in mind in writing any program that uses them. If a standard list abstraction from a library is to be used, the programmer must choose a version with performance characteristics appropriate to the program requirements. If a list, or some variation of it, is to be implemented directly within the program, the programmer must be aware of the techniques available and of the significant variations in performance that they involve.

These variations between possible list representations may be summarized as follows:

(a)   Contiguous representations of lists, in addition to the usual fixed storage allocation that they imply, impose an overhead on random insertions and deletions, due to the movement of list items involved. On the other hand, they are amenable to accelerated sorting and searching techniques such as Quicksort and the binary split search of ordered lists.

(b)   Chained representations are flexible in their use of storage and impose no overheads on random insertion and deletion. However, they involve the usual overhead in storage per item, which is doubled if chaining is used to give faster window movement. More significantly, they are less amenable to accelerated searching and sorting techniques, if strictly linear chaining is maintained.

In the next chapter we will study a pointer-based representation of ordered lists that enables faster searching by using a non-linear structure of chaining pointers.

EXERCISES

8.1 Express the stack and queue operators specified in Chapter 7 in terms of the list operators specified in this chapter.

8.2 Modify the list abstraction defined on page 174 to provide a two-way list in which window movement is possible in either direction. What implications would this change have for the implementations given as Listings 15 and 16?

8.3 Modify the bus depot control system of Chapter 7 so that it maintains a list, in ascending bus number order, of the buses currently out of the depot and the numbers of the routes they are serving, and will output this list on request.

8.4 Modify the selection sort and Quicksort procedures given on pages 201 and 204 to compute and output the number of item comparisons NC and number of item exchanges NE involved in any execution of the procedure. Use each of your modified procedures to sort the same randomly generated lists of 10, 100 and 1000 integers. How do the results compare with the predicted performance of each algorithm?

8.5 Implement the Quicksort algorithm using a doubly chained representation, as outlined on page 209.

8.6 Implement the *leaguetable* envelope of Exercise 6.4 using the list envelope developed in this chapter. What features of an ordered list abstraction would be used for the same purpose?

9

Packages:
an alternative abstraction mechanism

So far we have defined an abstract data type as an *envelope*, and then created individual objects of the abstract type as *instances* of that envelope. With this approach, automatic initialization and finalization of each object is provided by the envelope mechanism. Each object carries with it a set of operators that apply directly to its representation, and the operators provided (as starred procedures or functions) are the only ones applicable to objects of the abstract type. In general, these consequences of the envelope approach are desirable and enhance the simplicity and security of defining, creating and manipulating objects of an abstract data type.

However, the constraints which a language such as Pascal Plus imposes on the use of envelopes have an adverse affect on their use as abstract types in some situations. Three such constraints can be identified:

(a) Pascal Plus allows envelope instances to be declared only at block level, and not as a component of any other data structure that may be created. This means that objects of an abstract data type defined as an envelope cannot occur as components of other data types defined using the normal structured types of Pascal.

(b) Pascal Plus also precludes the use of an envelope identifier within the block that defines that envelope. This has the effect that none of the starred procedures and functions in an envelope may take parameters that are instances of the envelope itself, and hence an envelope defining an abstract data type cannot define corresponding operators that operate on two or more objects of the type. Implicitly, the operators only apply to the object whose name is used to invoke them.

(c) In Pascal, certain basic operators, such as assignment, are assumed to apply to all types defined by the language (with one exception which we will consider in a moment). In Pascal Plus, however, the assignment or copying of one envelope instance to another is not provided. Indeed, there are no standard operators applicable to instances of envelopes. In most cases, this restriction is desirable and is one of the motives for introducing the envelope concept.

In practice, a general definition of the meaning of assignment for envelopes would be difficult to provide as its effect would depend on the nature of the data representations used within the envelope, and any general copying scheme chosen would not necessarily be meaningful for particular envelopes. Pascal itself excludes assignment between file variables for similar reasons. In some cases, however, operations such as assignment may be meaningful for an abstract data type and the representation chosen for it may allow this operation to be realized using the standard Pascal assignment operator. In such cases, direct use of the assignment operator itself between instances of the abstract data type is the natural notation to provide, and it could be made available if the abstract type were allowed to inherit the operations applicable to its representation.

PACKAGES

An alternative to the envelope approach, which overcomes the restrictions outlined, is the approach supported by the Ada *package* concept. From the point of view of its user, an abstract data type may be thought of as a type definition and a collection of operators expressed as procedures and functions which operate on objects of that type. Given such a type definition and a set of procedures and functions we may group them as the visible attributes of a module or package which still hides the details of the representation and structure of the type and the implementation of the operators. In Pascal Plus this can be achieved by an envelope module of the following general form:

> **envelope module** *ADTpackage*;
>
> **type** **ADT* = . . . {*representation chosen*} . . .
>
> **procedure** **op*1 (**var** *d* : *ADT*; . . .) . . .
>
> **procedure** **op*2 (**var** *d* : *ADT*; . . .) . . .

With such a module the user program can declare variables using the visible type name (*ADT*) and then apply the operators defined by the visible procedures, *op*1, *op*2, etc., passing the variables as parameters to these procedures as required.

Consider, for example, our abstract type *multiset*, which could be re-defined in package format, as follows:

> **envelope module** *multisetpackage*;
>
> **type** *multiset = . . .
>
> **procedure** *initialize (**var** *s* : *multiset*); . . .
>
> **procedure** *clear (**var** *s* : *multiset*); . . .
>
> **function** *empty (**var** *s* : *multiset*): *Boolean*; . . .
>
> **procedure***insert (**var** *s* : *multiset*; *i* : *basetype*); . . .
>
> . . .
>
> **begin**
> ***{*no initial or final actions*}
> **end** {*multisetpackage*};

With this package module, the user program can then declare set variables, as follows:

> **var** *s*1,*s*2 : *multisetpackage.multiset*;

and then manipulate these variables by procedure calls such as follows:

> *multisetpackage.initialize* (*s*1);
> *multisetpackage.initialize* (*s*2);
> .
> .
> .
>
> *multisetpackage.insert* (*s*1,*x*);
> *multisetpackage.insert* (*s*2,*x*);
> .
> .
> .

Note, however, that explicit initialization of the set variables by use of the procedure *initialize* is now required, and that this operation is not necessarily identical to the operator *clear* used subsequently. In the latter case the component variables of the multiset representation have defined values which may require processing, e.g. to dispose of an existing chained representation, whilst in the former case the component variables are undefined and must be treated accordingly.

Each operation on a multiset variable now involves use of the module name *multisetpackage* to identify the procedure involved, and the passing of the particular set variable as an additional procedure parameter. In practice, the repeated use of the module name can be avoided by the use of a with-statement enclosing the entire body of each block that uses the package facilities, as follows:

```
with multisetpackage do
begin
    initialize (s1);
    initialize (s2);
    .
    .
    .
    insert (s1, x);
    remove (s2, x);
    .
    .
    .
end;
```

Thus the package approach imposes greater responsibility on the user in that initialization and any necessary finalization of objects of the abstract type must be explicitly programmed, and it involves a slightly more cumbersome notation for denoting operations on objects of the abstract type. However, it does overcome the possible disadvantages listed earlier for the envelope approach. Thus an object of our packaged *multiset* type can be embedded as a component of another structure, perhaps as follows:

```
client = record
            name : spelling;
            interests : multisetpackage.multiset
         end;
```

As we will see in the modular concordance program, this ability is important in programs involving multi-level abstractions.

The package approach also allows polyadic operators, that is operators that take more than one object of the abstract type as operands or parameters, to be defined within the package itself. Thus, if we have an appropriate definition for the union of two *multiset* objects, the package might provide a union operator, as follows:

```
procedure *union (op1, op2 : multiset;
                  var result : multiset);
```

so that the *multiset* equivalent of the Pascal set operation:

  s3 := *s1* + *s2*

could be expressed as:

  multisetpackage.union (*s1, s2, s3*)

The package approach also allows the concept of inherited operators to be provided. However, our *multiset* example illustrates how the inherited operators may be implementation dependent and, according to the implementation chosen, may or may not correspond to the desired operation on the abstract objects involved. Consider first, the array representation of our *multiset* type whose package declaration would be as follows:

  envelope module *multisetpackage*;

  type *multiset = **record**
                                 size : 0 . . *max*;
                                 member : **array** [1 . . *max*] **of** *basetype*
                             end;
     . . .

In this case each *multiset* object is represented as a Pascal record and the assignment operator which Pascal provides for record types will have the expected effect for the *multiset* objects themselves. Thus, the assignment:

  s1 := *s2*

will copy the size and members of the set *s2* to the set *s1* so that immediately thereafter the two sets have equal set values with independent representations, as shown in Fig. 9.1(a).

  However, if we now consider the chained representation of *multisets* whose package declaration would be as follows:

  envelope module *multisetpackage*;

  type *memberpointer* = ↑*memberrecord*;
        memberrecord = **record**
                                      value : *basetype*;
                                      nextmember : *memberpointer*
                               end;
        *multiset = *memberpointer* {*to first member*};
     . . .

the effect of an assignment:

   $s1 := s2$

is quite different, in that it merely copies the value of the pointer to the first member of set $s2$ as the corresponding pointer value for $s1$, as shown in Fig. 9.1(b). Immediately thereafter, the values of $s1$ and $s2$ will be equal as expected, but they will share the *same* chained representation, so that any subsequent modification of $s2$ will also affect $s1$ and vice versa. Thus, the

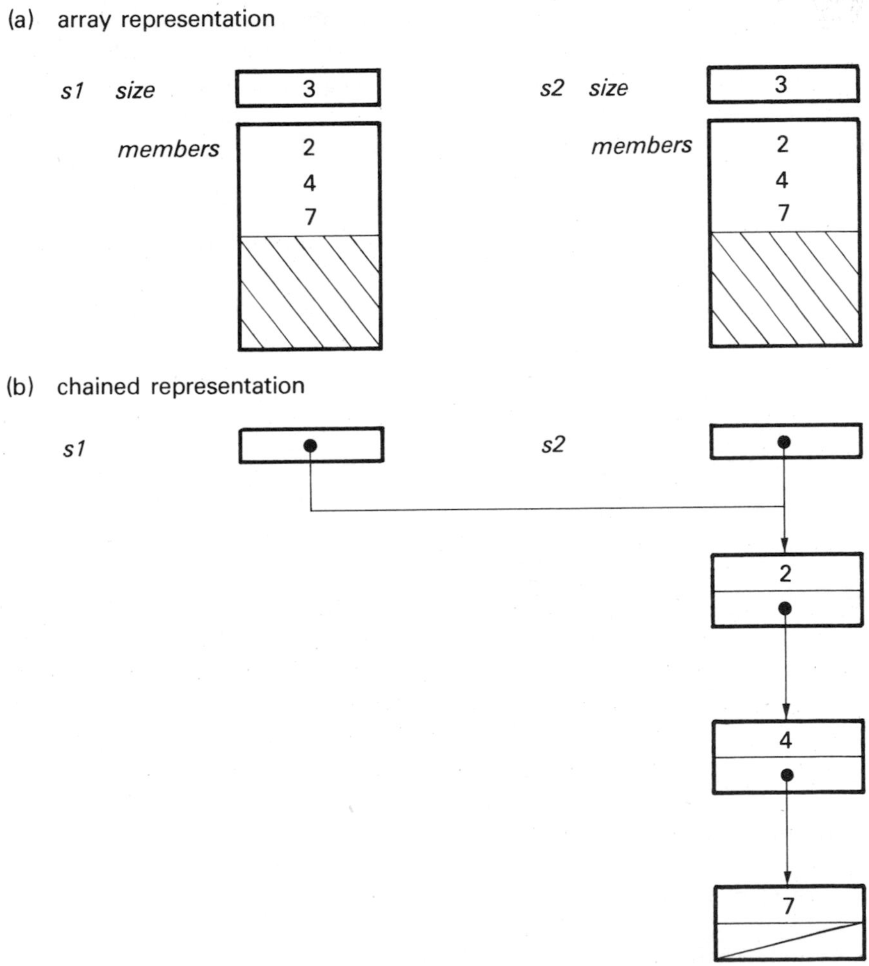

(a) array representation

(b) chained representation

Figure 9.1   Assignment of multiset representations

inherited assignment operator for the chained representation of multisets does not have the required effect for the abstract *multiset* objects and should not be used in this case.

The chained representation of multisets also illustrates how an abstract data type may inherit unwanted operators through the package approach. With this representation, each set value is represented as a pointer to its first member and, since Pascal allows the operators = and <> to be used with pointer types, tests such as:

> **if** $s1 = s2$ **then** . . .

are valid with this representation, though they do not have the expected meaning in terms of the abstract types so implemented.

These examples of operators inherited by abstract data types show that the package approach to their implementation must be used with caution. The language Ada, in which the package is the only means of implementing abstract data types, provides additional language features specifically to control operator inheritance. Pascal Plus takes a simpler approach. Whether or not the properties of a type exported by an envelope module can be exploited by the using program is determined solely by the starred and unstarred identifiers of the module. Any operation that requires use of an unstarred identifier for its expression is excluded, while any operation that can be expressed without the use of unstarred identifiers is valid.

As we have already noted, the only operation applicable to record types in Pascal is assignment and the components of a record can only be accessed by the use of a field identifier. Thus, in Pascal Plus all operations but assignment and parameter passing can be excluded for any exported type by encapsulating it as a record, possibly with a single field. For example, the chained representation of *multisets* might be expressed as follows:

> **envelope module** *multisetpackage*;
>
>   **type** *memberpointer* = ↑*memberrecord*;
>   . . .
>   **multiset* = **record**
>   *firstmember* : *memberpointer*
>   **end**;
>
>   . . .

With this form the test:

> **if** $s1 = s2$ **then** . . .

is excluded and the pointer to the *firstmember* of any set object cannot be obtained without use of the unstarred identifier *firstmember*. However, the assignment:

$s1 := s2$

remains valid even though it is not consistent with the abstract concept concerned. To exclude the assignment of abstract data types in Pascal Plus, the envelope rather than the package approach must be used for their implementation.

HIERARCHIC ABSTRACTIONS

We have seen that the multiset *envelope* abstraction, as defined in Chapter 6, can be rewritten as a multiset *package* abstraction, with some loss of succinctness and security, but some gain in flexibility. The same is true of the stack, queue and list abstractions defined in Chapters 7 and 8. Each of these can be recast in a package form which is more flexible, but less succinct and less secure in its use.

In effect, the package is a lower level abstraction mechanism than the envelope, and in Pascal Plus it is feasible to provide both levels of abstraction in the library of abstract data types that we build up.

Consider for example the list abstraction defined in Chapter 8. In package form this would be provided in a Pascal Plus library as follows:

envelope module *listpackage*;

{*assumes* **type** *itemtype = type of items in lists*,
    with := applicable}

type **list = . . .*;

procedure **initialize* (**var** *l:list*);
    {*initializes list l to empty, with inlist (l) false*}

function **length* (**var** *l:list*) : *integer*;

function **empty* (**var** *l:list*) : *Boolean*;
    . . .

Apart from the new operator *initialize* the operators provided as procedures and functions are identical to those defined in Chapter 8, except that they take an additional variable parameter which is the particular list on which they are to operate.

Given such a list package in our library, the higher level list envelope abstraction defined in Chapter 8 can now be redefined using the library package as follows:

    envelope *list*;
        {*assumes* **type** *itemtype* = *type of items in list*,
                                   with := *applicable*}

        envelope module *listpackage* **in** *library*;

        var *thislist* : *listpackage.list*;

        function **length* : *integer*;
          begin *length* := *listpackage.length* (*thislist*) **end**;

        function **empty* : *Boolean*;
          begin *empty* := *listpackage.empty* (*thislist*) **end**;
        . . .

        begin
          listpackage.initialize (*thislist*);
          * * *
        end {*list*};

Thus the *list* envelope declares a single variable of the type provided by *listpackage*, and implements each of its operators by invoking the corresponding *listpackage* operator on this variable. Automatic initialization of the list is provided by calling the additional *listpackage* operator *initialize* before the inner statement in the body of the envelope.

From now on we will assume that the abstract data types we have defined so far, and those that we define in subsequent chapters, are available both in package and in envelope form. For each application we can then choose between the succinctness and security of the envelope and the flexibility of the package, according to the needs of the particular application.

THE CONCORDANCE PROGRAM (YET AGAIN!)

To illustrate the choice between envelopes and packages we can now reconsider the concordance program as originally defined in Chapters 4 and 5, that is the program which prints an ordered list of the words in the text together with a list of the line numbers at which each word occurs.

Because the list of occurrences for each word must be embedded in the word list record for the word itself, we need the flexibility of the list package to represent the lists of occurrences, while we can retain the security of the list envelope for the word list itself.

Thus the *occurrences* module shown in Listing 5, which exports a type *listofoccurrences*, can be re-expressed, using the library module *listpackage* to implement the list of line numbers required. Each of its exported procedures, *initoccurrences*, *recordoccurrence* and *printoccurrences*, are then directly expressible in terms of the *listpackage* operators *initialize*, *precede* and *traverse*, as shown in Listing 18.

Listing 18

```
envelope module occurrences;

{ assumes const linemax = maximum output line length; }
{              indent  = left margin for printing a  }
{                        list of occurrences;        }
{         type linenumber = integer (or subrange of); }
{                                                     }
{ This module enables the creation and printout of   }
{ lists of occurrences, i.e. line numbers.           }

envelope module listpackage in library
  (where type itemtype = linenumber; );

type *listofoccurrences = listpackage.list;

procedure *initoccurrences = listpackage.initialise;

procedure *addoccurrence(newline: linenumber;
                         var l: listofoccurrences);
  begin listpackage.precede(l, newline) end;

procedure *printoccurrences(occurrences: listofoccurrences;
                            var printfile: text);
  var spaceleftonline: 0..linemax;

  procedure printlinenumber(var line: linenumber);
    begin
      if spaceleftonline < 6
      then begin
             writeln(printfile);
             write(printfile, ' ': indent);
             spaceleftonline := linemax - indent
           end;
      write(printfile, line: 6);
      spaceleftonline := spaceleftonline - 6
    end {printlinenumber};
```

continued on page 226

Listing 18 continued

```
  begin
    write(printfile, ' ': indent);
    spaceleftonline := linemax - indent;
    listpackage.traverse(occurrences, printlinenumber);
    writeln(printfile)
  end {printoccurrences};

procedure *disposeoccurrences(var l: listofoccurrences);
  begin
    with listpackage do
      begin
        locatefront(l);
        while not empty(l) do delete(l)
      end
  end {disposeoccurrences};

begin
  ***
end {occurrences};
```

Using the *listofoccurrences* type exported by this module, the *wordlist* module based on our standard list envelope can now be extended to record and print lists of occurrences for each word, as shown in Listing 19.

Listing 19

```
envelope module wordlist;

{ This envelope creates and prints an ordered list of words }
{ each with an associated list of linenumber occurrences    }
{                                                           }
{ assumes type wordspelling = any string type;             }
{              linenumber = 1 .. some maximum;             }

const linemax = 60;
      indent = 6;

envelope module occurrences in library;

type wordrecord = record
                    spelling: wordspelling;
                    occurred: occurrences.listofoccurrences
                  end;

envelope module list in library
  (where type itemtype = wordrecord; );

procedure *recordword(word: wordspelling; line: linenumber);
  var entry: wordrecord;
```

```
  function notless(w: wordrecord): Boolean;
    begin notless := (w.spelling >= word) end;

  procedure insertword;
    var entry: wordrecord;
    begin
      with entry do
        begin
          spelling := word;
          occurrences.initoccurrnces(occurred);
          occurrences.addoccurrence(line, occurred)
        end;
      list.precede(entry)
    end {insertword};

  begin
    with list do
      begin
        locatefront;
        locate(notless);
        if inlist
        then begin
                content(entry);
                if entry.spelling = word
                then begin
                        occurrences.addoccurrence
                          (line, entry.occurred);
                        replace(entry)
                     end
                else insertword {before window}
             end
        else insertword {at end of list}
      end
  end {recordword};

procedure *printwords(var printfile: text);

  procedure printword(var w: wordrecord);
    begin
      with w do
        begin
          writeln(printfile, spelling);
          occurrences.printoccurrences(occurred, printfile)
        end
    end {printword};

  begin list.traverse(printword) end;

begin
  ***
end {wordlist};
```

The two modules shown in Listings 18 and 19 are exactly equivalent, both in interface and in function, to those shown as Listings 5 and 6 in Chapter 5. The overall concordance program shown as Test 6 can therefore be recreated using these modules, with identical effect. The important difference is that the actual manipulation of words and occurrences is now expressed entirely in terms of our standard library list abstractions, with no explicit use of arrays or pointers in the concordance program itself, or in the *wordlist* and *occurrences* modules created specifically to support it. As such the program is more concise, more transparent, more reliable and more easily adapted to changes in the requirements of its use.

SUMMARY

In this chapter we have considered the package concept, which is a slightly lower-level but more flexible approach to the modular definition of abstract data types. This flexibility allows objects of the abstract type involved to be treated exactly like variables of a normal language-defined type, by imbedding them in other structures, assigning them, etc. The cost of this flexibility is a possible loss in security of the abstraction involved, through overlooked initialization, or unwanted inherited operators.

In Pascal Plus the module variant of the envelope concept allows either approach to be taken within a single notation, but with limited facilities for controlling operator inheritance. In other languages, such as Ada, the package is the standard means of defining abstract types, though a data module can be created (as a package which exports operators but no types) if only a single instance is required.

Whatever notation is available, it is important that the programmer is aware of the two approaches to data abstraction. On the one hand, an 'envelope' module that creates and hides a data structure, and exports only the operators applicable to it, is an elegant and secure means of representing the major data structures within a program.

On the other hand, a 'package' module that defines and exports a data type, together with the operators applicable to variables of that type, is a flexible means of realizing those abstract items which may occur in a variety of data contexts. Either concept may be the more appropriate in particular situations.

EXERCISES

9.1 Define a module *queuepackage* which exports a type *queue* together with operators equivalent to those provided by the queue abstraction defined in Chapter 7. How could a program using your package ensure that all storage occupied by unwanted queues is recovered?

9.2 Express the set abstraction developed for Exercise 6.3 in the form of a package. Extend the range of operators provided to include:

   (a)   set union, intersection, and relative complement operators;

   (b)   set equality and containment operators.

9.3 Define a module *complexnumbers* which exports a type *complex* whose values are complex numbers. The package should enable:

   (a)   complex values to be created from component parts expressed in either Cartesian or polar co-ordinates;

   (b)   such components to be extracted from existing complex values;

   (c)   addition, subtraction and multiplication of complex values to produce complex results.

   What limitation of Pascal adversely affects the form in which some features of your package are provided?

9.4 Define a module *matrixpackage* which exports a type matrix whose values are $N \times N$ matrices of real elements. The package should include facilities to enable:

   (a)   assignment and access to individual elements of a matrix;

   (b)   addition, subtraction, and multiplication of matrices;

   (c)   application of a specified operation to each element of a matrix, or of a specified row or column, in some suitable order;

   (d)   calculation of the determinant of a matrix.

9.5 Implement the module *listpackage* outlined on page 223.

9.6 An office block accommodates employees in rooms occupied by one or more people, each room having one telephone. An internal telephone directory for the block is available on a file, each record of the file containing an employee's name (a 16 character string) and his telephone number. The file is in alphabetic order of employees' names.

Use the *listpackage* module to write a program which will read the directory and output a series of lists of the employees in each room (together with the number of the telephone in that room). The lists are to be output in ascending order of telephone number, and the names of the employees in each room are to be output in alphabetic order.

9.7   A polynomial in a single variable with integer coefficients, e.g.,

$$4x^3 + 3x^2 - 1$$

may be represented as a sequence of (coefficient, degree) pairs of integers preceded by an integer specifying the number of such pairs, i.e., for the above polynomial,

$$3 \quad 4\ 3 \quad 3\ 2 \quad -1\ 0$$

Write a package to support polynomial manipulation which includes the following facilities:

(a)   a procedure to input a polynomial in the above form from a given file;

(b)   addition, subtraction, and multiplication operators;

(c)   a differentiation operator;

(d)   a function which evaluates a polynomial given the value of the variable concerned;

(e)   a procedure to output a polynomial to a specified file in a suitable form, e.g., the above polynomial might be output in the form

$$4x\uparrow 3 + 3x\uparrow 2 - 1$$

Implement your package using the *listpackage* module. How could your package be extended to handle polynomials in two variables?

9.8   A program is required to generate personalised standard letters using a basic letter held in a text file, with the adjustable parts enclosed in angle brackets, e.g.,

> *Dear <name>,*
>   *Thank you very much for the <item>. That is the best <classification> present that I have ever received. Really <name>, you are too good to me.*
>   *Yours <tone>,*
>   *<sender>*

Separate files then contain the expansions of the named fields required for particular letters, e.g., one such file might contain

<name>	*<John>*
<item>	*<exercise bicycle>*
<classification>	*<get-well-soon>*
<tone>	*<over the moon>*
<sender>	*<Jack>*

Implement a string handling package providing operations suitable for the construction of the above program. Use your package to implement the letter writing program.

10

Trees

In Chapters 7–9 we have considered various forms of sequence. Sequences are classed as *linear data structures*. A linear data structure is one in which each component of the structure has a unique predecessor component, and a unique successor component, if they exist. In this and the following chapter we consider *trees* and *graphs* which, in contrast to sequences, are *non-linear data structures*—they contain components which may have more than one successor and more than one predecessor. In this chapter we concentrate on trees.

A tree is a non-linear structure of which each component, or *node*, has one and only one predecessor node (except for the *root node*, which has none) but has zero or more successor nodes.

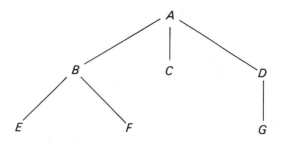

Figure 10.1 An example tree

An example of a tree structure is shown in Fig. 10.1. Every non-empty tree contains a distinguished node which has no predecessors (the node A in

the above tree) which is called the *root node* of the tree. A node (such as
C,E,F, or *G*) which has no successors is known as a *terminal node* or a *leaf* of
the tree. All other nodes are *non-terminal nodes*. The *degree* of a non-
terminal node is the number of direct successors which it has (e.g., the degree
of *A* is 3, the degree of *D* is 1). In the above tree we refer to *A* as the *parent* of
B,C, and *D*, which in turn are the *children* of *A*. The nodes *B*, *C*, and *D* are
siblings, with *B* as the eldest sibling. The arcs connecting the nodes are, for
obvious reason, called *branches*.

A familiar example of a tree is a genealogical tree which shows the
descendants of a particular person. The tree of Fig. 10.2 represents the
descendants of the late King George VI of England.

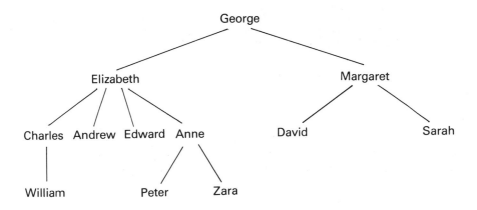

Figure 10.2 A family tree

Such a tree is known as an *ordered* tree since the ordering of the
offspring nodes at the various levels in the tree is significant. For the
purposes of establishing the line of succession to the throne, male children
take precedence over female children, and so the male children appear as
elder siblings (in tree terminology!) of all female children. As we shall see,
the line of succession may be determined from such an ordered tree by
traversing it in a particular way.

A tree is an inherently recursive structure in that each node can be
regarded as the root of a subsidiary tree comprising that node, and its
successors, their successors, and so on. Formally a tree is usually defined by a
correspondingly recursive definition, which states that a tree of node values
of some type *T* either:

(a)   is empty, or

(b)   consists of a node of type *T* and a finite number of disjoint trees of
       values of type *T*, which are the sub-trees of that node.

The tree in Fig. 10.1 consists of a node A and three sub-trees BEF, C, and DG ; the sub-tree BEF in turn consists of a node B and sub-trees E and F; and so on. As we shall see, this recursive view of tree structure is a significant conceptual aid to programming the manipulation of trees.

From now on we shall concentrate our attention upon ordered trees of degree less than or equal to 2, which are known as *binary trees*. A binary tree is a tree in which each node has exactly two (possibly empty) subtrees called the left and right subtrees of the node.

It is possible to convert a tree of any degree to a binary tree. The rules of conversion are as follows:

(a)   for each node its eldest child becomes the root of its left subtree;

(b)   its next eldest sibling becomes the root node of its right subtree.

Hence the family tree given earlier in Fig. 10.2 may be converted into the binary tree of Fig. 10.3.

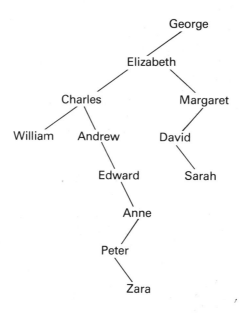

Figure 10.3   A family tree in binary form

An arithmetic expression involving dyadic operators (i.e., infix operators with two operands), may be conveniently represented as a binary tree. The binary tree in Fig. 10.4 represents the expression

$$(a + b*c)*(d/e - f)$$

The tree structure reflects the precedence of the operators, and the parentheses thus become redundant. The operands appear in terminal nodes of the tree while the operators are at non-terminal nodes.

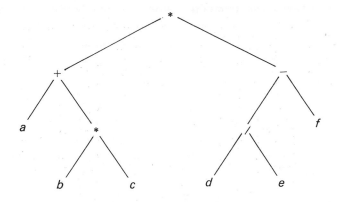

Figure 10.4 An expression tree

We saw earlier that the Quicksort process imposed an implicit recursive structure on the array being sorted—each partition being split into two sub-partitions with certain relative properties. The same implicit structure is exploited by the binary split search technique for searching a pre-sorted array. This implicit structure can be made explicit by holding sorted data in the form of a so-called *binary search tree*. A binary search tree is a binary tree on which an extra condition is imposed, namely that, for each node,

(a)   all values in the left subtree are less than the value at the node, and

(b)   all values in the right subtree are greater than the value at the node.

The tree of integer values shown in Fig. 10.5 is a binary search tree.

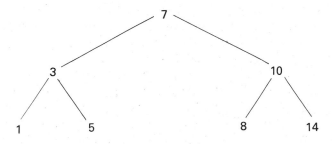

Figure 10.5 A binary search tree

Binary trees are generally used to build up lists of data in some significant sorted order. The location of an arbitrary value is obtained via a search path which switches left or right as the search progresses down through the tree, depending on the value encountered at each node. Provided that the tree is balanced (i.e., the numbers of nodes in the left and right subtrees of any non-terminal node are approximately equal) the time taken to find a given value in a list of n items held in a balanced search tree is proportional to $\log_2 n$. Hence the binary search tree is a suitable data structure for holding the ordered lists described in the previous chapter. A binary search tree has the additional and important advantage that the insertion of new values into a tree does not require any repositioning of existing items.

In many uses of trees we wish to perform the same operation P on each node of a tree—the process of visiting all the nodes of a tree is known as *tree traversal*. For binary trees there are three main orders in which one might

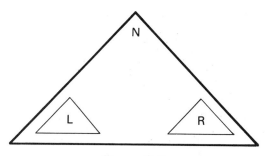

Figure 10.6

visit the nodes during a tree traversal. In terms of the tree shown in Fig. 10.6, where N denotes a node and L and R are its left and right subtrees, these orderings are:

(a)   preorder—N,L,R (i.e., visit node before each of its subtrees);

(b)   inorder—L,N,R (i.e., visit node between visiting its subtrees);

(c)   postorder—L,R,N (i.e., visit node after visiting its subtrees).

For example, visiting the nodes of the tree in Fig. 10.5 in each of these orders gives:

(a)	preorder	7	3	1	5	10	8	14
(b)	inorder	1	3	5	7	8	10	14
(c)	postorder	1	5	3	8	14	10	7

Obviously inorder traversal of a binary search tree is appropriate for dealing with its values in sorted order. However, preorder and postorder traversal are equally appropriate in other contexts. Thus, for a genealogical tree such as that in Fig. 10.2 or 10.3, preorder traversal is required to determine the order of succession to the throne. For evaluation of an expression tree such as that shown in Fig. 10.4, postorder traversal is appropriate, since the subtrees defining its operands must be evaluated before any operator node can be evaluated.

TREE REPRESENTATION OF ORDERED LISTS

As a first example of how trees are manipulated, we consider the use of a binary search tree as a means of representing an ordered list. Initially we will consider a simple subset of an ordered list abstraction suggested in Chapter 8, which we define as follows:

envelope *orderedlist* (**function** *inorder* (*i*1, *i*2 : *itemtype*) : *Boolean*);

    {*assumes* **type** *itemtype* = *type of items in list,*
                with := *applicable*}

    function *empty : *Boolean*;

    function *inlist : *Boolean*;

    procedure *locatevalue (*i* : *itemtype*);
      {*moves window to list item w such that*
       inorder(*i*, *w*) **and** *inorder*(*w*, *i*)
       if w exists, otherwise inlist is false}

    procedure *contents (**var** *i* : *itemtype*);
      {*if inlist then i* := *window item else error*}

    procedure *insert (*i* : *itemtype*);
      {*adds item i to list*}

    procedure *traverse (**procedure** *p* (*i* : *itemtype*));
      {*applies procedure p to each item in list,*
       in order determined by function inorder}

    begin
      {*list is initially empty*}
      * * *
    end {*orderedlist*};

In this restricted abstraction we have deliberately excluded the ability to delete or replace items, and to move the window from a list item to its successor, for reasons that will be apparent in due course. In practice such a restricted abstraction is sufficient for some applications, and the particularly simple implementations that it permits justify the restrictions imposed. It is this simple tree implementation strategy that we now consider.

The basic approach to representing trees using pointers is applicable to all data structures that can be defined recursively (including sequences). In this, each recursive component of such a structure is represented by a pointer to its value, rather than the value itself. Using the pointer value **nil** to denote an empty tree, the necessary type definitions to describe a binary search tree of *itemtype* values are

> **type** *node* = ↑*noderecord*;
> *noderecord* = **record**
> *nodevalue* : *itemtype*;
> *left, right* : *node*
> **end**;

A tree is then represented as a pointer to its root node, and the node window as a pointer to the appropriate node.

> **var** *root, window* : *node*;

and so the abstract tree of Fig. 10.5 is represented as shown in Fig. 10.7.

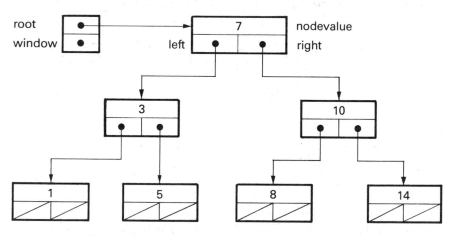

Figure 10.7   Pointer representation of a binary tree

For processing recursively defined data structures, the significant programming tool is the recursive procedure. For instance, the *locatevalue* operation can be implemented by means of a recursive procedure *search* which inspects the value at a node (starting from the root node). If this is not a node containing the required value, the procedure calls itself recursively to search either the left or right subtree (whichever is appropriate). This recursive process terminates either when the required node is found or the edge of the tree is reached. The form of this search procedure is:

```
procedure search (t : node);
  begin
    if t = nil
    then {no such node exists} window := nil
    else with t↑ do
         if not inorder (nodevalue, i)
         then search (left)
         else if not inorder (i, nodevalue)
              then search (right)
              else {required node has been found} window := t
  end {search};
```

and the locate operation simply consists of a call

```
search (root)
```

·The insertion procedure is similar, except that it searches its way through the tree until it reaches an edge (i.e., a subtree denoted by a **nil** pointer value) at which point it creates a new node in place of the empty subtree. Insertion is thus implemented as a call

```
insertin (root)
```

of a recursive procedure *insertin* local to the *insert* operator.

```
procedure insertin (var t : node);
  begin
    if t = nil
    then begin
           new (t);
           with t↑ do
           begin
             nodevalue := i;
             left := nil; right := nil
           end
         end
    else with t↑ do
         if inorder (nodevalue, i)
         then insertin (right)
         else insertin (left)
  end {insertin};
```

Note that *insertin* has a variable node parameter since the insertion process assigns a new value to the node component which previously had the **nil** value.

These processes of searching and insertion do not involve any retracing of the tree structure already scanned, and can therefore be implemented as non-recursive loops. Such loops may be slightly faster than the equivalent recursive procedures, but are less natural and less obviously correct. The iterative version of the *locatevalue* operator is as follows:

```
procedure locatevalue (i : itemtype);
  var t : node;
  begin
    window := nil;
    t := root;
    while (t <> nil) and (window = nil) do
      if not inorder (t↑.nodevalue, i)
      then t := t↑.left
      else if not inorder (i, t↑.nodevalue)
          then t := t↑.right
          else window := t
  end {locatevalue};
```

In contrast, tree traversal involves retracing of the tree structure and therefore can only be readily expressed as a recursive procedure. For example, inorder traversal of a binary search tree is performed by a call

```
travinorder (root)
```

of the recursive procedure *travinorder*:

```
procedure travinorder (t : node);
  begin
    if t <> nil
    then with t↑ do
        begin
          travinorder (left);
          p (nodevalue);
          travinorder (right)
        end
  end {travinorder};
```

The remaining operators of our restricted ordered list abstraction (*empty*, *inlist* and *contents*) are easily implemented in terms of the root and window pointers, leading to the complete implementation shown in Listing 20.

Listing 20

```
envelope orderedlist(function inorder(i1, i2: itemtype): Boolean);

{ This envelope maintains an ordered list of items of type     }
{ itemtype, in the form of a binary tree, with a window for    }
{ item access. Operators provided are locatevalue, content,    }
{ insert and traverse, with predicates empty and inlist to     }
{ test the list and window status.                             }
{                                                              }
{ It assumes type itemtype = any type with := applicable       }

type node = ^noderecord;
     noderecord = record
                      nodevalue: itemtype;
                      left, right: node
                  end;

var root, window: node;

function *empty: Boolean;
  begin empty := (root = nil) end;

function *inlist: Boolean;
  begin inlist := (window <> nil) end;

procedure *locatevalue(i: itemtype);

  procedure search(t: node);
    begin
      if t = nil
      then
            {no such node exists}
            window := nil
      else with t^ do
              if not inorder(nodevalue, i)
              then search(left)
              else if not inorder(i, nodevalue)
                   then search(right)
                   else
                         {required node found}
                         window := t
    end {search};

  begin search(root) end {locatevalue};

procedure *content(var i: itemtype);
  begin
    if window = nil
    then error('no window for content')
    else i := window^.nodevalue
  end {content};
```

continued on page 242

Listing 20 continued

```
procedure *insert(i: itemtype);


  procedure insertin(var t: node);
    begin
      if t = nil
      then begin
             new(t);
             with t^ do
               begin
                 nodevalue := i;
                 left := nil;
                 right := nil
               end
           end
      else with t^ do
             if inorder(nodevalue, i)
             then insertin(right)
             else insertin(left)
  end {insertin};


  begin insertin(root) end {insert};


procedure *traverse(procedure p(i: itemtype));


  procedure travinorder(t: node);
    begin
      if t <> nil
      then with t^ do
             begin
               travinorder(left);
               p(nodevalue);
               travinorder(right)
             end
  end {travinorder};


  begin travinorder(root) end {traverse};


procedure disposetree(t: node);
  begin
    if t <> nil
    then begin
           disposetree(t^.left);
           disposetree(t^.right);
           dispose(t)
         end
  end {disposetree};
```

```
begin
  root := nil;
  window := nil;
  ***;
  disposetree(root)
end {orderedlist};
```

The significant feature of this implementation is the ease with which the basic tree structure and its manipulation has been expressed in terms of pointers and recursive procedures. Indeed, the implementation has been included mainly to demonstrate these techniques. As a useful abstraction to be included in a software library the implementation has two significant limitations.

(a) The basic reason for adopting a binary tree representation of an ordered list is that the time taken either to locate or to insert an item in a list of n items varies as log n. In practice, however, this property holds only if the resultant tree is *balanced*, i.e. if the number of items in the left and right subtrees of any node are approximately equal, as in Fig. 10.5. The present implementation, however, makes no effort to ensure that this is so, and its actual performance depends on the order in which items are inserted. The worst case is when items arrive in monotonically increasing or decreasing value order. Thus if the item values from Fig. 10.5 are inserted in the order 1,3,5,7,8,10,14, then the 'tree' produced is in effect a linear list as shown in Fig. 10.8, and the time to locate or insert an item varies as n rather than log n.

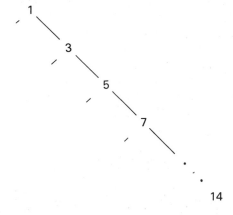

Figure 10.8 Worst case insertion in a binary tree

For many applications the order in which items are inserted in a value ordered list is sufficiently random to produce a reasonably balanced binary tree (and hence a performance which approximates to log n) without explicit effort to ensure a balanced tree. For those applications where this is not so, however, a binary tree representation of an ordered list is advantageous only if the insertion mechanism includes explicit logic to maintain tree balance. It is left as an exercise to the reader to investigate techniques by which this might be done.

(b)   A more serious limitation of our restricted ordered list is the set of operations that it does not provide. The significant omissions are:

   (i)   the ability to replace, and thus update, an existing list item with the necessary guarantee of order preservation;

   (ii)   the ability to delete an existing item;

   (iii)   the ability to move the list window to the next item in value order.

Even (iii) requires a feature not provided by the simple representation chosen so far, namely the ability to identify the parent of the current window item in the tree. To do so without a traversal of the entire tree requires either that

   (i)   each node record carries an additional pointer to its parent, or

   (ii)   each window moving operation creates or updates a record of the sequence of nodes on the path from the root node to the current window.

Solution (i) implies a significant increase in tree storage overheads, and some processing overheads in the *insert* operator. Solution (ii) implies significant processing overheads in all window moving operators, particularly in the *locatevalue* and *insert* operators. The impact of these will be considered further in the implementation of a general binary tree abstraction, which we now define.

A GENERAL BINARY TREE ABSTRACTION

The tree representation of an ordered list which we have just considered is not a tree abstraction in that the user is not aware of the tree structure, only of the possible improvement in performance that it provides. We now define a general abstraction of a binary tree, in which the user is explicitly aware of the tree structure involved, and expresses the operations on the tree accordingly.

The abstraction must provide facilities for

(a)   moving around an existing tree, usually called *tree walking*;

(b)   inspecting and altering the item values at any tree node;

(c)   inserting and deleting nodes;

(d)   general tree traversals.

We will retain the concept of a *window* for tree walking and node manipulation. At any moment a single node is in the window, except when the window has moved off the tree, or the tree is empty. The first interface requirement is therefore a function to reflect the window state:

function **intree* : *Boolean*;

intree will return *true* when a node is in the window, and false otherwise.
   The origin of a treewalking sequence will be the root node, so we provide an operation to position the window on the root node, if the tree is not empty:

procedure **locateroot*;

If the tree is empty *locateroot* has no effect, and *intree* remains false.
   From any node the window may move either left or right to the root nodes of the left or right subtrees of the current node, for which purpose we provide operators

procedure **nextleft*;

procedure **nextright*;

If the left or right subtree is empty, these operators may move the window off the tree, leaving *intree* false. In practice, however, it is often preferable to avoid such movements, so we provide additional functions to detect that the subtrees of the window node are empty as follows:

function **emptyleft* : *Boolean*;

function **emptyright* : *Boolean*;

For some tree applications the ability to move from the root node towards the leaf nodes is sufficient, but for others the need to move back towards the root is also necessary. We therefore provide an additional window movement operator:

procedure **nextparent*;

which moves the window to the parent of the current node. From the root node this operator will move the window off the tree, so for convenience we provide a further function:

function **onroot* : *Boolean*;

which allows this condition to be detected before a backward movement is requested.

With the four operators *locateroot*, *nextleft*, *nextright*, *nextparent* and the test functions *emptyleft*, *emptyright*, *onroot*, the treewalking sequence required by any tree application can be simply and conveniently expressed.

The item value at the window node can be inspected and updated using *contents* and *replace*, operators which are identical in form to those defined for lists:

procedure **contents* (**var** *i* : *itemtype*);

procedure **replace* (*i* : *itemtype*);

Insertion and deletion of tree nodes are the most difficult operations to define for a general tree abstraction. One option, which we will follow, is to allow insertion only at available leaf positions, and to define deletion in terms of complete subtrees rather than individual nodes. Thus we provide operators:

procedure **insertleft* (*i:itemtype*);

procedure **insertright* (*i:itemtype*);

which will insert a new node with item value *i* as the left or right subtree of the window node, but only if the condition *emptyleft* or *emptyright*, respectively, holds before the insertion is requested. Neither of those operators is applicable when inserting the root node of an empty tree so we must also provide a further operator:

procedure **insertroot* (*i* : *itemtype*);

which is applicable only to an empty tree.

The operator

procedure **delete*;

is defined to delete the window node *and* its left and right subtrees. As such it can be used to delete individual leaf nodes (which have empty left and right subtrees) but not to delete internal non-terminal nodes. In general, the tree rearrangement required following such deletions depends on the application involved and cannot be anticipated within a general tree abstraction. It should be noted, however, that the programming of such rearrangements, using the operators provided so far, is extremely clumsy.

The possibility of a lower level abstraction which facilitates such tree rearrangements is discussed later in this chapter.

The complete abstraction of a general binary tree which we have arrived at is as follows:

envelope *generalbinarytree*;

> {*assumes* **type** *itemtype = type of items held at tree nodes,*
> *with := applicable*}

type **treeorder* = (**preorder, *inorder, *postorder*);

function **empty* : *Boolean*;

function **intree* : *Boolean*;
{*is window on tree node?*}

function **onroot* : *Boolean*;
{*is window on root node?*};

function **emptyleft* : *Boolean*;
{*if not intree then error else*
is left subtree
of window node empty?}

function **emptyright* : *Boolean*;
{*if not intree then error else*
is right subtree
of window node empty?}

procedure **locateroot*;
{*if not empty then position window on root node*}

procedure **nextleft*;
{*if not intree then error else*
if emptyleft then intree := false else
window moves to root node of its left subtree}

procedure **nextright*;
{*if not intree then error else*
if emptyright then intree := false else
window moves to root node of its right subtree}

```
procedure *nextparent;
   {if not intree then error else
    if onroot then intree := false else
    window moves to its own parent node}

procedure *contents (var i : itemtype);
   {if not intree then error else
    i := item at window node}

procedure *replace (i : itemtype);
   {if not intree then error else
    item at window node := i}

procedure *insertroot (i : itemtype);
   {if not empty then error else
    create root node with item value i}

procedure *insertleft (i : itemtype);
   {if not intree then error else
    if not emptyleft then error else
    create node with item value i as left subtree of window}

procedure *insertright (i : itemtype);
   {if not intree then error else
    if not emptyright then error else
    create node with item value i as right subtree of window}

procedure *delete;
   {if not intree then error else
    delete window node and its left and right subtrees}

procedure *traverse (order : treeorder;
                         procedure p (var i : itemtype));
   {apply p to each item in tree, in order specified}

procedure *locate (order : treeorder;
                      function test (i : itemtype) : Boolean);
   {set window on first node encountered by traversal
    in order specified, whose item value satisfies test;
    if none is found intree := false}

begin
   {tree is empty; intree is false}
   ***
end {generalbinarytree};
```

To implement this general binary tree abstraction we will use the same pointer technique as before, except that each node record will include a pointer to its parent node, to support the *delete* and *nextparent* operators. With this modification, the complete range of operators specified by our abstraction is easily implemented as shown in Listing 21. Recursive procedures are used in the *delete* operator to dismantle the subtrees deleted, and in the *traverse* and *locate* operators, with a separate procedure for each traversal order. In the case of *locate* recursive searching is interrupted on finding the item required, by use of a non-local **goto** statement.

Listing 21

```
envelope generalbinarytree;

{ This envelope maintains a general binary tree of        }
{ items of type itemtype, with a window for item          }
{ insertion and inspection.                               }
{                                                          }
{ It assumes type itemtype = any type with := applicable }

type node = ^noderecord;
     noderecord = record
                     item: itemtype;
                     left, right, parent: node
                  end;
     *treeorder = (*preorder, *inorder, *postorder);

var root, window: node;

function *empty: Boolean;
  begin empty := (root = nil) end;

function *intree: Boolean;
  begin intree := (window <> nil) end;

function *onroot: Boolean;
  begin onroot := (window = root) and (root <> nil) end;

function *emptyleft: Boolean;
  begin
    if window = nil
    then error('no window for emptyleft')
    else emptyleft := (window^.left = nil)
  end {emptyleft};

function *emptyright: Boolean;
  begin
    if window = nil
    then error('no window for emptyright')
    else emptyright := (window^.right = nil)
  end {emptyright};
```

continued on page 250

Listing 21 continued

```
procedure *locateroot;
  begin window := root end;

procedure *nextleft;
  begin
    if window = nil
    then error('no window for nextleft')
    else window := window^.left
  end {nextleft};

procedure *nextright;
  begin
    if window = nil
    then error('no window for nextright')
    else window := window^.right
  end {nextright};

procedure *nextparent;
  begin
    if window = nil
    then error('no window for nextparent')
    else window := window^.parent
  end {nextparent};

procedure *contents(var x: itemtype);
  begin
    if window = nil
    then error('no window for contents')
    else x := window^.item
  end {contents};

procedure *replace(x: itemtype);
  begin
    if window = nil
    then error('no window for replace')
    else window^.item := x
  end {replace};

procedure makenode(x: itemtype; parentnode: node;
                   var newnode: node);
  begin
    new(newnode);
    with newnode^ do
      begin
        item := x;
        left := nil;
        right := nil;
        parent := parentnode
      end
  end {makenode};
```

```
procedure *insertroot(x: itemtype);
  begin
    if root <> nil
    then error('root already present for insertroot')
    else makenode(x, nil, root)
  end {insertroot};

procedure *insertleft(x: itemtype);
  begin
    if window = nil
    then error('no window for insertleft')
    else if window^.left <> nil
         then error('left node already present on insertleft')
         else makenode(x, window, window^.left)
  end {insertleft};

procedure *insertright(x: itemtype);
  begin
    if window = nil
    then error('no window for insertright')
    else if window^.right <> nil
         then error('right node already present on insertright')
         else makenode(x, window, window^.right)
  end {insertright};

procedure deletenodes(n: node);

  { used by *delete and finalisation }

  begin
    if n <> nil
    then begin
         deletenodes(n^.left);
         deletenodes(n^.right);
         dispose(n)
       end
  end {deletenodes};

procedure *delete;
  begin
    if window = nil
    then error('no window for delete')
    else begin
         if window = root
         then root := nil
         else with window^.parent^ do
                 if left = window
                 then left := nil
                 else right := nil;
         deletenodes(window);
         window := nil
       end
  end {delete};
```

continued on page 252

Listing 21 continued

```
procedure traversenodes(order: treeorder; procedure p(n: node));

  { used by *traverse and by *locate }


    procedure travinorder(t: node);
      begin
        if t <> nil
        then with t^ do
                begin
                  travinorder(left);
                  p(t);
                  travinorder(right)
                end
      end {travinorder};

    procedure travpreorder(t: node);
      begin
        if t <> nil
        then with t^ do
                begin
                  p(t);
                  travpreorder(left);
                  travpreorder(right)
                end
      end {travpreorder};

    procedure travpostorder(t: node);
      begin
        if t <> nil
        then with t^ do
                begin
                  travpostorder(left);
                  travpostorder(right);
                  p(t)
                end
      end {travpostorder};

  begin
    case order of
      inorder : travinorder(root);
      preorder : travpreorder(root);
      postorder : travpostorder(root)
    end
  end {traversenodes};

procedure *traverse(order: treeorder; procedure p(var i: itemtype));

  procedure applyp(n: node);
    begin p(n^.item) end;
```

```
  begin traversenodes(order, applyp) end {traverse};

procedure *locate(order: treeorder;
                  function test(i: itemtype): Boolean);
    label 99;

    procedure testnode(n: node);
      begin
        if test(n^.item)
        then begin
                window := n;
                goto 99
             end
      end {testnode};

    begin
      traversenodes(order, testnode);
      window := nil;
      99:
    end {locate};

begin
  window := nil;
  root := nil;
  ***;
  deletenodes(root)
end {tree};
```

As we noted earlier, the general binary tree abstraction implemented as Listing 21 is still restrictive in the sense that it provides only for insertion at available leaf positions and for deletion of complete subtrees. Unfortunately any other insertion or deletion implies some structural rearrangement of the remaining tree nodes, which can only be determined by the particular application involved, and must therefore be carried out by the user program itself. The problem is that such structural rearrangements are difficult, if not impossible, to express in terms of the abstraction provided so far. Unfortunately a much lower level abstraction is necessary to enable such rearrangements. The abstraction required is in effect a package for the creation, destruction, copying and linkage of tree nodes on an individual basis. As such it is little higher in level, and no more secure against misuse, than the pointer facilities of Pascal itself. The same effect could be achieved by starring the identifiers *node*, *item*, *left*, *right*, *parent*, *root* and *window* in Listing 21. The user program can then rearrange the existing structure at will, but the abstraction can no longer guarantee that the inherent tree structure is maintained.

When the structural rearrangements required after deletion are implied by the higher level abstraction itself, a secure implementation can be provided. This is the case for deletion of items from an ordered list held as a binary search tree. In this case deletion of an item which is not occupying a leaf position can be accomplished by replacing it by the leftmost value in its right subtree (or the rightmost value on its left subtree) and then 'deleting' the latter. If the subtree is not completely balanced the replacement value is not necessarily in a leaf position either, but recursive application of this deletion strategy quickly leads to the deletion of a leaf node.

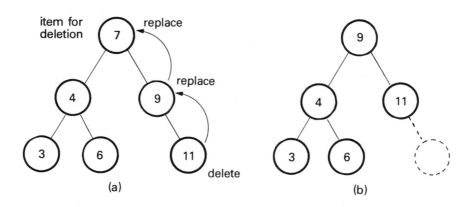

(a)   (b)

Consider for example the tree fragment shown in Fig. 10.9(a), where the item value 7 is to be deleted. Since it is not in a leaf position we locate the leftmost value in its right subtree and use this to replace the value 7. The leftmost value in the right subtree is the value 9, which is not in a leaf position either. However, applying the deletion strategy recursively to item value 9 we replace it by item value 11 and 'delete' the latter. This value is now a leaf position and can be deleted without further rearrangement, leading to the fragment shown in Fig. 10.9(b).

It is left as an exercise for the reader to extend the implementation given in Listing 20, using this deletion strategy and the representation adopted in Listing 21, to provide a complete implementation of the ordered list abstraction defined in Chapter 8.

CASE STUDY: AN ANIMAL GUESSING PROGRAM

To illustrate the use of our general binary tree abstraction we now consider its use to represent a decision tree. A decision tree is one in which each internal node represents a choice or decision to be made between alternatives, and each leaf node represents the net result of a sequence of decisions.

The particular application that we will consider is a 'learning' program which tries to identify the animal that its human opponent has thought of, by asking questions. Each question will have a yes or no answer, and on receiving each answer the program will either decide to ask another question or make a guess at the animal concerned. If this guess is wrong, the program will add to its knowledge by asking its opponent to supply a further question which distinguishes the new animal from the wrong guess. A typical dialogue between the program and its opponent would be as follows:

Program: Think of an animal . . .
            Has it four legs?
Opponent: Yes
Program: Are you thinking of A CAMEL?
Opponent: No
Program: I give up—what is your animal?
Opponent: AN ELEPHANT
Program: What question can I ask to identify AN ELEPHANT?
Opponent: Has it a trunk?
Program: Would you like another turn?
                . . .

The overall form of the program required is clearly a loop to conduct a sequence of question and answer sessions with its opponents, and can be expressed as follows:

```
begin {animalguessingprogram}
    startanimals;
    repeat
        writeln; writeln;
        writeln ('Think of an animal . . .');
        determineanimal;
        writeln ('Would you like another turn?');
        getreply (reply)
    until reply = no;
    writeln ('OK, bye for now')
end {animalguessingprogram}.
```

The procedure *getreply* merely obtains a yes/no answer from the opponent in response to the question just output, and is easily implemented. The procedure *startanimals* initializes the program's knowledge of animals in some appropriate way. The procedure *determineanimal* uses this knowledge to conduct a question and answer session leading to a guess at the animal thought of by its opponent, and adds to this knowledge if the guess is wrong.

Before we can refine these procedures further, we must make some decisions on how the program's knowledge of animals is to be represented.

The program will hold its knowledge as a binary tree in which each internal node is a question and each leaf node is an answer, i.e. an animal. Before the session illustrated earlier, for example, the program's very

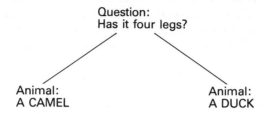

Figure 10.10   Initial state of animal tree

limited knowledge might be as shown in Fig. 10.10. After the above session, however, its knowledge will have been extended as shown in Fig. 10.11.

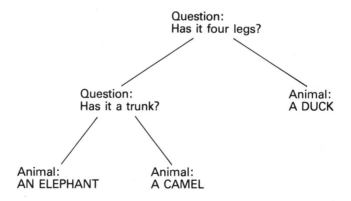

Figure 10.11   Extended animal tree

The data at any node of this tree may be described by the following Pascal definitions:

```
const
    questionlength = . . . ;
    namelength     = . . . ;
```

```
type
  nodeform      = (aquestion, ananimal);
  animalname    = packed array[1 . . namelength] of char;
  questionstring = packed array[1 . . questionlength] of char;
  nodedata      = record
                    case form : nodeform of
                    aquestion : (question : questionstring);
                    ananimal : (name : animalname)
                  end;
```

Using the general binary tree abstraction the knowledge tree can then be declared as follows:

> **envelope module** *animaltree = generalbinarytree* **in** *library*
> (*where* **type** *itemtype = nodedata;*);

The procedure *startanimals* might be written to retrieve the knowledge gained from some previous session from a knowledge file, and techniques for doing so will be discussed in Chapter 13. Alternatively, the program may start each session with the minimum knowledge possible, and rely entirely on the session itself to build up its knowledge of animals. To provide an initial well-formed decision tree, the minimum knowledge required is that of a single animal, arbitrarily chosen. Thus the procedure *startanimals* in its simplest form can be written as follows:

```
procedure startanimals;
  var firstanimal : nodedata;
  begin
    with firstanimal do
    begin
      form := ananimal;
      name := 'A DUCK'
    end;
    animaltree.insertroot (firstanimal)
  end {startanimals};
```

The procedure *determineanimal* starts at the root of the existing animal tree and follows a path of question/answer exchanges through the tree until a leaf node is reached. This is most simply expressed using a local recursive procedure, *trythisnode*, as follows:

```
procedure determineanimal;

  procedure trythisnode; . . .

  begin
    animaltree.locateroot;
    trythisnode
  end {determineanimal};
```

The procedure *trythisnode* extracts the contents of the current (window) node of the animal tree and acts accordingly. If it is an animal node a guess is made, and if this is incorrect a new animal (and question) is added to the tree. If the node is a question *trythisnode* asks the question, and on the basis of the reply moves the window to the left or right subtree, before calling itself recursively. By convention yes answers lead left, no answers lead right, so procedure *trythisnode* becomes:

```
procedure trythisnode;

    var thisnode : nodedata;
        reply : areply;

begin
    animaltree.contents (thisnode);
    with thisnode do
      if form = ananimal
      then begin
              writeln ('Are you thinking of ', name);
              getreply (reply);
              if reply = no
              then addanimal
              else writeln ('I win - thank you for the game')
           end
      else begin
              writeln (question);
              getreply (reply);
              if reply = yes
              then animaltree.nextleft
              else animaltree.nextright;
              trythisnode
           end
end {trythisnode};
```

The procedure *addanimal* must obtain from the opponent the new animal's name and a question which distinguishes it from the animal wrongly guessed, i.e. a question to which yes implies the new animal, no implies the old. As illustrated in Fig. 10.10 this new knowledge is accommodated in the tree by

(a)   inserting a copy of the old animal on the right of the current node;

(b)   inserting the new animal on the left; and

(c)   replacing the original node contents by the new question.

Thus procedure *addanimal* is expressed as follows:

> **procedure** *addanimal*;
>
> > **var** *oldanimal, newanimal, newquestion : nodedata*;
> >
> > **begin**
> > > *{copy old animal to right (no) path}*
> > > *animaltree.contents (oldanimal)*;
> > > *animaltree.insertright (oldanimal)*;
> > >
> > > *{set up new animal on left (yes) path}*
> > > *newanimal.form := ananimal*;
> > > *getanimal (newanimal.name)*;
> > > *animaltree.insertleft (newanimal)*;
> > >
> > > *{set up new question as current node}*
> > > *newquestion.form := aquestion*;
> > > *getquestion (newquestion.question)*;
> > > *animaltree.replace (newquestion)*
> > **end** *{addanimal}*;

The procedures *getanimal* and *getquestion* simply prompt the opponent with suitable questions and then copy the response into their variable parameter strings. Listing 22 shows a complete version of the animal guessing program that results.

Listing 22

```
program animalguessing(input, output);

   { This program plays an animal guessing game with its human      }
   { opponent. Initially it knows only one animal, but by learning  }
   { from its opponent it builds up its knowledge of animals        }
   { in the form of a binary decision tree.                         }

   const questionlength = 60;
         namelength = 16;

   type nodeform = (aquestion, ananimal);
        animalname = packed array [1..namelength] of char;
        questionstring = packed array [1..questionlength] of char;
        nodedata = record
                      case form: nodeform of
                          aquestion: (question: questionstring);
                          ananimal: (name: animalname)
                   end;
        areply = (yes, no);
```

continued on page 260

Listing 22 continued

```
envelope module animaltree = generalbinarytree in library
  (where type itemtype = nodedata; );

var reply: areply;

procedure startanimals;
  var firstanimal: nodedata;
  begin
    with firstanimal do
      begin
        form := ananimal;
        name := 'A DUCK
      end;
    animaltree.insertroot(firstanimal)
  end {startanimals};

procedure skiptoletter;
  begin while not (input^ in ['a'..'z', 'A'..'Z']) do get(input)
  end {skiptoletter};

procedure getreply(var reply: areply);
  var replych: char;
  begin
    skiptoletter;
    readln(replych);
    while not (replych in ['n', 'N', 'y', 'Y']) do
      begin
        writeln('?');
        skiptoletter;
        readln(replych)
      end;
    if replych in ['y', 'Y']
    then reply := yes
    else reply := no
  end {getreply};

procedure getstring(var string: packed array [m..n: integer] of char);
  var i: integer;
  begin
    i := m;
    skiptoletter;
    repeat
      read(string[i]);
      i := i + 1
    until eoln(input) or (i > n);
    for i := i to n do string[i] := ' ';
    readln
  end {getstring};
```

```
procedure determineanimal;

   { This procedure uses the recursive procedure trythisnode  }
   { to conduct a question and answer session determined      }
   { by the animal tree until a leaf (animal) node is reached }
   { If the animal so determined is wrong, a new animal is    }
   { added by further dialogue with the human opponent.       }


   procedure trythisnode;
      var thisnode: nodedata;
          reply: areply;

      procedure addanimal;

         { The window is over the rejected animal node.    }
         { The animal entry must be replaced by a question }
         { with a new animal node placed to the left and   }
         { the old animal node to the right                }

         var oldanimal, newanimal, newquestion: nodedata;

         procedure getanimal(var newname: animalname);
            begin
              writeln;
              writeln('I give up - What is your animal?');
              getstring(newname)
            end {getanimal};

         procedure getquestion(var question: questionstring);
            begin
              writeln;
              writeln
                ('What question can I ask to identify your animal?');
              getstring(question);
              writeln('Thank you for your help.')
            end {getquestion};

         begin

           { copy old animal to right (no) path }
           animaltree.contents(oldanimal);
           animaltree.insertright(oldanimal);

           { set up new animal on left (yes) path }
           newanimal.form := ananimal;
           getanimal(newanimal.name);
           animaltree.insertleft(newanimal);
```

continued on page 262

Listing 22 continued

```
            { set up new question as current node }
            newquestion.form := aquestion;
            getquestion(newquestion.question);
            animaltree.replace(newquestion)
         end {addanimal};

    begin
      animaltree.contents(thisnode);
      with thisnode do
        if form = ananimal
        then begin
               writeln('Are you thinking of  ', name);
               getreply(reply);
               if reply = no
               then addanimal
               else writeln('I win - thank you for the game ')
             end
        else begin
               writeln(question);
               getreply(reply);
               if reply = yes
               then animaltree.nextleft
               else animaltree.nextright;
               trythisnode
             end
      end {trythisnode};

  begin
    animaltree.locateroot;
    trythisnode
  end {determineanimal};

begin
  startanimals;
  repeat
    writeln;
    writeln;
    writeln('Think of an animal ....');
    determineanimal;
    writeln('would you like another turn?');
    getreply(reply)
  until reply = no;
  writeln('OK, bye for now')
end {animalguessing}.
```

The tree manipulation code required in the animal guessing program is particularly simple because the data held at each node implies the status of the node itself—an animal node is always a leaf, while a question node is always internal. We could, in fact, have omitted the tag field *form* from the node data records and instead used the tree operators *emptyleft* or *empty-right* to decide whether a given node represented a question or an animal, but the procedure *trythisnode* would be significantly less transparent as a result.

CONTIGUOUS TREE REPRESENTATIONS

So far we have considered only representations of binary trees using pointers. Given the non-linear structures involved, using pointers is a natural choice. In general, contiguous representation of a tree involves storing explicit links to other nodes in each element of a node array and is thus equivalent to the pointer representation.

Under one condition, however, a contiguous representation which does not involve explicit links can be used. The condition required is that the maximum depth of the tree, i.e. the maximum number of nodes on any path from root to leaf will not exceed some acceptable limit *maxdepth*. In this case the total number of items in a binary tree cannot exceed:

$$maxitems = 2^{\,maxdepth} - 1$$

and the tree can be represented in an array of *maxitems* elements as follows:

```
type nodeindex = 1 . . maxitems;
     node = packed record
                    case empty : Boolean of
                    true : ( );
                    false : (itemvalue : itemtype)
                 end;
     tree = array [nodeindex] of node;
```

Within an array *T:tree* representing a binary tree

(a)   element $T[1]$ represents the root node;

(b)   the children of a non-empty node represented by element $T[i]$, where $1 < i < maxitems$ **div** 2, are represented by elements $T[2*i]$ and $T[2*i+1]$.

Note that for a non-empty node $T[i]$, where $i > maxitems$ **div** 2, the depth condition guarantees that both children are empty, and so need no representation. Note also that the parent of any node $T[i]$, where $i > 1$, is represented by $T[i$ **div** $2]$.

Fig. 10.12 shows how the binary search tree originally shown in Fig. 10.5 may be stored as an array of 7 elements using this technique.

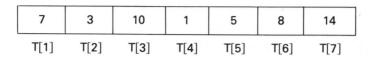

7	3	10	1	5	8	14
T[1]	T[2]	T[3]	T[4]	T[5]	T[6]	T[7]

Figure 10.12   Contiguous tree representation

For some item types the empty tag required in each packed node record may be accommodated without storage overhead. Alternatively, if item values require a significant amount of storage, and the tree on average holds significantly less than its maximum number of items, it may be more economical to represent it as an array of pointers to item values, as follows:

> *nodeindex* = 1 . . *maxitems*;
> *node*   = ↑*itemtype*;
> *tree*   = **array** [*nodeindex*] **of** *node*;

In this case empty nodes are represented by **nil** pointers, and storage for items is allocated only when required, i.e. for the non-empty nodes.

It is left as an exercise for the reader to implement one of our previous tree abstractions, using this contiguous array representation.

SUMMARY

Trees are important non-linear data structures which are used both to mirror real world data with an inherent hierarchical structure, and for the efficient implementation of other structures, such as ordered lists, which are not inherently tree-structured. In this chapter we have confined our attention to binary trees, but the concepts and implementation techniques so introduced can be generalized to trees of higher degree.

At the implementation level we have seen that the pointer is a natural means of representing tree structures, the only significant choice being whether to include a backward pointer to the parent of each tree node. Contiguous representations are a practical alternative only for trees that are both limited in size and regular in form.

For the examples we have considered, the window mechanism (which permits access to a single tree node at any time) has proved an adequate and secure access, but for some tree rearrangements a single window could prove a limitation.

In Chapter 11 we consider graph structures (of which trees are a special case) and use an alternative access mechanism to the nodes involved, which is more flexible but less secure.

EXERCISES

10.1 Use the *orderedlist* envelope to implement the *wordlist* module of the concordance program.

10.2 Extend the binary tree implementation of an ordered list given as Listing 20 to provide

(a) a *replace* operator, which requires that the new and old values of a list item are equal, where equality is defined as for the operator *locatevalue*;

(b) a *delete* operator, using the strategy illustrated in Fig. 10.9. Make sure the window position after deletion is consistent with the definition of the delete operator given in Chapter 8.

10.3 Show how a catalog of all the files existing in an operating system may be organised as a list ordered according to file names, using the ordered list abstraction (as extended in Exercise 10.2). For each file the date of its last access is encoded as an integer (e.g., 830726 denotes July 26, 1983). Write procedures which

(a) update the last access date in a file entry;

(b) go through the catalog and delete all files whose last access was before a certain date.

10.4 Use the *generalbinarytree* envelope to implement the *orderedlist* envelope.

10.5 Define instances of the *generalbinarytree* envelope suitable for the representation of

(a) a Royal family tree;

(b) an arithmetic expression.

Write procedures to output the line of succession to the throne, and the value of an arithmetic expression, respectively.

10.6   A family tree, such as that shown in Fig. 10.2, can be represented as an indented text, thus:

> *George*
> > *Elizabeth*
> > > *Charles*
> > > > *William*
> > >
> > > *Anne*
> > > > *Peter*
> > > >
> > > > *Zara*
> > >
> > > *Andrew*
> > >
> > > *Edward*
> >
> > *Margaret*
> > > *David*
> > >
> > > *Sarah*

Write a procedure *readfamily* which reads such a text and constructs a family tree, (in the equivalent binary tree form illustrated in Fig. 10.3) using the *generalbinarytree* envelope.

Write a procedure *printgrandchildren* which reads the name of one person in the family tree (assume the name is unique) and prints out the names of all grandchildren of that person.

10.7   Implement the *generalbinarytree* envelope using a contiguous representation, as outlined on page 263.

11

Graphs

In Chapter 10 we considered trees as a particular class of non-linear data structures in which each component has multiple successors, but no more than one predecessor. The more general non-linear structure, in which each component may have zero or more successors and predecessors, is usually referred to as a *graph* structure, and in this chapter we consider the basic principles of defining, representing and using such structures.

DIRECTED GRAPHS

A *directed graph* is a data structure consisting of a number of items, or nodes, where those nodes that have a certain relationship are connected together by directed *arcs* (sometimes called *edges*).

A first example of a directed graph is a project plan. A project may be made up of a number of separate activities, many of which must be com-

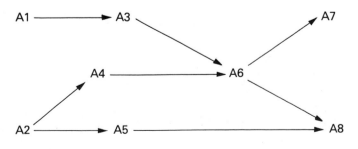

Figure 11.1 A project plan

pleted before other activities may commence. Such a project may be represented as a directed graph as shown in Fig. 11.1, where the activities, represented as nodes and arcs, connect an activity to other activities which cannot begin until it has been completed. Such a graph may be analysed to determine the sequencing and timing of the activities necessary for the project to be completed in the shortest possible time.

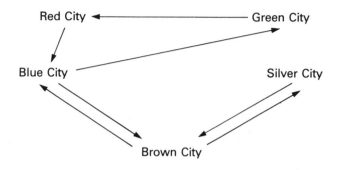

Figure 11.2   An airline route map

Another example of a directed graph is an airline route map (Fig. 11.2), consisting of a number of nodes (cities) where those cities which have a direct air connection are linked together by an arc. An arc from node A to node B indicates there is a direct flight from city A to city B. In some cases the arcs may have extra information associated with them (e.g. the airline flying the route, the flight time, etc.).

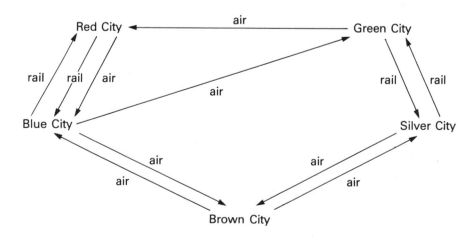

Figure 11.3   A composite route map

In general nodes may have a number of different relationships with each other, e.g. we might extend our route map to indicate not only air connections but also direct rail connections (Fig. 11.3), in which case each arc must be labelled to indicate whether it denotes an air or rail connection.

To demonstrate the basic principles of graph manipulation we will confine ourselves to consideration of (unlabelled) directed graphs, in which there is at most one arc from node i to node j, and in which arcs do not have extra information associated with them; information is held only at nodes. Such graphs may be viewed as a generalization of all those data structures in which there is a defined relationship or connection between some or all components. Hence the various categories of sequence considered in Chapters 7 and 8, and the trees considered in Chapter 10, are particular restricted cases of our general graph structure.

A Directed Graph Abstraction

A general abstraction of a directed graph whose nodes hold items of some given type must provide operators for the creation and deletion of nodes, for the inspection and updating of node items, for the creation and deletion of arcs, and for moving around the graph structure in a manner determined by the arcs available. As such, these requirements are similar to those already considered for lists and trees, but in practice the form in which we provide them is somewhat different because of the greater generality of the graph abstraction.

For lists and trees we adopted the concept of a window to represent the current point of attention in the data structure concerned. At any moment at most one component was accessible via this window, and the user program had no means of remembering or operating on other components of the structure without moving the window, except by complete traversal operations. For most applications of lists and trees the single focus of attention provided by the window mechanism is an adequate, efficient and secure means of enabling item manipulation.

For graphs, however, the window concept is inadequate for the description of arcs, and window movement is difficult to define for the unbounded multiplicity of arcs that may lead to and from each node. Instead, therefore, we adopt an alternative technique that enables the user program to obtain and store *references* to nodes within the graph. Arcs can then be described by pairs of node references, and the multiplicity of predecessors and successors of any node can be expressed as sets of node references.

This alternative technique is enabled by exporting, from the graph abstraction envelope, a type whose values are references to nodes of the graph, thus:

> **envelope** *graph*;

> **type** **node* = . . .;

For the manipulation and comparison of node references, we will assume that the assignment and test of equality operators, := and =, apply to values of type *node*.

By declaring and using a variable of type *node*, the user program can then express the creation of a new node with a specified item value by use of an operator:

> **procedure** **newnode* (**var** *n* : *node*; *i* : *itemtype*);

and can express the inspection, updating or deletion of a previously referenced node by the operators:

> **procedure** **contents* (*n* : *node* ; **var** *i* : *itemtype*);

> **procedure** **replace* (*n* : *node* ; *i* : *itemtype*);

> **procedure** **delete* (*n* : *node*);

The *delete* operator deletes the referenced node from the graph together with any arcs leading to or from that node.

The explicit node reference *n* required by the *contents*, *replace* and *delete* operators replaces the implicit window concept used by the corresponding operators for lists and trees. It is the user's responsibility to obtain, store and supply the appropriate reference value for each operator. The security of this mechanism will be discussed later in this chapter.

Given references to the nodes concerned, the creation or deletion of individual arcs can be expressed using the following operators:

> **procedure** **setarc* (*n*1, *n*2 : *node*);

> **procedure** **deletearc* (*n*1, *n*2 : *node*);

How do we enable the location and manipulation of the successors or predecessors of a given node? For the moment we will adopt a minimal interface which provides the ability to traverse the successors or predecessors of a given node *n* performing a given operation *p* on each in turn, as follows:

> **procedure** **foreachsuccessor* (*n* : *node* ; **procedure** *p* (*x* : *node*));

> **procedure** **foreachpredecessor* (*n* : *node* ; **procedure** *p* (*x* : *node*));

Note that these operators take a procedure parameter *p* whose own parameter is a node reference, not an item. This allows the operators to be used for systematic processing both of arcs connecting nodes and of the items held at nodes, since the latter can be accessed within the actual parameter *p* using the *contents* and *replace* operators.

The ability to traverse the successors or predecessors of a given node is equally applicable to the entire graph itself. We therefore provide a corresponding operator:

procedure **traverse* (**procedure** *p* (*n* : *node*));

which applies its parametric procedure *p* to every node in the graph, in some arbitrary order.

For some applications it is necessary to locate an arbitrary graph node which satisfies a specified condition, and a corresponding *locate* operator is therefore defined. In the absence of a window concept, the *locate* operator returns the result of its search as a Boolean flag indicating success or failure, together with a node reference when successful:

procedure **locate* (**function** *test* (*n* : *node*) : *Boolean*;
                  var *found* : *Boolean* ; **var** *n* : *node*);

Again the parameter to the *test* function is a node reference rather than an item value, so that *locate* may be used to search for nodes with properties specified in terms of either arcs or item values.

Finally, for general graph manipulation it is convenient to be able to test the cardinality, or emptiness, of a graph as a whole, or of the successors or predecessors of any node. For maximum generality we therefore define three functions:

function **nodecount* : *integer*;

function **successorcount* (*n* : *node*) : *integer*;

function **predecessorcount* (*n* : *node*) : *integer*;

Our initial graph abstraction is summarized by the following envelope interface:

envelope *graph*;

    {*assumes* **type** *itemtype* = *type of item at each node*,
                                with := *applicable*}

    type **node* = . . .;

    procedure **newnode* (**var** *n* : *node* ; *i* : *itemtype*);

procedure **deletenode* (*n* : *node*);

procedure **locate* (**function** *test* (*n* : *node*) : *Boolean*;
                 var *found* : *Boolean* ; **var** *n* : *node*);

procedure **contents* (*n* : *node* ; **var** *i* : *itemtype*);

procedure **replace* (*n* : *node* ; *i* : *itemtype*);

procedure **setarc* (*n1,n2* : *node*);

procedure **deletearc* (*n1,n2* : *node*);

procedure **foreachsuccessor* (*n* : *node* ; **procedure** *p* (*x* : *node*));

procedure **foreachpredecessor* (*n* : *node* ; **procedure** *p* (*x* : *node*));

procedure **traverse* (**procedure** *p* (*x* : *node*));

function **nodecount* : *integer*;

function **successorcount* (*n* : *node*) : *integer*;

function **predecessorcount* (*n* : *node*) : *integer*;

begin
  {*graph is empty*}
  * * *
end {*graph*};

GRAPH MANIPULATION

To assess the adequacy of our initial graph abstraction, we now consider some of the typical graph manipulation required in practical applications, namely graph input, path analysis, and topological sorting.

Graph Input

Many of the graphs that arise in practical applications are models of real world situations such as the activity diagram in Fig. 11.1 or the airline network in Fig. 11.2. Before such graphs can be analysed they must be input by some means.

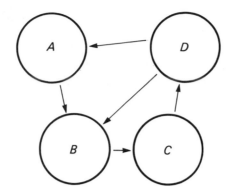

Figure 11.4   A graph with node labels only

   The simplest case of graph input is when the only data held at each node is a 'label' value which reflects its real world significance. Consider the simple graph shown in Fig. 11.4. The letters A,B,C,D distinguish the nodes of the graph, and no other data is associated with each node. Such a graph can be described simply by listing the node label pairs that define its arcs, thus:
   AB, BC, CD, DA, DB.

In general, however, the items held at the nodes of a graph are composite data items that cannot be used directly to denote the start and end point of each arc. For example, the data held at each node of an activity diagram such as that shown in Fig. 11.1 might be defined as follows:

itemtype = **record**
           activitynumber : 1 . . 100;
           duration : . . .;
           manpower : . . .;
           cost : . . .;
           startdate : . . .;
       end;

For such graphs it is necessary to separate the input of the data held at the nodes from the input of the arcs that connect them. For convenience, we will assume that two separate files are used to hold the node and arc data, in which case a procedure to input the graph may be defined as follows:

      procedure *readgraph* (**var** *nodefile,arcfile* : *text*;
                           instance *g* : *graph*);
       . . .
      begin
        readnodes (*nodefile*);
        readarcs (*arcfile*)
      end {*readgraph*};

Reading the nodes involves a straightforward file reading loop which calls the *newnode* operator for each node item read:

```
procedure readnodes (var nodefile : text);

    var i : itemtype;
        n : g.node;

    begin
      reset (nodefile);
      while not eof (nodefile) do
      begin
        readitem (nodefile,i);
        g.newnode (n,i)
      end
    end {readnodes};
```

The procedure *readitem* must read a single item value from the file specified, leaving *eof* true when the last item has been read. Note that the references to the nodes created at this stage are discarded, and must be re-determined by searching the graph during input of the arc data.

To read the arcs we must introduce a new type, *nodelabel*, whose values are used to distinguish the nodes within the arc data. For the activity diagram with node items as above we might use the activity number fields to distinguish nodes, and define:

nodelabel = 1 . . 100;

With such a *nodelabel* type a procedure to read a sequence of label pairs and create the corresponding arcs in the graph *g* can now be programmed.

```
procedure readarcs(var arcfile : text);
    var l1, l2 : nodelabel;
        n1, n2 : g.node;
    begin
      reset (arcfile);
      while not eof (arcfile) do
      begin
        readlabelpair (arcfile, l1, l2);
        findnode (l1, n1);
        findnode (l2, n2);
        g.setarc (n1, n2)
      end
    end {readarcs};
```

The procedure *readlabelpair* must read the next pair of label values from the specified file leaving *eof* true when the last pair is read. The procedure *findnode* must locate an existing node in the graph *g* which has the label specified, and return a corresponding node reference. If we assume a function *haslabel* which determines whether a specified item value corresponds to a specified label, thus:

function *haslabel* (*i* : *itemtype* ; *l* : *nodelabel*) : *Boolean*;

the procedure *findnode* can be expressed using the *locate* operator of our graph abstraction, as follows:

procedure *findnode* (*l* : *nodelabel* ; **var** *n* : *g.node*);

    var *found* : *Boolean*;

    function *labelsought* (*n* : *g.node*) : *Boolean*;
      var *i* : *itemtype*;
      begin
        g.contents (*n, i*);
        labelsought := *haslabel* (*i,l*)
      end {*labelsought*};

    begin
      g.locate (*labelsought,found,n*);
      if not *found* **then** *error* (*'invalid label in arc'*)
    end {*findnode*};

On definition of the auxiliary type *nodelabel*, the procedures *readitem*, *readlabelpair* and the function *haslabel*, a graph manipulation program can use this procedure to input any graph defined, using our graph abstraction envelope.

Path Analysis

Much graph manipulation involves the analysis of paths between graph nodes. Consider first the problem of determining which nodes are reachable from a given node by paths that follow the directed arcs of the graph. Formally, we say that a node *b* is reachable from a node *a* if:

(a)   *b* and *a* are the same node, or

(b)   *b* is reachable from any node that is a successor of *a*.

This recursive definition immediately suggests an algorithm for identifying the nodes reachable from any node:

```
procedure consider (n : g.node);
  begin
    {n is reachable};
    g.foreachsuccessor (n,consider)
  end {consider};
```

If called with node *a* as its initial parameter, the procedure *consider* will in principle visit each graph node that is reachable from *a*. In practice, however, it is defective in two ways:

(a)   if a node *b* is reachable from *a* by two or more distinct paths, consideration of *b* and all nodes reachable via *b* will occur more than once;

(b)   if any path from *a* includes a cycle, i.e. leads back onto itself, the procedure will not terminate.

To overcome these defects the procedure must record all nodes reached and avoid reconsideration of any node already reached. The nodes reached at any stage may be thought of as a set of nodes. For the moment we will assume that such a set can be defined as a Pascal set (of node references), thus

```
setofnodes = set of g.node;
```

In practice, the validity of this depends on how the type *g.node* is implemented, a point we will return to later.

Using such a set to represent the nodes concerned, we can now construct a procedure that determines all nodes reachable from a given node, thus:

```
procedure reachablenodes (a : g.node ;
                              var nodesreachable : setofnodes);

  procedure consider (n : g.node);
    begin
      if not (n in nodesreachable) then
      begin
        {n is now reachable};
        nodesreachable := nodesreachable + [n];
        g.foreachsuccessor (n,consider)
      end
    end {consider};
```

```
  begin
    nodesreachable := [ ];
    consider (a)
  end {reachablenodes};
```

A function to determine whether a specific node *b* is reachable from node *a* can be constructed using a similar recursive procedure, as follows:

```
function reachable (a,b : g.node) : Boolean;

  label 1;

  var nodesreached : setofnodes;

  procedure consider (n : g.node);
    begin
      if not (n in nodesreached) then
      begin
        if n = b then
        begin reachable := true ; goto 1 end;
        nodesreached := nodesreached + [n];
        g.foreachsuccessor (n, consider)
      end
    end {consider};

  begin
    nodesreached := [ ];
    consider(a);
    reachable := false;
  1:
  end {reachable};
```

If procedure *consider* encounters node *b* the traversal of nodes reachable from *a* is interrupted by a goto statement, to return result *true*. If the traversal terminates without such interruption then *b* is not reachable from *a*, so result *false* is returned.

Identifying a path from node *a* to node *b*, i.e. determining the sequence of intermediate nodes involved, can also be programmed using the same basic algorithm. Depending on the application concerned, the path finding algorithm may be required to:

(a) find any path from *a* to *b*, or

(b) find all paths from *a* to *b*, or

(c) find a path from *a* to *b* that satisfies some specific criterion determined by the application, which may be a function of the number of arcs involved, or of the item values at the nodes on the path.

In practice, all of these objectives can be catered for by a general path finding procedure which constructs each possible path, and calls a parametric procedure *pathfound*, with the path found as parameter, each time a new path has been constructed, thus:

> **procedure** *findpaths* (*a*,*b* : *g.node*;
> > **procedure** *pathfound* (*p*:*path*))

In case (a) the actual procedure supplied as *pathfound* will interrupt the path finding process (by not returning control). In case (b) the procedure must copy or output the path represented in its parameter and then allow path finding to resume. In case (c), the procedure must evaluate the path in its parameter against the criterion involved, and decide whether or not to resume the path finding process.

Internally, the path finding algorithm differs from the reachability algorithm in two significant ways:

(a)   Since distinct paths from *a* to *b* that intersect at some intermediate node must be separately identified, the discriminating test at entry to the recursive procedure only excludes further consideration of those nodes already on the current path, thus avoiding cyclic and potentially infinite paths,

(b)   in determining a path by trial and error the algorithm records the sequence of nodes that lead to the current point of attention. This involves adding node *n* to the sequence before investigating all paths leading from *n* (i.e. at entry to the recursive procedure concerned), and removing *n* from the sequence when this investigation is complete (i.e. at exit from the recursive procedure).

How should a path be represented? The user program sees a path as a sequence of node references which can be inspected in order. During its construction by trial and error the path finding algorithm adds nodes and removes nodes, one by one, at the end of an initially empty path. The necessary operations on a path are thus summarized by the following envelope interface:

> **envelope** *path*;
>
> > **function** **length* : *integer*;
> > **procedure** **clearpath*;
> > **procedure** **addnode* (*n* : *g.node*);
> > **procedure** **removenode*;
> > **procedure** **traversepath* (**procedure** *p* (*n* : *g.node*));

```
begin
  {path is clear, with length 0}
  ***
end {path};
```

Assuming the existence of such an envelope the path finding algorithm is easily programmed as follows:

```
procedure findpaths(a, b : g.node;
                        procedure pathfound (instance p : path));

  instance pathnow : path;
  var pathnodes : setofnodes;

  procedure extendpath (n : g.node);
    begin
      if not (n in pathnodes) then
      begin
        pathnow.addnode (n);
        pathnodes := pathnodes + [n];
        if n = b
        then pathfound (pathnow)
        else g.forallsuccessors (n, extendpath);
        pathnodes := pathnodes − [n];
        pathnow.removenode
      end
    end {extendpath};

  begin {findpaths}
    pathnow.clearpath;
    pathnodes := [ ];
    extendpath (a)
  end {findpaths};
```

Note that the procedure again uses an internal set of nodes to enable convenient avoidance of cyclic paths.

All of our path analysis procedures so far have shared a common algorithmic strategy based on a recursive procedure which performs a depth-first analysis of the possible paths from any node. By depth-first we mean that all nodes reachable via the first successor of any node are investigated before the next successor is considered—Fig. 11.5 shows a graph fragment with nodes numbered to show the order in which they may be visited in a depth-first search from node 0.

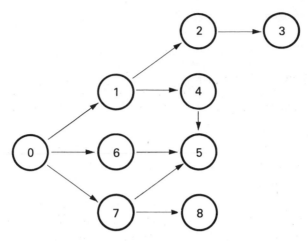

Figure 11.5   Depth-first traversal of graph nodes

Note that with the depth-first strategy nodes 2,3,4,5 are considered before
nodes 6 or 7, even though they are more remote from node 0, and that the
path that leads to consideration of node 5 (via nodes 0,1,4,5) is not the
shortest path (which is via node 6 or 7).

An alternative breadth-first strategy, which considers the nodes reachable from a given node in increasing order of remoteness, can also be
implemented. Figure 11.6 shows the same graph fragment with nodes numbered in the order in which they might be visited by a breadth-first traversal.

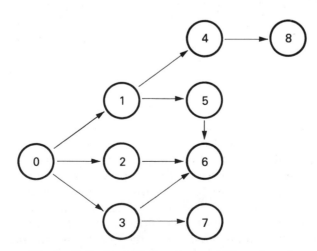

Figure 11.6   Breadth-first traversal of graph nodes

To illustrate the use of a breadth-first strategy we will reconsider our procedure *reachablenodes*, which determines the set of all nodes reachable from a given node. The algorithm involved, which is known as Warshall's algorithm, is a standard graph manipulation algorithm and as such is a good test of the adequacy of our graph abstraction.

If we use the term *reachable in n* to describe those nodes reachable by traversing n arcs but not reachable by less, then our breadth-first algorithm must have the general form:

> **for** $n := 0$ **to** *somelimit* **do**
>   *add nodes reachable in n to reachable nodes*

though we do not as yet know how the repetition will terminate or how to compute the nodes reachable in n.

A little reflection, however, shows that the nodes reachable in n must be successors of nodes reachable in $n-1$, but excluding any such successors that are themselves reachable in $n-1$ or less. By similar reasoning, our repetition may terminate when the set of nodes reachable in n is empty, since all further sets reachable in $n+1$, etc. must also be empty. The algorithm can thus be reformulated as follows:

> *reachablenodes* := [ ];
> *newnodes* := [a];
> **repeat**
>   *reachablenodes* := *reachablenodes* + *newnodes*;
>   *newnodes* := *allsuccessorsof* (*newnodes*) − *reachablenodes*
> **until** *newnodes* = [ ]

Computing the set *allsuccessorsof* (*newnodes*) is in principle accomplished as follows:

> *allsuccessors* := [ ];
> **for** *each node n in newnodes* **do**
>   *allsuccessors* := *allsuccessors* + *successorsof* (*n*)

If we assume:

(a)   a set iteration statement **for** *m in s* **do,** which executes the following statement for each member value m in s, and

(b)   that our graph abstraction allows the successors s of a node n to be extracted in a single operator *g.getsuccessors* (*n,s*)

then our procedure *reachablenodes* can be expressed in the following form:

```
procedure reachablenodes (a : g.node ;
                          var nodesreachable : setofnodes);

    var newnodes, allsuccessors, successorsofn : setofnodes;
        n : g:node;

    begin
      nodesreachable := [ ];
      newnodes := [a];
      repeat
        nodesreachable := nodesreachable + newnodes;
        allsuccessors := [ ];
        for n in newnodes do
        begin
            g.getsuccessors (n, successorsofn);
            allsuccessors := allsuccessors + successorsofn
        end;
        newnodes := allsuccessors − nodesreachable
      until newnodes = [ ]
    end {reachablenodes};
```

Without the *getsuccessors* operator the inner loop of this procedure would be written as:

```
for n in newnodes do
    g.foreachsuccessor (n, addtosuccessors)
```

where *addtosuccessors* is a local procedure defined as follows:

```
procedure addtosuccessors (x : g.node);
    begin allsuccessors := allsuccessors + [x] end;
```

The *getsuccessors* operator clearly simplifies the expression of this algorithm and is consistent with the set arithmetic approach that it involves. Whether it improves the efficiency of the algorithm depends on the relative efficiencies of the implementations chosen for the operators *foreachsuccessor* and *getsuccessors*, and on the efficiency of the set arithmetic actually available, a point which we will return to in due course.

Topological Sorting

A directed graph that contains arcs between some but not all pairs of nodes defines a partial ordering between the nodes, in the sense that a node *a* from which an arc leads to node *b* is said to *precede* node *b*. We may consider the ordering relationship established by each arc as a transitive operator if we extend our definition to say that a node *a* precedes node *b* if any path leads from node *a* to node *b*. Clearly, this transitive ordering is strict only for a graph that is *acyclic*, i.e. contains no cyclic paths.

For such a graph it is possible to arrange the nodes in a sequential order that reflects the partial ordering defined by its arcs—a process known as *topological sorting*.

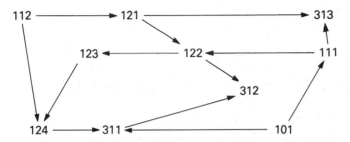

Figure 11.7   A graph of prerequisites between course units

Consider for example a university degree course in which certain course units are prerequisite for the taking of other units. The prerequisite relationships between course units may be represented as arcs in a graph of the course—Figure 11.7 represents a complicated set of course units in this way. The topological sort of such a graph embeds the partial order defined by its arcs in a linear order or, in graphical terms, it arranges the node in a line such that all arcs go from left to right as shown in Fig. 11.8.

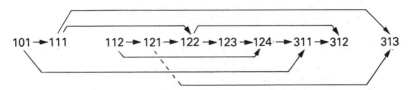

Figure 11.8   A topologically sorted prerequisite graph

For a course graph such a topological sort is useful in that:

(a)   it establishes that no cyclic prerequisites exist, and

(b)   it provides guidance for the course organiser in time-tabling the course units, and for students in choosing a sequence of units to take.

Topological sorting has a similar role to play in many other applications that involve graph-structured data. For this reason, it is again a good test of the adequacy of our graph abstraction to consider its impact on algorithms for topological sorting.

How can topological sorting of a graph be accomplished? We will derive a number of algorithms in the form of a general sort procedure whose effect is to apply a parametric procedure *p* to each node item of a graph *g* in topologically sorted order, i.e. such that *p* is applied to all predecessors of any node *n* before it is applied to *n* itself:

> **procedure** *topsort* (**instance** *g* : *graph*;
> **procedure** *p* (*n* : *g.node*));

If we adopt a simple selection strategy for sorting the graph analogous to the straight selection sort for lists, we may immediately write down an outline topological sorting algorithm:

> **repeat**
>   *search graph for a sortable node*;
>   *sort this node*
> **until** *all nodes sorted*

where sorting a node means applying procedure *p* to it. In topological sorting terms a sortable node is one that has not yet been sorted but whose predecessors, if any, have already been sorted. We must remember, however, that if the graph is cyclic a sortable node may not be found, and in this case the sort must fail. We therefore reformulate our basic algorithm as follows:

> **repeat**
>   *search graph for a sortable node*;
>   **if** *a node is found* **then** *sort it*
> **until** *none is found*;
> **if** *unsorted nodes remain* **then** *sort has failed*

Using the *locate* operator of our graph abstraction, this can immediately be expressed in the following more precise form:

> **repeat**
>   *g.locate* (*sortablenode, found, n*);
>   **if** *found* **then** *sort node n*
> **until not** *found*;
> **if** *unsorted nodes remain* **then** *error* (*'sort failed : graph is cyclic'*)

How we implement the tests *sortablenode* and *unsorted nodes remain* and the step *sort node n* depends on whether or not we have the freedom to destroy the graph as we sort it.

If we have that freedom, then we can adopt the simple strategy of *deleting* each node as it is sorted, and *sort node n* becomes

   $p\ (n)\ ;\ g.delete\ (n)$

With the deletion of sorted nodes, a node is sortable if it has no predecessors remaining in the graph, so we have:

```
function sortablenode (n : g.node) : Boolean;
   begin
      sortablenode := (g.predecessorcount(n) = 0)
   end {sortablenode};
```

With all sorted nodes deleted, the test *unsorted nodes remain* is simply a test to see if any nodes remain in the graph, so our first and simplest topological sorting algorithm can be implemented as follows:

```
procedure topsort1(instance g : graph;
                        procedure p (n : g.node));

   var found : Boolean;
       n : g.node;

   function sortablenode (n : g.node) : Boolean;
      begin sortablenode := (g.predecessorcount (n) = 0) end;

   begin {topsort1}
      repeat
         g.locate (sortablenode, found, n);
         if found then
         begin p (n) ; g.delete (n) end
      until not found;
      if g.nodecount <> 0 then error ('sort failed : graph is cyclic')
   end {topsort1};
```

If we cannot destroy the graph during sorting, the effects required by our basic algorithm are achieved by maintaining a set of all nodes sorted so far, together with a count of nodes sorted to simplify the final completeness test:

```
procedure topsort2 (instance g : graph;
                        procedure p (n : g.node));

   var sortednodes : setofnodes;
       sortedcount : integer;
       found : Boolean;
       n : g.node;
```

```
function sortablenode(n : g.node) : Boolean; . . . {see below}
```

```
begin {topsort2}
  sortednodes := [ ];
  sortedcount := 0;
  repeat
    g.locate (sortablenode, found, n);
    if found then
    begin
      p(n);
      sortednodes := sortednodes + [n];
      sortedcount := sortedcount + 1
    end
  until not found;
  if sortedcount <> g.nodecount
  then error ('sort failed : graph is cyclic')
end {topsort2};
```

In this case, however, implementation of the test *sortablenode* is affected by
the graph interface chosen. If our abstraction provides an operator to extract
the predecessors *p* of a node *n* by a single operator *g.getpredecessors(n,p)*,
the test can be expressed directly as a set containment test:

```
function sortablenode (n : g.node) : Boolean;
  var predecessors : setofnodes;
  begin
    g.getpredecessors (n, predecessors);
    sortablenode := (predecessors <= sortednodes)
  end {sortablenode};
```

If, however, we have only the ability to traverse the predecessors one by one,
as provided by our initial graph abstraction, the test is most economically
implemented in the following somewhat clumsy manner:

```
function sortablenode (n : g.node) : Boolean;

  label 1;

  procedure checkifsorted (p : g.node);
    begin
      if not (p in sortednodes) then
      begin sortablenode := false; goto 1 end
    end {checkifsorted};
```

```
    begin
        g.foreachpredecessor (n, checkifsorted);
        sortablenode := true;
        1:
    end {sortablenode};
```

Thus the *getpredecessors* operator enables a much clearer and more concise expression of the *sortablenode* test in our non-destructive topological sorting algorithm. Whether it is more efficient again depends on the relative efficiencies of the implementations chosen for the operators *getpredecessors* and *foreachpredecessor* and of the set containment operator actually available.

The strategy used to identify each sortable node in these topological sorting algorithms is a simple scan of the entire (remaining) graph, using the *locate* operator. Since the number of nodes examined by each call of *locate* must be proportional to n, the total number of nodes in the graph, it follows that the total number of *sortablenode* tests carried out in a complete sort varies as n^2, and for large n these tests will dominate the total time taken.

An improvement on this n^2 behaviour can be achieved by recognizing that during a topological sort each node either

(a)   is initially sortable, i.e. has no predecessors in the original graph, or

(b)   becomes sortable as the result of sorting a node which is its last unsorted predecessor.

By

(a)   creating an initial set of sortable nodes from which all nodes for sorting are taken, and

(b)   examining the successors of each node sorted for possible inclusion in the sortable set,

a significant reduction in the number of *sortablenode* tests can be achieved. In outline the algorithm involved is as follows:

```
        create an initial set of sortable nodes;
        while sortable nodes <> [ ] do
        begin
            select any node n from sortable nodes;
            sort node n;
            for each successor s of n do
                if s is sortable then add s to sortable nodes
        end;
        if unsorted nodes remain then sort has failed
```

Using the same non-destructive techniques as we used in *topsort2*, we can expand this into the following procedure:

```
procedure topsort3 (instance g : graph;
                         procedure p (n : g.node));

    var sortablenodes, sortednodes : setofnodes;
        sortedcount : integer;
        n : g.node;

    function sortablenode (n : g.node) : Boolean; . . {as for topsort2}

    procedure addifsortable (n : g.node);
      begin
        if sortablenode (n) then
            sortablenodes := sortablenodes + [n]
      end;

    begin
        sortednodes := [ ];
        sortedcount := 0;
        sortablenodes := [ ];
        g.traverse (addifsortable);
        while sortablenodes <> [ ] do
        begin
            take n from sortablenodes;
            p(n);
            sortednodes := sortednodes + [n];
            sortedcount := sortedcount + 1;
            g.foreachsuccessor (n, addifsortable)
        end;
        if sortedcount <> g.nodecount
        then error ('sort failed : graph is cyclic')
    end {topsort3};
```

The initial set of sortable nodes is formed by using the *traverse* operator to examine every node. For simplicity, we have used the same examination procedure for this and for the subsequent examination of the successors of each node sorted, though the initially sortable nodes can be identified by the simpler function *sortablenode* used in *topsort1*, which merely tests if the predecessor count of the node is zero.

We have also retained the abstract notation **take** *m* **from** *s* for the operation of identifying and removing an arbitrary member *m* from a set *s*. This set operator is not provided in Pascal, and has to be simulated by a clumsy loop to search for a member in the set. It is, however, a commonly required operator in many set applications, and on many machines it can be implemented more efficiently than its Pascal simulation achieves. For these reasons, we retain it as an identifiable requirement of the set arithmetic associated with the graph manipulation.

How does the performance of our new topological sorting algorithm compare with the previous algorithm? In creating the initial set of sortable nodes the *sortablenode* test is applied to every node in the graph, i.e. n times. Thereafter, it is applied to the successors of each node as it is sorted. If the average number of successors per node is c this will involve $n \times c$ applications, so the total number of sortable node tests involved is:

$$n \times (1 + c)$$

How c, the average number of successors per node, varies with n, the number of nodes in the graph, depends on the application involved. For some applications c is effectively independent of n; for others c may increase slowly with n, usually at a rate much less than linear proportionality. There are few graph applications where c increases as rapidly as n, or even as log n. For most applications, therefore, the topological sorting algorithm embodied in *topsort*3 offers a much better potential performance on large graphs than that embodied in *topsort*1 and *topsort*2. Whether this potential performance advantage is realized in practice depends on the relative implemented efficiencies of the graph and set operators involved.

A REVISED GRAPH ABSTRACTION

Our investigation of algorithms for graph input, path analysis and topological sorting has shown, as we might have expected, that all of these typical graph manipulation algorithms can be expressed in terms of the initial graph abstraction defined on p.271. However, in the case of path analysis and topological sorting we may make the following significant observations:

(a)   The algorithms all rely on the creation and manipulation of sets of graph nodes, and the efficiency of the algorithms is directly dependent on the efficiency of the set operations involved, as detailed in (b) and (c).

(b)   The algorithms for depth-first path analysis rely only on set operations for adding, removing, or testing the presence of, a single member m in a set s, which we denote in Pascal as follows:

```
s := s + [m]
s := s - [m]
m in s
```

(c)   The algorithms for breadth-first path analysis and for non-destructive topological sorting rely on more advanced operators for set union, set difference and set containment, for iterating over members of a set, and for extracting an arbitrary member from a set. These we have denoted as follows:

$s3 := s1 + s2$
$s3 := s1 - s2$
$s1 <= s2$
for m **in** s **do** . . .
take m **from** s

The first three are directly available for Pascal sets, but the last two can only be simulated, using a **for** or **while** loop and the **in** operator, with much less than their potential efficiency.

(d)   The breadth-first path analysis and topological sorting algorithms are also significantly improved if the successors or predecessors of a given node can be extracted as a set of nodes by a single operation, rather than by iterating over the members one by one.

On the basis of these observations we make the following extensions to our initial graph abstraction:

(a)   The abstraction will define and export a type *setofnodes* whose values are sets of the node reference values of type *node*. This type *setofnodes* must be implemented to allow manipulation of sets in as efficient and flexible a way as possible. In practical terms this means that the type should be implemented as a Pascal set type whenever possible, thus allowing the user program to exploit the built-in facilities of the language. Otherwise it should be implemented in a way such that the user is aware of the cost of the set operations possible, as these costs may directly influence the choice of graph manipulation algorithms.

(b)   The abstraction will define operations for extracting the successors or predecessors of a given node as sets, as well as the traversal operators already defined:

procedure **getsuccessors* (n : *node*; **var** s : *setofnodes*)

procedure **getpredecessors* (n : *node*; **var** s : *setofnodes*)

We will not define any other set manipulation facilities as part of the graph abstraction interface but, depending on the representation of *setofnodes* chosen for a particular implementation of the graph envelope, a corresponding package of set manipulation facilities may be included in the library.

Similarly, we will not include any higher level facilities for graph input, path finding or topological sorting within the basic graph abstraction. These too can be provided as separate library units which assume the existence of this basic abstraction, and of any set manipulation package required. In this way, the user can mix and match the facilities required according to the nature of the application and the graph processing it involves.

The final form of our graph abstraction envelope, therefore, is as follows:

envelope *graph*;

    {*assumes* **type** *itemtype = type of item at each graph node,*
                                 with := *applicable*}

    type **node = {values are references to graph nodes,*
                 with := *and* = *applicable, otherwise*
                 implementation-defined};

       *setofnodes = {values represent sets of nodes as above,
                   in implementation-defined manner};

    procedure **newnode* (**var** *n* : *node* ; *i* : *itemtype*);
      {*returns reference to new node containing item i*}

    procedure **deletenode* (*n* : *node*);
      {*deletes node n and all associated arcs*}

    procedure **locate* (**function** *test* (*x* : *node*) : *Boolean*;
                    var *found* : *Boolean* ; **var** *n* : *node*);
      {*locates arbitrary node n satisfying test if one exists,*
       otherwise found is false}

    procedure **contents* (*n* : *node* ; **var** *i* : *itemtype*);
      {*returns value of item at node n*}

    procedure **replace* (*n* : *node* ; *i* : *itemtype*);
      {*replaces item at node n by value i*}

    procedure **setarc* (*n1, n2* : *node*);
      {*creates arc from node n1 to node n2*}

    procedure **deletearc* (*n1, n2* : *node*);
      {*deletes arc from node n1 to node n2*}

procedure **foreachsuccessor* (*n* : *node* ; **procedure** *p* (*x* : *node*));
  {*applies procedure p to each successor of node n*}

procedure **foreachpredecessor* (*n* : *node* ; **procedure** *p* (*x* : *node*));
  {*applies procedure p to each predecessor of node n*}

procedure **getsuccessors* (*n* : *node* ; **var** *s* : *setofnodes*);
  {*returns set of successor nodes of node n*}

procedure **getpredecessors* (*n* : *node* ; **var** *s* : *setofnodes*);
  {*returns set of predecessor nodes of node n*}

function **successorcount* (*n* : *node*) : *integer*;
  {*returns number of successors of node n*}

function **predecessorcount* (*n* : *node*) : *integer*;
  {*returns number of predecessors of node n*}

procedure **traverse* (**procedure** *p* (*x* : *node*));
  {*applies procedure p to every node in graph*}

function **nodecount* : *integer*;
  {*returns number of nodes in graph*}

begin
  {*graph is empty*}
  * * *
end {*graph*};

CONTIGUOUS REPRESENTATION OF GRAPHS

Provided that some upper limit can be placed on the number of nodes in a graph at any time, we may represent the graph using an array containing one element for each possible node. Each element of this node array must, at a minimum, consist of two fields. The first is the item value held at the node concerned; the second is the successors of the node, i.e. the set of indices of node array elements that represent nodes to which arcs from the node concerned exist.

Conceptually we may depict this tabular representation of the graph shown on the left of Fig. 11.9 as the array shown on the right.

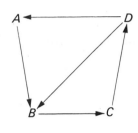

nodes		
	node value	successors
1	*A*	{2}
2	*B*	{3}
3	*C* ·	{4}
4	*D*	{1,2}

Figure 11.9 A tabular graph representation

In practice, we will consider two contiguous representations based on this basic tabular model. The first may be regarded as a *minimal contiguous representation*, which stores only the minimum information necessary for representing the graph, and takes no account of Pascal's special facilities for set manipulation or of the limitations that Pascal implementations impose on sets. As such it is the appropriate contiguous representation for very large graphs, but cannot provide maximum efficiency either in the graph operators it provides or in the set arithmetic associated with their use.

The second contiguous representation we consider is deliberately designed to allow exploitation of Pascal's facilities for set manipulation and to achieve the most efficient implementation of the graph operators themselves, by storage of redundant information if necessary. As such it provides the most efficient graph processing consistent with a contiguous representation, but may be impractical for the representation of large graphs either because of its high storage requirements or because of the size restrictions imposed on sets by Pascal implementations.

Consider first the minimal contiguous representation, which we derive by further refinement of our simple tabular model. The successors field for each node in the tabular representation is a set whose members index other elements of the node array. To avoid the possible limits imposed by Pascal implementations on the base type of sets, we use an equivalent Boolean array of the form:

packed array [*nodeindex*] **of** *Boolean*

to represent the *successors* field.

Because nodes may be created and deleted dynamically, we must also keep track of the node array elements in use at any time. This we do by including an additional tag field *inuse* in each element of the node array.

If the maximum number of nodes is given as a constant *maxnodes*, say, we may summarize these decisions in the following Pascal declarations:

```
type nodeindex = 1 . . maxnodes;
     setofindices = packed array [nodeindex] of Boolean;

var nodes : array [nodeindex] of
            record
              case inuse : Boolean of
              false : ( );
              true : (nodevalue : itemtype;
                        successors : setofindices)
            end;
```

The representation of the graph illustrated in Fig. 11.9 may now be depicted as in Fig. 11.10.

nodes			
	inuse	node value	successors 1 2 3 4 5 . . .
1	T	A	F T F F F . . .
2	T	B	F F T F F . . .
3	T	C	F F F T F . . .
4	T	D	T T F F F . . .
5	F		
:	:		

Figure 11.10 A minimal contiguous representation

From Fig. 11.10 we see that the arcs connecting graph nodes are effectively represented by a two-dimensional Boolean array in which each row represents the nodes to which arcs lead from a particular node, i.e. its successors. We could have chosen to represent the arcs separately from the node values by an explicit two-dimensional array. Such a *connectivity matrix* has the property that the *i*th row represents the successors of the *i*th node, while the *i*th column represents its predecessors. In practice, however, there is little advantage in defining the representation in matrix form, since the techniques used to represent two-dimensional arrays make manipulation of rows more efficient than columns, or vice versa. In Pascal, for example, we can extract a complete row by a singly subscripted variable access, but to extract a complete column it must be copied element by element using double subscripting for each. Thus our decision to distribute the *successors* arrays within the corresponding node array elements, which follows naturally from stepwise refinement of the data structure involved, is no less efficient for arc processing in general than the connectivity matrix technique. It is biased towards convenient manipulation of successors rather than predecessors, but the techniques for representing two-dimensional arrays inevitably impose a similar or opposite bias if a connectivity matrix is used.

We have now determined the internal representation of our graph structure using contiguous storage techniques. How should the exported types *node* and *setofnodes* be defined for use by the user program? For the time being, we will ignore the problem of error security and concentrate on providing efficient graph manipulation.

Ignoring problems of security, each node reference passed to the user can simply be the index of the element in the nodes array that represent the node concerned. Thus we define:

*node = nodeindex;

Likewise, the sets of nodes manipulated by the user program can be represented in the same way as the successors field within each element of the nodes array, so we have:

*setofnodes = setofindices;

With these decisions on how a graph shall be represented the operators defined by our graph abstraction are easily implemented. Listing 23 shows the complete implementation that results, but the following notes may clarify the techniques used.

(a)   The *newnode* operator searches the *nodes* array for an element which is not in use. If none exists the graph has exceeded the upper limit on the number of nodes, and an error is reported. Otherwise, the chosen element is suitably initialized, and its index passed back as the reference to the newly created node.

(b)   The *delete* operator clears the *inuse* flag for the specified node, but must also remove any references to the node from the *successors* fields of other graph nodes.

(c)   The *locate* operator examines each node array element in use until one is found whose *nodevalue* field satisfies the function *test*, and returns its index as the reference to the required node.

(d)   The *contents*, *replace*, *setarc* and *deletearc* operators are trivially expressed in terms of the *nodevalue* and *successors* fields of the node array element indexed by their parameters.

(e)   The *getsuccessors* operator simply involves extracting the *successors* field of the node array element referenced. In contrast, the *get-predecessors* operator involves building the required set of nodes by traversal of the entire graph. This is equivalent to extracting a column from a connectivity matrix, and the additional processing required reflects the asymmetry of any contiguous representation, as discussed earlier.

(f)   The *foreachsuccessor* and *foreachpredecessor* operators are implemented by a complete traversal of a 'row' or 'column' of the connectivity matrix formed by the *successors* fields, calling the procedure *p* for each true value encountered. The *successorcount* and *predecessorcount* functions are implemented by traversing a row or column to count the true values, and the *nodecount* function is similarly implemented by counting the true *inuse* flags in the complete node array.

Listing 23

```
envelope graph;

{ This envelope maintains a graph of up to maxnodes nodes, }
{ each holding a value of type itemtype.                    }
{                                                            }
{ It assumes const maxnodes = maximum number of nodes;      }
{              type itemtype = any type with := applicable   }




type nodeindex = 1..maxnodes;
     setofindices = packed array [nodeindex] of Boolean;
     *node = nodeindex;
     *setofnodes = setofindices;




var nodes:
     array [nodeindex] of
       record
         case inuse: Boolean of
           false: ();
           true:
             (nodevalue: itemtype;
               successors: setofindices)
       end;
     j: node;
     emptyset: setofindices;
```

```
procedure *newnode(var n: node; i: itemtype);
  label 1;
  var j: nodeindex;
  begin
    for j := 1 to maxnodes do if not nodes[j].inuse then goto 1;
    error('too many nodes in graph');
    1:
      with nodes[j] do
        begin
          inuse := true;
          nodevalue := i;
          successors := emptyset
        end;
    n := j
  end {newnode};

procedure *deletenode(n: node);
  var j: nodeindex;
  begin
    nodes[n].inuse := false;
    for j := 1 to maxnodes do
      with nodes[j] do if inuse then successors[n] := false
  end {deletenode};

procedure *locate(function test(x: node): Boolean;
                  var found: Boolean; var n: node);
  label 1;
  var j: nodeindex;
  begin
    for j := 1 to maxnodes do
      with nodes[j] do
        if inuse
        then if test(j)
              then begin
                      found := true;
                      n := j;
                      goto 1
                   end;
    found := false;
    1:
  end {locate}:

procedure *content(n: node; var i: itemtype);
  begin i := nodes[n].nodevalue end;

procedure *replace(n: node; i: itemtype);
  begin nodes[n].nodevalue := i end;

procedure *setarc(n1, n2: node);
  begin nodes[n1].successors[n2] := true end;
```

continued on page 298

Listing 23 continued

```
procedure *deletearc(n1, n2: node);
  begin nodes[n1].successors[n2] := false end;

procedure *foreachsuccessor(n: node; procedure p(x: node));
  var j: nodeindex;
  begin
    with nodes[n] do
      for j := 1 to maxnodes do if successors[j] then p(j)
  end {foreachsuccessor};

procedure *foreachpredecessor(n: node; procedure p(x: node));
  var j: nodeindex;
  begin
    for j := 1 to maxnodes do
      with nodes[j] do if inuse then if successors[n] then p(j)
  end {foreachpredecessor};

procedure *getsuccessors(n: node; var s: setofnodes);
  begin s := nodes[n].successors end;

procedure *getpredecessors(n: node; var s: setofnodes);
  var j: nodeindex;
  begin
    for j := 1 to maxnodes do
      with nodes[j] do
        if inuse
        then s[j] := successors[n]
        else s[j] := false
  end {predecessors};

function *successorcount(n: node): integer;
  var count: integer;
      j: nodeindex;
  begin
    count := 0;
    with nodes[n] do
      for j := 1 to maxnodes do
        if successors[j] then count := count + 1;
    successorcount := count
  end {successorcount};

function *predecessorcount(n: node): integer;
  var count: integer;
      j: nodeindex;
  begin
    count := 0;
    for j := 1 to maxnodes do
      with nodes[j] do
        if inuse then if successors[n] then count := count + 1;
    predecessorcount := count
  end {predecessorcount};
```

```
function *nodecount: integer;
  var count: integer;
      j: nodeindex;
  begin
    count := 0;
    for j := 1 to maxnodes do
      if nodes[j].inuse then count := count + 1;
    nodecount := count
  end {nodecount};

procedure *traverse(procedure p(x: node));
  var j: nodeindex;
  begin for j := 1 to maxnodes do if nodes[j].inuse then p(j)
  end {traverse};

begin
  for j := 1 to maxnodes do
    begin
      nodes[j].inuse := false;
      emptyset[j] := false
    end;
  ###
end {graph};
```

At this point it is worthwhile to consider the cost in storage and in time of this minimal contiguous representation.

For simplicity, we will consider the representation of a graph of n nodes, where n is predetermined, and we may ignore storage wastage through unused elements in the *nodes* array. Each element of the array consists of:

(a)   an *inuse* field requiring a minimum of 1 bit,

(b)   a *nodevalue* field whose storage requirement depends on the application involved, and

(c)   a *successors* field requiring a minimum of n bits.

Thus, if we ignore the application-dependent storage requirement for the node values themselves, the minimum storage cost of our minimal contiguous representation is $n(n + 1)$ bits. For large n this storage requirement is dominated by the n^2 bits used to represent the connectivity matrix.

Now consider the time taken to execute the operators provided for graph manipulation, or rather how this time varies with the graph size n. For graph building the operators *newnode* and *deletenode* each have overheads that vary directly with n, because of the searching for an unused node, or the removal of arcs from the deleted node's predecessors, that is involved. The operators *setarc* and *deletearc*, however, have overheads that are independent of the graph size n. The significance of these properties of the graph building operators depends on the application involved. For many applications the graphs involved are relatively static, i.e. they are built initially and then repeatedly analysed without further modification. In such cases the efficiency of the graph building operators is not significant compared to the efficiency of the remaining operators for graph analysis.

Of the analytic operators *locate* and *traverse* have overheads proportional to the size of the graph, a property that is inevitable for any representation. The significant feature for analysis is that of the remaining analytic operators, only *getsuccessors* has overheads that are not directly proportional to the graph size n. The others, *foreachsuccessor*, *foreachpredecessor*, *getpredecessors*, *successorcount*, *predecessorcount* and *nodecount*, all have overheads directly proportional to n, because of the element-by-element inspection of n Boolean array elements involved in each case.

In assessing any graph representation we must also consider the efficiency of the secondary set manipulation enabled by the exported type *setofnodes*. With the minimal contiguous representation of a graph of n nodes this is effectively:

   setofnodes = **packed array** $[1 \, . \, . \, n]$ **of** *Boolean*;

With this representation, the simple set membership operations:

   $s := s + [m]$
   $s := s - [m]$
   m **in** s

are efficiently implemented as the updating or inspection of a single Boolean element. However, the operations:

   $s1 + s2$
   $s1 - s2$
   $s1 <= s2$
   for m **in** s
   take m **from** s

all involve element-by-element traversal of the Boolean arrays involved, and thus have overheads proportional to the graph size n.

In summary, the distinctive characteristics of the minimal contiguous representation are as follows:

(a)   its storage overhead is approximately n^2 bits for large n;

(b)   all graph analytic operators except *getsuccessors*, and all advanced set operators, have overheads directly proportional to n.

This direct variation with *n*, the graph size, in the cost of many graph and set operators must be borne in mind when choosing graph analysis algorithms to be used in conjunction with the minimal contiguous representation.

Now consider our fast contiguous representation based on the tabular model. The data structure involved differs from the minimal contiguous representation in three significant ways:

(a) To allow direct use of Pascal's set manipulation facilities the *setofnodes* concept is represented as a Pascal set type both inside and outside the implementation, thus:

> *setofindices* = **set of** *nodeindex*;
> **setofnodes* = *setofindices*;

(b) To avoid the overheads in computing counts each node record contains fields to hold the successor count and predecessor count for that node. Similarly, an additional variable is introduced to hold the node count for the graph as a whole.

(c) To avoid the asymmetry in the efficiency of extracting successors and predecessors two sets are held within each node record, one for the successors and one for the predecessors of that node. Note, however, that this implies a complete duplication of the connectivity matrix within the representation!

These changes in the data structures used by our fast representation are summarized in the following data declarations:

> **type** *nodeindex* = 1 . . *maxnodes*;
> *setofindices* = **set of** *nodeindex*;
> **node* = *nodeindex*;
> **setofnodes* = *setofindices*;

> **var** **nodecount* : *integer*;
> *nodes* : **array** [*nodeindex*] **of**
> **record**
> **case** *inuse* : *Boolean* **of**
> *false* : ( );
> *true* : (*nodevalue* : *itemtype* ;
> *successors, predecessors* : *setofindices*;
> *succcount, predcount* : *integer*)
> **end**;

The three design changes described above are all intended to improve the efficiency of graph processing, at the expense of either the generality of the implementation, or of the storage it consumes. As such, the resultant representation is an opposite extreme to the minimal contiguous representation described earlier. It is worth noting, however, that the three design changes involved are essentially independent of one another. Thus, in practice, a spectrum of intermediate representations is possible, each of which incorporates some but not all of the design changes listed, and gives a corresponding variation in the performance achieved.

The code changes required in the implementation of the graph operators follow directly from these representation changes. They are:

(a)   additional code to create and maintain the *predecessors*, *predcount* and *succcount* field of each node record, and the variable *nodecount*, during the creation or deletion of nodes and arcs;

(b)   the use of set rather than Boolean operators in maintaining and scanning the *successors* and *predecessors* fields;

(c)   simplification of the operators *getpredecessors*, *successorcount* and *predecessorcount* to exploit the extra fields, and the elimination of the function *nodecount*, by starring the corresponding variable now available.

Listing 24 shows the implementation that results.

Listing 24

```
envelope graph;

{ This envelope maintains a graph of up to maxnodes nodes, }
{ each holding a value of type itemtype.                    }
{                                                           }
{ It assumes const maxnodes = maximum number of nodes;      }
{               type itemtype = any type with := applicable  }

type nodeindex = 1..maxnodes;
     setofindices = set of nodeindex;
     *node = nodeindex;
     *setofnodes = setofindices;

var *nodecount: integer;
    nodes:
      array [nodeindex] of
        record
          case inuse: Boolean of
            false: ();
            true:
              (nodevalue: itemtype;
               successors, predecessors: setofindices;
               succcount, predcount: integer)
        end;
      j: node;
```

```
procedure *newnode(var n: node; i: itemtype);
  label 1;
  var j: nodeindex;
  begin
    for j := 1 to maxnodes do if not nodes[j].inuse then goto 1;
    error('too many nodes in graph');
    1:
      with nodes[j] do
        begin
          inuse := true;
          nodevalue := i;
          successors := [];
          predecessors := [];
          succcount := 0;
          predcount := 0
        end;
    nodecount := nodecount + 1;
    n := j
  end {newnode};

procedure *deletenode(n: node);
  var j: nodeindex;
  begin
    with nodes[n] do
      begin
        for j := 1 to maxnodes do
          begin
            if j in successors
            then with nodes[j] do
                   begin
                     predecessors := predecessors - [n];
                     predcount := predcount - 1
                   end;
            if j in predecessors
            then with nodes[j] do
                   begin
                     successors := successors - [n];
                     succcount := succcount - 1
                   end
          end;
        inuse := false
      end;
    nodecount := nodecount - 1
  end {deletenode};

procedure *locate(function test(x: node): Boolean;
                  var found: Boolean; var n: node);
  label 1;
  var j: nodeindex;
```

continued on page 304

Listing 24 continued

```pascal
  begin
    for j := 1 to maxnodes do
      with nodes[j] do
        if inuse
        then if test(j)
              then begin
                      found := true;
                      n := j;
                      goto 1
                   end;
    found := false;
    1:
  end {locate};


procedure *replace(n: node; i: itemtype);
  begin nodes[n].nodevalue := i end;


procedure *content(n: node; var i: itemtype);
  begin i := nodes[n].nodevalue end;


procedure *setarc(n1, n2: node);
  begin
    with nodes[n1] do
      begin
        successors := successors + [n2];
        succcount := succcount + 1
      end;
    with nodes[n2] do
      begin
        predecessors := predecessors + [n1];
        predcount := predcount + 1
      end
  end {setarc};


procedure *deletearc(n1, n2: node);
  begin
    with nodes[n1] do
      begin
        successors := successors - [n2];
        succcount := succcount - 1
      end;
    with nodes[n2] do
      begin
        predecessors := predecessors - [n1];
        predcount := predcount - 1
      end
  end {deletearc};
```

```
procedure *foreachsuccessor(n: node; procedure p(x: node));
  var j: nodeindex;
  begin
    with nodes[n] do
      for j := 1 to maxnodes do if j in successors then p(j)
  end {foreachsuccessor};

procedure *foreachpredecessor(n: node; procedure p(x: node));
  var j: nodeindex;
  begin
    with nodes[n] do
      for j := 1 to maxnodes do if j in predecessors then p(j)
  end {foreachpredecessor};

procedure *getsuccessors(n: node; var s: setofnodes);
  begin s := nodes[n].successors end;

procedure *getpredecessors(n: node; var s: setofnodes);
  begin s := nodes[n].predecessors end;

function *successorcount(n: node): integer;
  begin successorcount := nodes[n].succcount end;

function *predecessorcount(n: node): integer;
  begin predecessorcount := nodes[n].predcount end;

procedure *traverse(procedure p(x: node));
  var j: nodeindex;
  begin for j := 1 to maxnodes do if nodes[j].inuse then p(j)
  end {traverse};

begin
  nodecount := 0;
  for j := 1 to maxnodes do nodes[j].inuse := false;
  ***
end {graph};
```

How does the fast contiguous representation compare in cost with the minimal contiguous representation?

In terms of storage the additional costs are the storage of two integer counts in each node element, and the duplication of the connectivity matrix by storing predecessor as well as successor sets. Each stored set has the same storage requirement as a corresponding packed Boolean array, i.e. n bits, so that for large n the storage overhead again varies as n^2, but is approximately $2n^2$ bits rather than n^2 bits.

The significant change in operator efficiency is, that the majority of analytic operators no longer have overheads directly proportional to n. In the case of the operator *getpredecessors* and the functions *successorcount*, *predecessorcount* and *nodecount*, the extra information maintained within the representation eliminates any dependence on the graph size n. In the case of the operators *foreachsuccessor* and *foreachpredecessor* the situation is more complex. If standard Pascal set operators are used in their implementation, as in Listing 24, the overheads remain proportional to n. However, if a properly implemented **for** m **in** s operator is available the overheads are in principle proportional to c, the average number of successors per node, rather than to n.

A similar improvement is achieved in the secondary set manipulation required by graph processing. The cost of operations

$$s1 + s2$$
$$s1 - s2$$
$$s1 <= s2$$

is now independent of n. With standard Pascal the operators

for m **in** s
take m **from** s

can only be simulated with an overhead proportional to n, but a proper implementation of these operators would give an overhead directly proportional to the number of members in the set in the first case, and independent both of n and of the number of set members in the second case.

The significant improvement in efficiency of the graph and set operators required for graph analysis is the major advantage of the fast contiguous representation. It is achieved, however, at the expense either of staying within the limitations on set sizes which implementations of Pascal-like set facilities may impose, or of a significant increase in the total storage required.

CHAINED REPRESENTATION OF GRAPHS

A graph can be represented using chained storage techniques by

(a)   using a dynamically allocated record to represent each node of the graph, and

(b)   using a chained list of node references to represent each set of nodes required.

In the chained analog of our fast contiguous representation each node record would hold the node item value itself, successor and predecessor counts and pointers to the chained lists of references (i.e. pointers) to the node records for the successors and predecessors of this node. Figure 11.11 shows the representation of a single node with three predecessors and one successor.

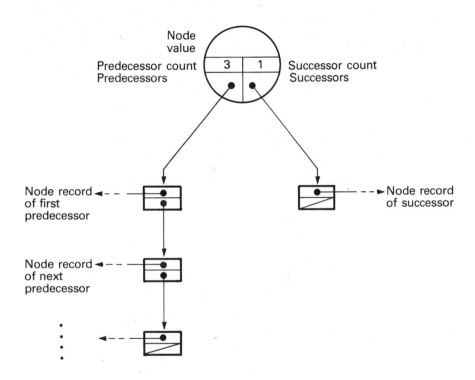

Figure 11.11 Chained representation of a graph node

In practice, the node records of the entire graph must also be connected together to enable the *traverse* and *locate* operators to be implemented. This could be done by including an extra pointer within each node record to form a linear chain, but a neater implementation of operators is obtained by using the chained representation for a set of nodes to represent the complete set of nodes in the graph as well. Figure 11.12 shows the overall representation of a graph of four nodes that results, but with details of the arcs between nodes, i.e. the successors and predecessors sets, suppressed.

This representation is described in Pascal as follows:

```
type  nodeptr = ↑ noderecord;
      memberptr = ↑ memberrecord;
    *node = nodeptr;
    *setofnodes = memberptr;
      noderecord = record
                        nodevalue : itemtype;
                        succcount, predcount : integer;
                        successors, predecessors : setofnodes
                   end;
      memberrecord = record
                        member : node;
                        nextmember : memberptr
                     end;

var  nodes : setofnodes;
   *nodecount : integer;
```

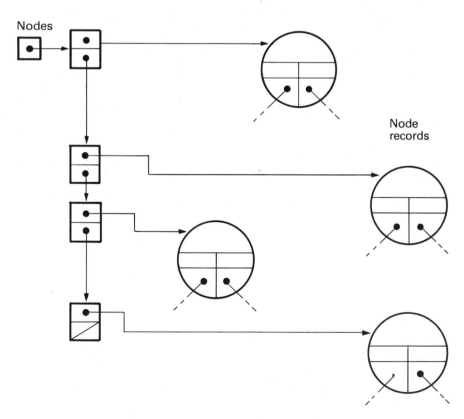

Figure 11.12   Overall organization of a chained graph representation

Implementation of this chained graph representation is left as an exercise for the reader. In practice, it requires the provision of a package of set manipulation operators for use with the chained representation of a set of nodes, as well as the graph abstraction itself.

It is possible, however, to predict the overall cost of such an implementation without its detailed inspection. Consider first the storage involved. Apart from the node value and successor and predecessor counts, each node requires four pointers for its representation—two within the node record itself represent the successor and predecessor sets, and two in the corresponding entry in the chain representing the complete set of nodes in the graph. Within the successor and predecessor set chains each member represented also requires two pointers. Since the average number of members in each set is c (the average number of successors per node in the graph), each node uses an average of $4c$ pointers within the representations of its successors and predecessors. Thus the storage overhead of the chained representation of graph connectivity is $4 + 4c$ pointers per node, i.e. a total of

$$4n \times (1 + c) \text{ pointers}$$

compared with $2n^2$ bits for the fast contiguous representation or n^2 bits for the minimal contiguous representation. Thus, for large graphs with a low average number of successors per node, the chained representation gives a much lower storage requirement.

This reduction in storage must be balanced against the possible loss of efficiency in graph analysis. With a chained representation of sets of nodes, all set operations, including the assignment or copying of a set value, have cost directly proportional to the number of members in the set. Thus the operators *getsuccessors*, *getpredecessors*, *foreachsuccessor* and *foreachpredecessor*, all have an average cost directly proportional to c, the average number of successors per node. The most significant impact, however, is on the secondary set manipulation required during graph analysis, where all operators (except **take** m **from** s) have a cost directly proportional to the number of members in the sets involved. If an algorithm uses a set s whose size varies as n, then the cost of even the simplest operations on this set, such as

$$s := s + [m]$$
$$s := s - [m]$$
$$m \text{ in } s$$

varies as n, with direct consequences for the efficiency of the algorithm itself.

Figure 11.13 summarizes how the storage requirement, and the efficiency of graph analysis and set operators, varies with graph size and connectivity for each of the representations we have discussed. For each

	minimal contiguous representation	fast contiguous representation	fast chained representation
storage required other than for node items	$n(n+1)$ bits	2n integers $+n(2n+1)$ bits	2n integers $+4n(1+c)$pointers
Graph operators:			
locate	n	n	n
traverse´	n	n	n
foreachsuccessor	n	c^*	c
foreachpredecessor	n	c^*	c
getsuccessors	1	1	c
getpredecessors	n	1	c
successorcount	n	1	1
predecessorcount	n	1	1
nodecount	n	1	1
Set operators:			
$s := s + [m]$	1	1	s
$s := s - [m]$	1	1	s
m **in** s	1	1	s
$s1 + s2$	n	1	s
$s1 - s2$	n	1	s
$s1 <= s2$	n	1	s
for m **in** s	n	s^*	s
take m **from** s	n	1^*	1

Figure 11.13   Variation of storage requirements and operator
efficiency with graph size and connectivity

operator the column entries have the following meaning:

1 means the operator cost is independent of graph size or connectivity;

n means the operator cost varies directly with the graph size;

c means the operator cost varies directly with the number of successors per node;

s means the operator cost varies directly with the number of members in the set involved.

The entries marked with an asterisk hold only if a direct implementation of the set operators **for** m **in** s or **take** m **from** s is available. If these are simulated, using standard Pascal set operators, the appropriate column entry is *n*.

In considering Fig. 11.13 it must be remembered that the entries reflect the variation of efficiency with graph size and connectivity, not the absolute efficiency involved. Thus two 1's in different columns do not imply that the operators concerned are equally efficient, only that their costs do not vary with size or connectivity. In general, the relative efficiency of operators will depend on the efficiency of the underlying implementation of sets, Boolean arrays or pointers and can be determined only for particular language implementations on particular machines.

NODE REFERENCE SECURITY

The implementations of our graph envelope in Listings 23 and 24 show clearly the basic principles for the contiguous representation of graphs, and how typical graph processing operations can be implemented with acceptable efficiency. From a data abstraction point of view, however, they are unsatisfactory in that they do not guarantee correct usage of the abstraction by the user program, since values passed by the program as node references are not checked for validity.

At first sight such checks are easily added, in that the *inuse* flags determine whether or not a value of type *node* is an index to a current graph node. A little further thought, however, shows that such checks are not sufficient, for two reasons:

(a)   since the exported node type is an integer subrange the user program may inadvertently 'forge' node references, by integer arithmetic, say, which may be acceptable by the *inuse* test;

(b)   the user program may obtain a reference to a node, request deletion of the node, and then request the creation of a new node. If the new node happens to re-use the node array element released by the previous deletion, the old reference will now seem valid by the *inuse* test, even though it was created for a node that has since been deleted.

The first problem, of 'forged' node references, can be overcome by the techniques described in Chapter 9 for protecting exported types. The second problem, however, is more difficult and is a fundamental one for all systems that release and re-allocate storage while allowing user programs to retain references to the storage involved. It arises in the implementation of Pascal itself since a program may dispose of a dynamic variable while retaining a pointer value that references it, a so-called *dangling* pointer. If the storage released by the disposed variable is re-allocated by a subsequent *new* operation, the existing pointer value may lead to misuse of the new variable unless the implementation takes active steps to prevent it. In practice, many Pascal implementations provide no such protection against dangling pointer references, but we will now consider a method of providing protection against dangling node references in the case of our graph abstraction.

The basic technique used is to generate a sequence of unique keys or values, each of which is associated with exactly one of the graph nodes created by the *newnode* operator. Nodes with disjoint lifetimes that happen to use the same element of the *nodes* array are then distinguished by the distinct key values involved. Provided this key value is also incorporated in the node references passed to the user program, the validity of their subsequent use can always be established.

In detail, the security provided by the key mechanism is illustrated by the following sequence of events:

(a)   A graph node is created by a user program call

   newnode (*r*1, *x*)

The node created is represented by element 40, say, of the *nodes* array and acquires a unique key value $k1$. This value is embedded both in the array element and in the node reference returned as $r1$ so that the resultant situation is as follows:

$r1$

index = 40- -	- - - - → *nodes*[40]	*inuse = true*
refkey = $k1$		*nodekey* = $k1$
		nodevalue = x
		successors = . . .

(b)   The node x is deleted and element 40 of the *nodes* array is re-used by a subsequent call:

   newnode (*r*2,*y*)

This call will obtain a new key value $k2$ which is again stored in the array element and in the node reference returned as $r2$, thus:

$r1$

index = 40 - -	- - ⊤ → *nodes*[40]	*inuse = true*
refkey = $k1$		*nodekey* = $k2$
		nodevalue = y
		successors = . . .

$r2$

index = 40 - -	- ⌐
refkey = $k2$	

At this stage, the user program holds a valid reference ($r2$) to the node represented at element 40 of the *nodes* array, and an invalid reference (*r*1) which also indexes element 40. Any attempt to use the invalid reference *r*1, however, is detected by the fact that its imbedded key value *k*1 does not match the key value now held at *nodes*[40].

Since the program can create and delete nodes at will, in principle an infinite sequence of distinct node keys is required. In practice, however, it is usually acceptable to put some adequately large bound on the number of key values provided. Thus if we use natural numbers as key values we can generate *maxint* distinct key values without difficulty, which will be adequate for most applications. Their generation is encapsulated in the following simple module:

```
envelope module uniquekeys;
  type *key = 0 . . maxint;
  var nextvalue : key;
  function *nextkey : key;
    begin
      nextkey := nextvalue;
      nextvalue := nextvalue + 1
    end {nextkey};
  begin
    nextvalue := 0;
    ***
  end {uniquekeys};
```

If a larger range of unique keys is necessary it can be provided in some analogous fashion. To provide security in the directed graph envelope a key value must be imbedded in each element of the *nodes* array and in each node reference passed to the user program. We therefore amend our definition of the type *node* as follows:

```
*node = record
          index : nodeindex;
          refkey : uniquekeys.key
        end;
```

and our definition of the *nodes* array (for the minimal contiguous representation) as follows:

```
nodes : array(nodeindex] of
          record
            case inuse : Boolean of
            false : ( );
            true : (nodekey : uniquekeys.key;
                     nodevalue : itemtype;
                     successors : setofnodes)
          end;
```

The procedure *newnode* is now programmed as follows:

```
procedure *newnode (var n : node ; i : itemtype);
  label 1;
  var j : nodeindex;
  begin
    for j := 1 to maxnodes do
    with nodes [j] do
      if not inuse then
      begin
        inuse := true;
        nodekey := uniquekeys.nextkey;
        nodevalue := i;
        successors := emptyset;
        with n do
        begin
          refkey := nodekey;
          index := j
        end;
        goto 1
      end;
    error ('too many nodes in graph');
  1:end {newnode};
```

Likewise, the operator *locate* must be amended to set its output parameter *n* with the *index* and *nodekey* of the node found.

All other operators which receive a node reference *n* from the user program can then validate the reference by checking that the array element indexed is in use *and* that the key values in the node reference and node element are the same. If the node element has been deleted and re-allocated since the reference was created, the latter test will fail. The valid node reference test is thus encapsulated in the following function:

```
function validreference (n : node) : Boolean;
  begin
    with n, nodes[index] do
      if not inuse
      then validreference := false
      else validreference := (refkey = nodekey)
  end {validreference};
```

With this function, all individual node references received from the user program can be checked by the operators that receive them.

The change in representation for node references required to achieve error security impacts on the user program in two ways. Firstly, the equality operator = is no longer directly applicable to node references. Hence to enable comparison of node references by the user program, the abstraction must export an equality function of the form:

function **samenode (n1,n2 : node) : Boolean*;

The most significant cost of node security, however, is not the creation and checking of node keys within the graph implementation or the clumsy node comparison in the user program. It follows from the fact that the required form of node, a record with fields which must be hidden from the user program, makes it impossible to use any form of efficient set manipulation for sets of nodes. With node references in record form the only way in which the *setofnodes* concept can be implemented is as a list of node references, with a significant loss of efficiency in the set manipulation required by many graph processing applications. It is this loss of efficiency in the secondary set manipulation required that makes a secure implementation of our graph abstraction unacceptable for many applications, rather than the direct cost of implementing the security within the graph operators themselves.

It is worth reiterating at this point that the problem of dangling node references follows directly from the need to allow the user program to obtain, store and return such references. For graph abstraction this is inevitable, but the consequent security problems that arise serve to emphasize the virtue of the window mechanism used for lists and trees. With these abstractions the user program has a single point of attention at all times (the window) and has no means of remembering an arbitrary position in the list or tree for subsequent re-use. By definition, therefore, the problem of dangling references cannot arise. While the window concept is sometimes constraining from the user's viewpoint, and makes some manipulation of lists and trees clumsier than it would otherwise be, the inherent security that the concept provides is valuable in precluding programming errors that are otherwise very difficult or very expensive to detect.

SUMMARY

Graphs are the most general form of data structure that we consider, and our earlier data abstractions, of trees, lists, queues and stacks, are effectively special cases of graphs. This generality itself creates problems for our modular approach to the definition of abstract data types:

(a)   Defining a general graph abstraction is difficult because of the wide variety of potential requirements arising from different graph applications. The abstraction that we have chosen is a minimal low-level abstraction on which the higher-level requirements of particular applications can be built, as required.

(b)   The very general structure permitted in a graph leads to graph manipu-
      lation algorithms of significant complexity, which are typified by the
      path analysis and topological sorting algorithms. The efficiency of such
      algorithms depends critically on the efficiency of the basic graph
      operators involved. As we have seen, this efficiency can vary signific-
      antly with the representation chosen for a graph abstraction. Inevi-
      tably, the implementation chosen for a graph must be tailored closely
      to the application requirements, if acceptable efficiency is to be
      achieved.

(c)   The possible manipulations required for graphs make it impractical to
      retain the single window concept as the means of graph node access.
      Instead we allow the user program to extract and store references to
      graph nodes, and to express subsequent manipulation in terms of these
      references. As we have seen, however, the storage of such references
      creates a significant insecurity against programming error. Detection
      of 'dangling' node references can be programmed within the
      implementation of our graph, but only at the sacrifice of efficiency for
      many of the basic graph operators, and particularly for the set-of-nodes
      manipulation required by many applications. Such inefficiency is unac-
      ceptable in most graph processing applications, and users must rely on
      some other means of verifying the validity of the graph manipulations
      they program.

Thus, the manipulation of graph structures presents a significant challenge
to the approach we have taken to abstract data types, both in defining an
abstraction that can be implemented independently of the programs that use
it, and in the incorporation of checks against incorrect usage by these
programs. Nevertheless, the abstractions we have defined and the
implementation techniques we have demonstrated provide a basis for the
implementation of graph manipulation programs. With appropriate tailor-
ing to the particular needs of the application concerned, such abstractions
can provide a significant aid to the generation of the programs required.

      The replacement of the window concept by storable node references is
also of relevance to the abstract data types we have defined previously. A
similar approach could have been taken to defining our list and tree abstractions in Chapters 8 and 10. The resulting abstractions would be more flexible
than those based on the window concept. The problem of dangling references would again arise, but the cost of their detection would be less
dramatic for most list and tree processing algorithms than for graphs. What is
significant, however, is that a large number of list and tree applications can
be programmed using the window mechanism. The resultant error security
at zero cost justifies the more restrictive abstraction involved. For those
cases where the window abstraction is too restrictive, alternative abstractions of lists and trees, using node references, can be provided. The definition and implementation of such abstractions is left as an exercise to the
reader.

EXERCISES

11.1 Using a Pascal set type to implement the set *setofnodes* and assuming
the existence of the graph abstraction specified on page 291, implement the path finding and topological sorting routines developed in
this chapter, in a form suitable for use as library procedures.

11.2 Write a program which constructs a graph whose nodes are the
squares of an 8×8 chessboard, and whose arcs are the legitimate
moves of a chess knight from each square (a knight's move consists of
moving two squares in any direction parallel to an edge of the board,
then one square at right angles). The program should use this graph

(a) to verify that a knight starting from any square on the board can
reach any other square by some sequence of moves;

(b) to find and print out the shortest sequence of moves by which a
knight can get from square a to square b where a and b are input
by the user. What advantages does this method have over others
which don't use a graph?

11.3 A group of international airlines offers a single price round the world
air ticket. A purchaser may stop for any period in any of the cities
served by the airlines, subject to the following conditions:

(i) on all flights taken by the purchaser the destination city must be
farther east than the city of departure, or farther west in the case
of those wishing to travel westwards (i.e., it is not possible to
backtrack);

(ii) only one circuit of the world is allowed and the purchaser must
return to the city from which he started out.

Two files contain data about the cities served and their longitudes,
and the cities connected by return flights, respectively, in a form
suitable for use by a graph input procedure similar to that given on
page 273. Write a program to determine the itinerary which permits a
traveller to visit the greatest number of cities on a round the world
trip.

11.4 Given a graph G, a *clique* C is a set of nodes of G which satisfies the
conditions:

(i) each node in C is connected to all other nodes in C (i.e., C is
completely connected);

(ii) there is no other node in G which could be added to C without
violating condition (i) (i.e., C is *maximal*).

Write a procedure which will find (and output) all cliques of a given
graph. Warning: Readers unfamiliar with graph theory may find this
exercise difficult.

12

Sparse Data Structures

Throughout this book we have used Pascal array types to model the contiguous storage representations of various abstract structures such as stacks, queues, lists, trees and graphs. This use of the array as a low-level storage mechanism reflects the fact that in implementations of Pascal there is a simple one to one relationship between the elements of an array and the storage occupied by them in the computer memory. Each array occupies a contiguous block of storage which is sufficient to accommodate all of the array elements, and within this storage elements are allocated successive storage locations according to their index values. Thus, if we have an array A declared as follows:

> **var** A : **array** [1 . . 10] **of** T;

A will be allocated a block of storage sufficient to hold 10 values of type T, and within this storage the individual elements $A[1]$, $A[2]$, etc. occupy consecutive storage locations, as shown in Fig. 12.1.

If the number of storage locations required for a single value of type T is S_T, then the array A will occupy a total of $10 \times S_T$ adjacent locations, and the first location of element $A[i]$ will be the $(i-1) \times S_T$th location from the start of the overall storage for A. Any element of A is thus accessible with equal efficiency, by a simple calculation that determines its storage position from its index value. This efficiency of element access, for both sequential and random processing of elements, is the distinctive feature of the contiguous representation of arrays.

Pascal sets are represented in a similar manner, but using contiguous storage on a bit-by-bit basis. If we have a set S declared as follows:

> **var** S : **set of** 1 . . n;

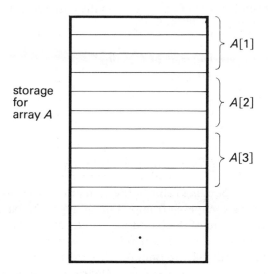

Figure 12.1 Contiguous representation of an array

S will be allocated sufficient storage to provide *n* consecutive bits, each of which may take value 0 or 1. The *i*th bit in this storage represents the presence or absence of member value *i* in the set *S*—a 0 means *i* is absent, a 1 means *i* is present. Thus the representation of *S* after execution of the statement:

$$S := [1,5 \; . \; . \; 7]$$

would be as follows:

    100011100 000   (*n* bits in all)

    In general, adding, removing, or testing the presence of, member value *i* in any set involves manipulation of the *i*th bit in the representation of the set. In addition, the 'bit parallel' operations, which are available on most machines for performing logical **and** and **or** operations between corresponding bits of multibit patterns, enable highly efficient implementation of operators such as union and intersection on sets represented in this way.

    These 'positional' representations of arrays and sets enable Pascal implementations to provide highly efficient manipulation of arrays and sets both on a sequential and on a random basis—the efficiency of accessing any element of the structure is independent of the order in which element access occurs. However, this efficiency is achievable only if it is both possible and economical to allocate storage to each potential element of the structure, whether it is used or not. For this reason, Pascal implementations impose restrictions on the index type of arrays and on the base type of sets. For most compilers the types:

> *largearray* = **array** [*integer*] **of** 0 . . 9;
> *largeset*   = **set of** *integer*;

are unacceptable, because of the impractical storage requirements of their positional representations.

At an abstract level, however, these types are quite valid. In abstract terms, an array value is a mapping from the values of a domain type (the index type) to an element type—within the mapping each value of the index type identifies a corresponding value of the element type. Similarly, we may think of a set value as a mapping from a domain type, the base type, to the type *Boolean*—each value of the base type identifies the value *true*, if that base value is a member of the set, or *false* if it is not.

Thus we have no difficulty in thinking of array or set types with infinite or very large domains. Nevertheless, it is clearly impractical to represent values of such types by storing the element values corresponding to the domain values if all the element values are distinct and independent at all times. It is, however, quite practical to represent such values if only a finite number of element values need to be stored. Thus it is practical to represent sets with an infinite domain type if we know that each set value that actually occurs only has a finite number of members. For example, the set value:

> [1, 1000, 1000000]

has an infinite base type (*integer*) but, with only three members, it is clearly representable in some suitable way. Similarly, representation of arrays over infinite domain types can be a practical proposition if only a finite number of elements have significant values (i.e. values different from some default value) at any time. Some finite representation of such sets or arrays is possible, even though representation of arbitrary values of their type is not. Arrays and sets of this form, which are potentially infinite but are known to contain only a finite number of significant element values at any time, are known as *sparse* data structures. In this chapter we consider techniques for representing such structures while maintaining their essential abstract characteristics as arrays or sets.

Arrays and sets whose domains are finite may also be regarded as sparse if the actual number of significant elements or members is at all times much less than the potential number allowed by their types. In the interests of storage economy such structures may also be handled by sparse structure techniques, rather than the standard representations for their types.

Familiar examples of sparse structures are the sparse vectors and matrices that occur frequently in mathematics and engineering. The matrix shown below contains only five non-zero values in a total of 36 elements.

$$
\begin{array}{cccccc}
0 & 0 & 0 & 1 & 0 & 2 \\
0 & 0 & 0 & 3 & 0 & 0 \\
0 & 0 & 0 & 0 & 0 & 1 \\
0 & 0 & 0 & 0 & 0 & 0 \\
0 & 0 & 0 & 0 & 0 & 2 \\
0 & 0 & 0 & 0 & 0 & 0
\end{array}
$$

Dealing with such matrices is a standard problem in numerical mathematics, but sparse structures also occur in many other computing applications.

Consider the problem of maintaining a register of motor car ownership in any country. If we consider car registration numbers consisting of three letters, three digits and a final letter, e.g. PNB 760W, then the cardinality or number of possible values of this car number type is over 500 million! However, if we need a program to manipulate the sets of cars owned by individuals, most sets will have only one member, and very few will have more than ten, say. The car sets are thus describable as set values of type:

type *carset* = {*sparse*} **set of** *carnumber*;

where we write {*sparse*} in front of the set definition to remind ourselves that *carset* is not an acceptable Pascal set type.

In the register of car ownership, each owner may be represented as a name string of adequate length, say:

type *owner* = **packed array** [1 . . 40] **of** *char*;

This *owner* type is effectively infinite, but in the register of car ownership only a finite number of the possible values of type *owner* (the names of actual car owners) have significant (non-empty) car sets. A suitable type for describing the register is thus:

type *register* = {*sparse*} **array** [*owner*] **of** *carset*;

Another example of a sparse structure arises in the compilation of computer programs written in a language like Pascal. For each identifier declared in a program the compiler must record its *attributes*, i.e. its class (constant, type, variable identifier, etc.), its type if it is a constant, variable, or function, and so on. Identifiers in Pascal are arbitrary sequences of letters and digits, and are thus values of an infinite type:

type *identifier* = . . . {*sequence of characters*} . . .

but the compiler needs significant attribute records only for those identifiers used in a program—the default attribute 'undeclared' being associated with all other unused identifiers. The information may thus be considered as an array:

> **type** *dictionary* = {*sparse*} **array** [*identifier*] **of** *attributes* ;

The need to insert and extract the attributes of individual identifiers in an arbitrary order during compilation is encapsulated in this sparse array description.

Multi-dimensional sparse arrays arise from the need to record information by multi-dimensional cross classification, i.e. the need to classify and process the same information by distinct components at different points in time. Such information can be thought of as a sparse multi-dimensional array over the ranges of components involved. For example, the following sparse array variable is a more general representation of the parent/children relationship between persons than the family tree:

> **var** *children* : {*sparse*} **array** [*person, person*] **of**
> {*sparse*} **set of** *person*;

where the first index refers to a mother and the second index to a father. Hence, for a given mother *m* and father *f*:

> *children*[*m,f*]

is the set of children of *m* and *f*. This set is itself a sparse set of all persons. Row *m* of this sparse matrix represents all offspring of mother *m*, while column *f* represents all offspring of father *f*.

A SPARSE ARRAY ABSTRACTION

Sparse arrays and sets require the same operations for their manipulation as the corresponding non-sparse structures, and so we may immediately define the following abstract data type *sparsearray* with a minimal set of operations:

> **envelope** *sparsearray* (*default* : *element*);
>
> {*assumes* **type**   *domain* = . . .;
>   *element* = . . .;
>   **function** *domainorder* (*d1, d2* : *domain*) : *Boolean*;
>   **function** *samevalue* (*e1, e2* : *element*) : *Boolean*;}

procedure **value* (*d* : *domain*; **var** *e* : *element*);

procedure **assign* (*d* : *domain*; *e* : *element*);

procedure **subscript* (*d* : *domain*;

$\qquad\qquad\qquad$ **procedure** *p* (**var** *e* : *element*));

procedure **traverse* (**procedure** *p* (*d* : *domain* ; *e* : *element*));

begin
$\quad${*all elements initialized to the value default*}
$\quad$ * * *
end; {*sparsearray*}

In general form the envelope assumes the existence of domain and element types. The type *domain* is assumed to be ordered, as defined by the function *domainorder*. An equality test function *samevalue* for the type *element* is also assumed—this is necessary to avoid the storage of default values within the representation. The default value is specified as a parameter when declaring an instance *A* of the *sparsearray* envelope, whose initialization implies the assignment of this value to all elements of *A*.

The operator *assign* may then be used to assign a new value *e* to element *d*, and is equivalent to the non-sparse operation:

$$A[d] := e$$

In general, the assigned value *e* may equal the default value. The operator *value* is used to extract the current value, default or otherwise, of element *d* and is thus equivalent to the non-sparse operation:

$$e := A[d]$$

To avoid multiple *value* and *assign* operations on the same element, the operator *subscript* may be used to apply procedure *p* to element *d*, and is thus equivalent to the non-sparse operation:

$$p(A[d])$$

Note that in general the value of $A[d]$ may be the default value either before or after the execution of *p*.

The operator *traverse* is slightly different from corresponding non-sparse operations in that it applies the procedure *p* to the index and value of those elements *that are significant* (i.e. differ from the default value), in the order of their corresponding domain values. In general, we cannot apply any operation to every element value (significant and non-significant) of a sparse array, since there may be an infinite number of such values. In practice, the ability to identify and apply some operation to the significant element values only is exactly what is required in most applications.

As an example of the use of the *sparsearray* data type, consider again the concordance program. The word list that records word frequencies may be thought of as a sparse array of the form:

{*sparse*} **array** [*wordspelling*] **of** 0 . . *maxint*

where only those entries that correspond to words actually occurring in the text have values other than the default value zero. The *wordlist* module may thus be rewritten using the *sparsearray* data type, viz:

```
envelope module wordlist;

    function wordorder (w1, w2 : wordspelling) : Boolean;
      begin
        wordorder := ( w1 < w2 )
      end {wordorder};

    function sameinteger (i1, i2 : integer) : Boolean;
      begin
        sameinteger := (i1 = i2)
      end {sameinteger};

    envelope sparsearray in library
      (where type domain = wordspelling;
                 element = integer;
             function domainorder = wordorder;
             function samevalue = sameinteger;);

    instance words : sparsearray(0);

    procedure *recordword (word : wordspelling);

      procedure increment (var e : integer);
        begin e := e +1 end;

      begin
        words.subscript (word, increment)
      end {recordword};

    procedure *printwords;
```

```
      procedure printword (w : wordspelling; n : integer);
        begin
          writeln (w,n)
        end {printword};

      begin
        writeln ('*** words ***'); writeln;
        words.traverse (printword)
      end {printwords};

  begin
    ***
  end {wordlist};
```

Note that the procedure *recordword* no longer has to distinguish between the first and subsequent occurrences of any word—it simply applies the *increment* operator to the (possibly zero) element for that word and the sparse array implementation does the rest. Likewise, the procedure *printwords* simply uses the *traverse* operator to supply the appropriate word and frequency values to the *printword* procedure for each significant element in the array, i.e. those that have a non-zero value due to previous *recordword* operations. In this example the sparse array abstraction reflects the precise requirement of the word list, which is to provide access to its significant entries in both random and sequential order.

REPRESENTATION OF SPARSE STRUCTURES

Sparse arrays are usually represented by keeping a record, in some form, of the elements that are significant at any moment, and of the default value for those that are not. Each element is represented as a record consisting of its subscript and its value. The subscript is known as the *key*, the value is known as the *information*, and their combination is known as an *entry*.

Sparse sets are similarly represented, except that no information need be held in each entry—the presence of an entry with a particular key value is sufficient to indicate that the value is a member of the set.

Figure 12.2 illustrates the general principle of representing a sparse array and a sparse set, without implying any particular organization for the significant entries involved.

Given any representation of a sparse array it is a simple matter to derive a corresponding sparse set representation, so from here on we consider only the representation of sparse arrays. Before looking in detail at how the

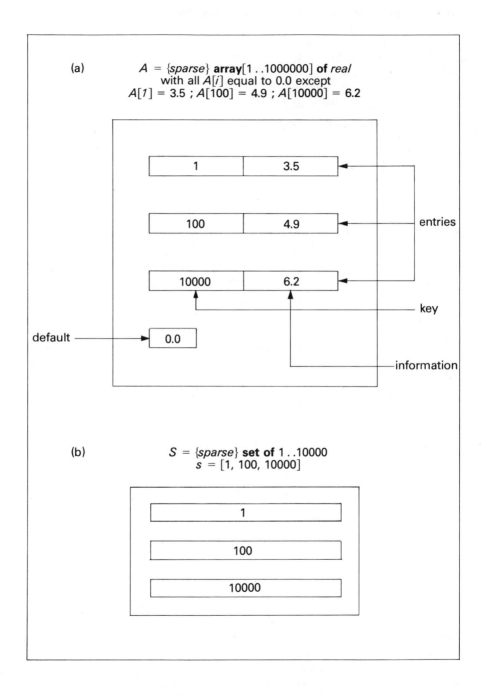

Figure 12.2   Representation of sparse structures

collection of significant entries involved in any representation may be organized, we note two basic principles:

(a)   At all times the collection should contain only entries for elements with non-default values. Thus, for a sparse array the assignment operator only adds an entry to the collection if the value being assigned is not the default value. Similarly, assignment of the default value to an element for which there is an entry in the significant collection implies removal of that entry. The *subscript* operation may also involve addition or removal of an entry, depending on its alteration, if any, of the element concerned.

(b)   The order in which entries are added to or removed from the collection of significant entries is not significant, and hence the order in which entries are held within the collection can be determined by the implementation. In particular the *traverse* operator can be implemented more easily if the collection of entries is held in some way that reflects the order of the key values concerned.

In practice, how the collection of entries representing the sparse structure is held depends on its size and the operations to be applied to it. The techniques which we shall describe are based upon, and extend, the list representation techniques introduced in Chapter 8. Hence, the first technique is a simple sequential list representation of significant entries.

Sequential Representation

The simplest representation of a sparse data type is as a list of significant entries, i.e., the type:

{*sparse*} **array** [*domain*] **of** *element*

is represented as a list of significant values of the type:

type *entry* = **record**
                    key : *domain*;
                    info : *element*
           end;

and the significant list is represented using any of the list representations described in Chapter 8. Figure 12.3 illustrates two possible representations of the sparse array of Fig. 12.2.

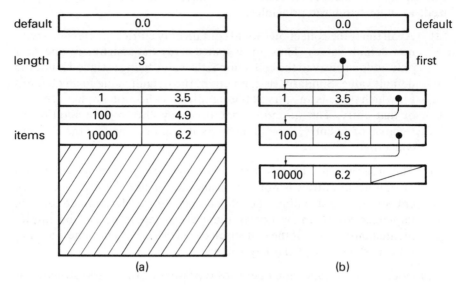

Figure 12.3 Sequential sparse array representations:
(a) contiguous representation;
(b) chained representation

Note that in both representations the entries are held in key order. This reduces the access time for non-significant entries, and simplifies implementation of the *traverse* operator. In the case of the contiguous representation the entries can be accessed by a binary split search.

These simple representations can be realized either by using the list abstractions defined in Chapter 8 to implement the sparse array abstraction, or by direct transcription of those parts of the list implementations that are required. These implementations are left as an exercise for the reader.

The implementations that result inevitably have the same advantages and disadvantages observed for sequential lists, but some of these are more significant for sparse arrays than for sequential list processing. In particular, the array abstraction suggests a free choice between the random access of elements in any order and their sequential processing in domain order. For Pascal arrays the two modes of access are equally efficient, because the contiguous representation enables the position of any element to be calculated directly from its index. For sparse arrays represented as sequential lists, however, access of an arbitrary element involves searching the list of significant entries for the index or key value involved. Whether this search is sequential or by binary splitting, its overheads inevitably make random access of sparse array elements significantly less efficient than sequential processing, and for applications that are dominated by random rather than sequential processing these overheads may be unacceptable. If sequential

processing of elements is not required *at all*, the following representation is
an attractive alternative which is used in many applications.

Hash Table Representation

When sequential processing of entries in key order is not required, a great
increase in both insertion and access speed may be achieved using a fixed
length array:

> **var** *table* : **array** $[1 \ . \ . \ n]$ **of** *entry*;

to hold the significant entries as a *hash table.*

   To organize the entries in a hash table some arbitrary *hashing* function is
chosen which maps all values of the domain type onto integers in the range
$1 . . n$ (necessarily a many-to-one mapping). When an entry is inserted it is
placed (if possible) at the position in the table indicated by hashing its key or
subscript, so that any subsequent access using the same hashing function
must find it there. Figure 12.4 shows a possible hash table representation of
the sparse array defined in Fig. 12.2.

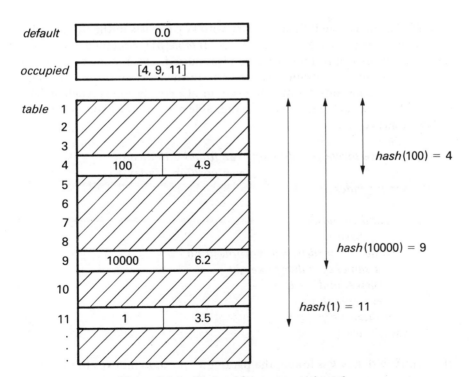

Figure 12.4   Hash table representation of sparse array

The component *occupied* is used to indicate which elements of *table* hold significant entries at any moment. It may be held as a set of the entry positions in *table*, i.e. a set of $1 . . n$, as a packed Boolean array, or alternatively, it may be represented by a Boolean field within each entry of *table* if this is convenient.

Because the hash function that determines the preferred position $p1$ for an entry with a given key k is necessarily a many-to-one mapping, position $p1$ may be occupied by an entry with a different key value. In this case a *collision* is said to occur, and must be resolved in some way. This involves calculating second, third, etc. choice positions $p2,p3, . . .$ for key k and trying each in turn, until either a vacant position or an entry with key k is found. This process of generating second and third choice positions for a given key is known as *rehashing*, and the sequence of positions $p1,p2,p3, . . .$ generated for any key k is known as its *probe sequence*.

Let us now try to define the process of locating an entry in a hash table more precisely.

The first step in locating an entry with a key k in the table is to calculate its preferred position p by applying the hash function to k.

$$p := hash(k)$$

If *table*[p] is unoccupied, then no entry with key k exists in the table, and if necessary a new entry may be made there. If *table*[p] is occupied, either it is the required entry or further inspection is required. This is done by applying a *rehash* procedure to compute second and third choice positions, etc., and applying the same consideration to each, until a conclusion is reached. The overall process of locating an entry in the table may thus be expressed as the following procedure:

```
procedure locate (k : domain; var found : Boolean;
                                var position : index);
    var p : index;
    begin
      found := false;
      p := hash(k);
      while occupied[p] and not found do
        if samekey (table[p].key,k)
        then found := true
        else rehash p;
      position := p
    end {locate};
```

If an entry with key k is found, the parameter *position* indexes this entry in the table. If no entry is found, *position* indexes the appropriate point of insertion for such an entry if required. With this property the sparse array operators *assign*, *value* and *subscript* are easily implemented, as we shall see.

The rehash process determines the second, third, etc., choice positions examined if the first choice position is occupied by an entry with another key value. To ensure full utilization of table storage, the sequence of positions generated by rehashing from any initial hash value should visit each entry position in the table. One simple way of doing so is to use a so-called *linear rehash* which tries successive table positions in turn, cycling back to the first table position after the last position has been tried. This is easily expressed, as follows:

$$p := p \bmod n + 1$$

However, the simple technique makes obvious one new problem. What happens if every table position is occupied, but not by the entry sought? To prevent looping, this condition must be detected within the *locate* procedure, but its significance depends on whether or not a subsequent insertion is required. We therefore modify the *locate* procedure to return a second Boolean result *full* to indicate when insertion is impossible, thus:

```
procedure locate1 (k : domain; var found, full : Boolean;
                                var position : index);
    var p,p1 : index;
    begin
      found := false; full := false;
      p1 := hash(k);
      p := p1;
      while occupied [p] and not (found or full) do
        if samekey (table[p].key, k)
        then found := true
        else begin
              p := p mod n + 1;
              if p = p1 then full := true
            end;
      if not full then position := p
    end {locate1};
```

One further problem remains with our hash table strategy. If the default value is assigned to a previously significant element of the sparse array, our basic representation principle requires that the element should no longer be represented in the collection of significant elements. However, we cannot simply mark its position in our hash table as unoccupied because if the position of its entry *e*1 lay on the probe sequence of an entry *e*2 made after itself, any search for *e*2 would now terminate incorrectly, at the unoccupied position. A compromise solution to this problem is to leave the entry in the table with its default value, but to re-use its position if it is found to lie on the probe sequence leading to the insertion of a new significant entry. Provided our rehashing process generates probe sequences that visit every position in the table, all such default entries will be overwritten with new significant entries before the table is deemed to be full. This strategy is implemented by the following version of our *locate* procedure:

```
procedure locate2 (k : domain; var keyfound, full : Boolean;
                                   var position : index);
var defaultfound, allexamined : Boolean;
    p,p1 : index;
begin
  keyfound := false; full := false;
  p1 := hash(k);
  p := p1;
  defaultfound := false; allexamined := false;
  while occupied[p] and not (keyfound or allexamined) do
    if samekey (table[p].key, k)
    then begin keyfound := true; position := p end
    else
    begin
      if not defaultfound then
        if samevalue (table[p].info, default) then
        begin defaultfound := true; position := p end;
      p := p mod n + 1;
      if p = p1 then
      begin full := not defaultfound; allexamined := true end
    end;
  if not (keyfound or defaultfound or allexamined) then position := p
end {locate2};
```

This version of *locate* is now sufficient for an implementation of our sparse array abstraction using a hash table to hold the significant entries. Before completing the implementation, however, the following points must be noted.

(a)   In general, the user program should determine the hash table size n and hence the table index type *index*.

(b)   The hash table mechanism implemented by *locate* requires an equality testing function *samekey* for key or domain values, rather than an ordering function. Since the hash table implementation cannot support the ordered traversal operator in any case, it is logical to replace the ordering function *domainorder* required by our previous abstraction by the function *samekey*.

(c) The hash function used to determine the first choice position of an entry is solely a function of its key value. Ideally, it should provide even distribution of positions for the range of key values involved. However, since the nature of keys is determined by the program using the table, in general the hash function must be supplied by the user program rather than within the table implementation itself.

With these decisions, the interface provided by our hash table implementation of a sparse array may be summarized as follows:

envelope *hashtable* (*default* : *element*);

    {*assumes* **const** *n* = *size of hash table to be used*;
            type *domain* =
                element =
            function *samekey* (*d1*, *d2* : *domain*) : *Boolean*;
            function *samevalue* (*e1*, *e2* : *element*) : *Boolean*;
            function *hash* (*d* : *domain*) : 1 . . *n*}

    procedure *value (*d* : *domain*; **var** *e* : *element*);

    procedure *assign (*d* : *domain*; *e* : *element*);

    procedure *subscript (*d* : *domain*; **procedure** *p* (**var** *e* : *element*));

    begin
      {*all elements* := *default*}
      ***
    end {*hashtable*};

Listing 25 shows a complete implementation of this abstraction using the hash table strategy. For maximum efficiency two versions of the procedure *locate* are used in this implementation. The operator *value*, in which no possibility of inserting a new entry is involved, uses *locatevalue* (which is a simplified version of *locate2*) to avoid the possibly expensive *samevalue* test for default entries. The operators *assign* and *subscript*, however, in which new entries may be inserted, use a procedure *locateposition* that is identical to the procedure *locate2* described earlier.

Note also that the operator *subscript* uses a local variable *n* to avoid making an entry in the table if the element concerned has the default value before and after the execution of procedure *p*. This avoids the possibility of an unnecessary array overflow. It also avoids the possibility of cluttering the table with default value entries if the user program uses the *subscript* operator, in cavalier fashion, to process default element values without altering their value.

Listing 25

```
envelope hashtable(default: element);

{ This envelope implements a sparse array with index of       }
{ type domain and elements of type element as a hash table. }
{                                                             }
{ It assumes const n = size of hash table to be used;         }
{         type domain = any type with := applicable;          }
{              element = any type with := applicable;         }
{         function samekey(d1,d2: domain): Boolean;           }
{         function samevalue(e1,e2: element): Boolean;        }
{         function hash(d: domain): 1..n                      }

type index = 1..n;




var table:
      array [index] of
        record
          key: domain;
          info: element
        end;
    occupied: packed array [index] of Boolean;
    i: index;




procedure locatevalue(k: domain; var found: Boolean;
                      var position: index);
  var p, p1: index;
      allexamined: Boolean;
  begin
    found := false;
    allexamined := false;
    p1 := hash(k);
    p := p1;
    while occupied[p] and not (found or allexamined) do
      if samekey(table[p].key, k)
      then begin
             found := true;
             position := p
           end
      else begin
             p := p mod n + 1;
             if p = p1 then allexamined := true
           end
  end {locatevalue};
```

```
procedure locateposition(k: domain; var keyfound, full: Boolean;
                          var position: index);
  var defaultfound, allexamined: Boolean;
      p, p1: index;
  begin
    keyfound := false;
    full := false;
    defaultfound := false;
    allexamined := false;
    p1 := hash(k);
    p := p1;
    while occupied[p] and not (keyfound or allexamined) do
      if samekey(table[p].key, k)
      then begin
              keyfound := true;
              position := p
           end
      else begin
             if not defaultfound
             then if samevalue(table[p].info, default)
                  then begin
                          defaultfound := true;
                          position := p
                       end;
             p := p mod n + 1;
             if p = p1
             then begin
                     full := not defaultfound;
                     allexamined := true
                  end
           end;
    if not (keyfound or defaultfound or allexamined)
    then position := p
  end {locateposition};

procedure insert(d: domain; e: element; position: index;
                 full: Boolean);
  begin
    if full
    then error('hash table overflow')
    else begin
            with table[position] do
              begin
                key := d;
                info := e
              end;
            occupied[position] := true
         end
  end {insert};
```

continued on page 336

Listing 25 continued

```
procedure *value(d: domain; var e: element);
  var found: Boolean;
      position: index;
  begin
    locatevalue(d, found, position);
    if found
    then e := table[position].info
    else e := default
  end {value};

procedure *assign(d: domain; e: element);
  var found, full: Boolean;
      position: index;
  begin
    locateposition(d, found, full, position);
    if found
    then table[position].info := e
    else if not samevalue(e, default)
         then insert(d, e, position, full)
  end {assign};

procedure *subscript(d: domain; procedure p(var e: element));
  var found, full: Boolean;
      position: index;
      n: element;
  begin
    locateposition(d, found, full, position);
    if found
    then p(table[position].info)
    else begin
           n := default;
           p(n);
           if not samevalue(n, default)
           then insert(d, n, position, full)
         end
  end {subscript};

begin
  for i := 1 to n do occupied[i] := false;
  ***
end {hashtable};
```

How are the hash functions defined for actual applications of such an implementation? For a program such as the concordance program, the key values are word spellings defined as:

wordspelling = **packed array** [1 . . *wordlength*] **of** *char*;

A possible function in this case has the form:

```
function hashword (w : wordspelling) : index;
    const factor = . . . ; k = . . . ;
    var h : index;
    begin
        h := 0;
        for i := 1 to k do
            h := (h*factor+ord(w[i])) mod n +1;
        hashword := h
    end {hashword};
```

After each iteration of the for loop h has a value in the range 1 to n determined by the first i characters of the wordspelling w. If *factor* is coprime with n, then all characters have an equal effect on the final hash value. In practice, the number k of characters used can be small, so limiting the cost of calculating the hash value. Similar, or even simpler, hash functions may be devised for keys of other types. For example, if a sparse array of the form:

{*sparse*} **array** [1 . . 1000000] **of** . . .

is to be represented, and the index values of its significant elements are randomly distributed over the range, then a simple modulo operation provides an adequate hash function:

hash := i **mod** $n +1$

How well does the hash table achieve its objective, which is to provide efficient random access to the elements of a sparse array? Using the linear rehash, and assuming a random distribution of hash values, it can be shown that the average number of key comparisons required to locate an entry in the hash table is approximately

$$(1 - \alpha/2) / (1 - \alpha)$$

where α is the *load factor* or *occupancy*, i.e. the ratio of the number of occupied entries in the table to the total table size n. Hence:

10% occupancy gives an average of 1.06 comparisons per search,
50% occupancy gives an average of 1.50 comparisons per search,
90% occupancy gives an average of 5.50 comparisons per search.

These example figures demonstrate two significant features of hash tables:

(a)   the average number of comparisons per search is remarkably low even at high occupancy levels;

(b)   the performance of the table varies inversely with the load factor rather than the absolute number of entries—by using a table of sufficient size, fast insertion and retrieval of entries can be assured, however many entries are involved.

In fact, the linear rehash used so far is not a good rehashing technique, as it suffers from *clustering*—occupied entries tend to cluster together in long sequences causing a more rapid fall off in performance. This clustering occurs because the probe sequences leading from each first choice position in the hash table are all cyclic rotations of a single sequence $1, 2, 3, \ldots, n$.

The table performance may be improved further by adopting an alternative rehash which guarantees probe sequences that are distinct permutations of the values $1 \ldots n$, even under cyclic rotation. One simple method of doing so is to choose a table size n such that $n+1$ is prime, and then generate probe sequence values by the recurrence relation:

$$p_{i+1} = (p_i + p_1) \bmod (n+1)$$

Provided $n+1$ is prime, this gives a distinct permutation of the values $1 \ldots n$ for each starting value $1 \ldots n$, before generating 0 as the $(n+1)$th value in every case.

With such a rehash, the average number of key comparisons required to locate an entry in the hash table is approximately:

$$\tfrac{1}{\alpha} \, log \, (1-\alpha)$$

so that:

10% occupancy gives an average of 1.05 comparisons per search,
50% occupancy gives an average of 1.39 comparisons per search,
90% occupancy gives an average of 2.56 comparisons per search!

AN INTERACTIVE CONCORDANCE PROGRAM

To illustrate a context in which a hash table representation of a sparse array is the appropriate choice, consider a variation on our previous concordance program in which an interacting user is able to query the frequency of occurrence of an arbitrary word in the text under investigation. At an abstract level the program may be defined as follows:

```
program wordqueries;

    type wordspelling = . . .;

    var frequency : {sparse} array [wordspelling] of integer;
        word : wordspelling;

begin
    construct frequency array from text;
    repeat
        input query word from user;
        output frequency[word]
    until user quits
end {wordqueries}.
```

In this case the order of updating and of retrieving word frequences in the array is arbitrary, and no processing of words in spelling order is required, so a hash table is a logical and efficient means of implementing the sparse array.

To do so, we must retrieve the hash table abstraction from the library as follows:

```
envelope wordcounts = hashtable in library
    (where const n = textmax;
            type domain = wordspelling;
                 element = integer;
            function samekey = sameword;
            function samevalue = sameinteger;
            function hash = hashword;);

instance frequency : wordcounts(0);
```

where textmax is greater than the maximum number of distinct words expected in the text, and the other types and functions are similar to those defined before.

We may use the envelope wordinput to handle both the initial text input that creates the frequency array, and the subsequent sequence of user queries, with an appropriate file parameter for each:

```
envelope wordinput in library;

instance textwords : wordinput (textfile);
         userwords : wordinput (input);
```

The body of our abstract word query program can then be re-expressed as

follows:

```
{construct frequencies from text file}
with textwords do
  while not endofwords do
  begin
    frequency.subscript (word, increment);
    getword
  end;

{process user queries}
with userwords do
  while not endofwords do
  begin
    frequency.value (word, count);
    writeln (word,' occurs', count,' times');
    getword
  end
```

Listing 26 shows the complete *wordqueries* program that results.

Listing 26

```
program wordqueries(textfile, input, output);

{ This program constructs a concordance of words extracted  }
{ from the file textfile, and then outputs the frequency of }
{ occurrence for each query word input on the standard      }
{ input file                                                }

const wordlength = 20;
      textmax = 5000;

type wordspelling = packed array [1..wordlength] of char;
     linenumber = 1..9999;

var textfile: text;

envelope wordinput in library;

instance textwords: wordinput(textfile);
         userwords: wordinput(input);

function sameword(w1, w2: wordspelling): Boolean;
  begin sameword := (w1 = w2) end;

function sameinteger(i1, i2: integer): Boolean;
  begin sameinteger := (i1 = i2) end;
```

```
function hashword(w: wordspelling): integer;
  const factor = 26;
  var h, i: integer;
  begin
    h := 0;
    for i := 1 to wordlength do
      if w[i] <> ' '
      then h := (h * factor + ord(w[i])) mod textmax + 1;
    hashword := h
  end {hashword};


envelope wordcounts = hashtable in library
  (where const n = textmax;
         type domain = wordspelling;
              element = integer;
         function samekey = sameword;
         function samevalue = sameinteger;
         function hash = hashword; );


instance frequency: wordcounts(0);


var count: integer;


procedure increment(var i: integer);
  begin i := i + 1 end;


begin

{ construct frequencies from text file }
with textwords do
  while not endofwords do
    begin
      frequency.subscript(word, increment);
      getword
    end;

  { process user queries }
  with userwords do
    while not endofwords do
      begin
        frequency.value(word, count);
        writeln(word, ' occurs', count, ' times');
        getword
      end
end {wordqueries}.
```

MULTI-DIMENSIONAL SPARSE ARRAYS

Sparse arrays of two or more dimensions can be represented using similar techniques to those for one-dimensional arrays, by regarding the set of subscripts that index a particular element as a composite key, of record form, say. Thus, an array of form:

{*sparse*} **array** [*domain*1,*domain*2] **of** *element*

can be regarded as an array of the form:

{*sparse*} **array** [*domainx*] **of** *element*

where

    domainx = **record**
                    *d*1 : *domain*1;
                    *d*2 : *domain*2
            end

and can be represented by storing the significant entries with keys of type *domainx*, as before.

However, the efficiency of sequential processing which the sequential representation provides for one-dimensional arrays does not extend to two- (or multi-) dimensional arrays such as these. Sorting the entries in some key order makes one subscript more significant than the other, with the result that entries are not correctly sorted in terms of the latter subscript, and efficiency of sequential access cannot be symmetric with respect to both.

With a normal two-dimensional array

A : **array** [1 . . *n*1,1 . . *n*2] **of** *element*;

we can process the elements of the *i*th row:

for *j* := 1 **to** *n*2 **do** $p(A[i,j])$

or of the *j*th column:

for *i* := 1 **to** *n*1 **do** $p(A[i,j])$

with equal efficiency. Similarly we can process the entire array row-by-row:

for *i* := 1 **to** *n*1 **do**
  for *j* := 1 **to** *n*2 **do** $p(A[i,j])$

or column-by-column:

> **for** $j := 1$ **to** $n2$ **do**
>   **for** $i := 1$ **to** $n1$ **do** $p(A[i,j])$

with equal efficiency. For a two-dimensional sparse array we might expect similar flexibility in processing the significant elements in rows or columns, as expressed by the following sparse matrix abstraction:

> **envelope** *sparsematrix* (*default* : *element*);
>
>   {*assumes* **type** *domain1* =
>   *domain2* =
>   *element* =
>   **function** *domain1order* (*d1, d2* : *domain1*) : *Boolean*;
>   **function** *domain2order* (*d1, d2* : *domain2*) : *Boolean*;
>   **function** *samevalue* (*e1, e2* : *element*) : *Boolean*}
>
>   **procedure** **assign* (*i* : *domain1*; *j* : *domain2*; *e* : *element*);
>
>   **procedure** **value* (*i* : *domain1*; *j* : *domain2*; **var** *e* : *element*);
>
>   **procedure** **subscript* (*i* : *domain1*; *j* : *domain2*;
>   **procedure** *p* (**var** *e* : *element*));
>
>   **procedure** **traverserow* (*i* : *domain1*;
>   **procedure** *p* (*j* : *domain2*; *e* : *element*));
>
>   **procedure** **traversecolumn* (*j* : *domain2*;
>   **procedure** *p* (*i* : *domain1*; *e* : *element*));
>
>   **procedure** **rowbyrow*(**procedure** *p*(*i* : *domain1*;
>   *j* : *domain2*;
>   *e* : *element*));
>
>   **procedure** **columnbycolumn*(**procedure** *p*(*i* : *domain1*;
>   *j* : *domain2*;
>   *e* : *element*));
>
>   **begin**
>   {*all elements* := *default*}
>   ***
>   **end** {*sparsematrix*};

The symmetry of access efficiency for rows and columns implied by this abstraction can be achieved using a grid representation, as illustrated in Fig. 12.5.

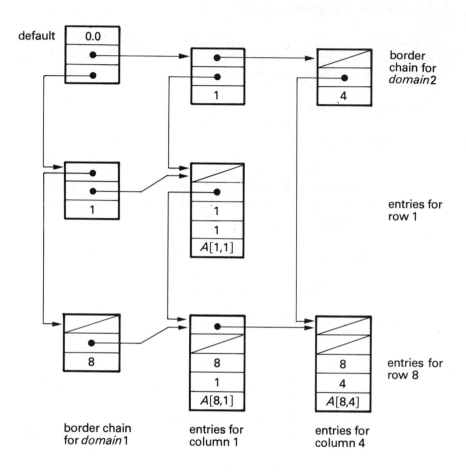

Figure 12.5   Grid representation of sparse matrix

For each value *i* of *domain*1 that actually occurs as a subscript of a significant element, an entry is created on a border chain for *domain*1, and each value *j* of *domain*2 that actually occurs is placed on a border chain for *domain*2. Each element in a border chain contains a pointer to a chained sequence of entries for elements with that subscript value. Each entry now has two pointers attached, one to the next entry for a significant element with the same *domain*1 subscript, the other to the next element with the same *domain*2 subscript. Thus each entry consists of these two pointers, the subscript values i and j, and the element value. Figure 12.5 illustrates the grid representation for a sparse array A containing just three significant entries, $A[1,1]$, $A[8,1]$, and $A[8,4]$.

Processing all elements of A with a given *domain*1 value, or all elements with a given *domain*2 value, can now be carried out with equal efficiency.

Although the *value* retrieval operation remains straightforward to implement, the multiple pointer chains that have to be maintained make the *assign* operation quite complex, in the case where a new grid entry and one or more new border chain entries have to be created. Detailed implementation of the sparse matrix abstraction using the grid representation is left as an exercise to the reader.

SUMMARY

The ability to view a finite collection of data as a large, possibly infinite, array or set in which the majority of elements are missing (or have some default value) is a significant conceptual aid when it is applicable. Many real-world data sets can be viewed in this way, and their manipulation can then be neatly expressed using array and set operators.

An abstraction of such sparse arrays or sets can be implemented easily, using the list and tree representations described in previous chapters, to allow both random and sequential access of the data elements concerned. In the case when sequential access in a particular order is not required, however, the hash table representation can be used to provide random access, with an efficiency which can be tailored to the data set concerned by adjusting the total amount of storage used. As such it is a fundamental tool in the representation of randomly accessed tables which arise in many computing applications.

EXERCISES

12.1   Implement the contiguous and chained sequential representations of
a sparse array, as outlined on page 328.

12.2   Use an ordered chained list representation to implement a sparse set
abstraction with the following interface:

> **envelope** *sparseset*;
> {*assumes* **type** *domain* = *any type with* := *applicable*;
>   **function** *domainorder* (*d1, d2* : *domain*) : *Boolean*}
> **procedure** **include* (*d* : *domain*);
> **procedure** **exclude* (*d* : *domain*);
> **function** **contains* (*d* : *domain*) : *Boolean*;
> **function** **empty* : *Boolean*;
> **procedure** **traverse* (**procedure** *p* (*d* : *domain*));

Use your implementation to write a program which reads sequences
of words from two input texts and prints out, in lexicographic order,
those words which occur in the second text but not in the first.

12.3   Implement the hash function suggested on page 337 to convert
alphabetic strings of up to 16 letters to a hash index in the range
1 .. 100. Use this in a test program to compute

(a)   the distribution of hash indices generated for the names of the
states of the USA;

(b)   the average number of comparisons required to locate a valid
state name in a hash table of size 100 which uses this function,
and a linear rehash to resolve collisions (assume any convenient
order of insertion for the state names, and that no entries other
than state names are present);

(c)   the average number of comparisons required to determine that
a state name is invalid.

12.4   An alternative method of resolving collisions in a hash table is for all
the entries whose key values map onto a particular table position to
be held as an ordered list or binary tree. Modify the *hashtable*
implementation given in Listing 25 to use either of these methods of
holding the table entries.

12.5   Implement the word queries program using

(a)   a linear list;

(b)   a binary tree;

(c)   a hash table

to hold the concordance involved. Measure either the time or the number of word comparisons required to construct the concordance from some substantial text, and the average time or number of comparisons taken to answer any query thereafter.

12.6   Use the *sparsematrix* envelope in a program which reads the contents of an input file and determines the pairs of characters which occur adjacent to each other in the text, together with a count of the occurrences of each adjacent pair. The results should be output in a legible form. Calculate the amount of storage used by your envelope for a sample text, and compare it with the storage used for the same purpose by a conventional Pascal two-dimensional array.

12.7   Implement the grid representation of a sparse matrix, as outlined on page 344.

13

Permanent Storage of Data Structures

In previous chapters we have considered how a variety of abstract data types may be represented using contiguous or chained storage, as provided by Pascal's array or pointer mechanisms. An underlying assumption of both these mechanisms is that all storage used by them is accessible with equal efficiency, a characteristic of the primary storage or memory provided on most computers. This primary storage has two significant disadvantages, however, which are as follows:

(a)   the amount of storage available is limited;

(b)   the data stored within it exists only for the duration of the program execution that creates it.

In many computer applications the data involved either exceeds the capacity of the primary storage available, or must persist beyond any particular execution of the programs that manipulate it, or both. For such data secondary storage, such as that provided by magnetic disks or tapes, must be used, with data being transferred between primary and secondary storage during processing, as required.

Secondary storage has the characteristics necessary to overcome the problems of primary storage, in that

(a)   the amount of secondary storage available can be very large, and effectively unlimited; and

(b)   the stored data persists until it is overwritten.

However, secondary storage has less desirable access characteristics in that data can only be transferred between primary and secondary storage at relatively low speed, usually in large fixed length units or *blocks*. Magnetic tape has the additional disadvantage that data can only be transferred in the sequence of its storage on the tape, and alteration of any stored data in general involves rewriting all data on the tape. Magnetic disks allow the access or rewriting of individual blocks of data in an arbitrary order, but the rate of data transfer may be reduced by the physical repositioning of the disk read/write devices required by such arbitrary access. Efficient use of secondary storage, or rather efficient performance of the programs that use it, can be achieved only if such access characteristics are taken into account by these programs.

Thus, while in principle the abstractions appropriate to the data stored on secondary storage media are no different from those used for data held in primary storage, in practice they must be, if efficient processing is to be achieved.

Pascal's sequential file concept is itself an extreme example of an abstract data type designed to take account of the access characteristics of backing store. The sequential processing of file components, one by one, and the inability to mix component input (reading) with component output (writing) are both consistent with the limitations of magnetic tapes as storage media. While most modern computer systems use magnetic disks as their secondary storage medium and need not therefore enforce such strict sequential access restrictions, the sequential file remains a fundamental concept in secondary storage organization which is simple to provide and to use.

Many basic data processing applications can be implemented satisfactorily using sequential files as the only form of secondary storage, but many others cannot, particularly those requiring random access to large data sets with fast and equally fast access to all components. The study of the data abstractions involved in such applications, and the representations used for their implementation, is beyond the scope of this text. The reader is referred to Elder [1984] for an in depth treatment of this topic in a similar style. In this final chapter we confine ourselves to the problem of storing and retrieving from secondary storage those data structures which can be held in primary storage during their manipulation, but which persist from one program execution to the next.

For simplicity, we will use Pascal's sequential file abstraction as the means of organizing the secondary storage involved. The sequentialization of the representation that this implies is not a significant overhead in this case, since it affects only the storage and retrieval operations and not the efficiency of the data structure during its existence in primary storage.

ABSTRACTION OF STORAGE AND RETRIEVAL FACILITIES

Two basic approaches can be taken to the provision of storage and retrieval facilities for abstract data types.

One is to define the storage and retrieval facilities as a separate auxiliary package to be incorporated in a user program if required, using the operators of the abstract type itself to implement the storage and retrieval processes.

Such a package would define a file type appropriate for the storage of the abstract data type concerned, and provide *save* and *retrieve* operators, each of which takes an instance of the abstract data type and a file variable as parameters.

Thus, if we have an abstract data type *ADT* defined in our library, a package for the storage and retrieval of instances of type *ADT* would have the following form:

> **envelope module** *filedADTpackage*;
>
> {*assumes* **envelope** *ADT as in library*;
>   **type** *itemtype etc . . . as assumed by ADT*}
>
> **type** **filedADT* = **file of** . . .;
>
> **procedure** **save* (**instance** *i* : *ADT*; **var** *f* : *filedADT*);
>
> **procedure** **retrieve* (**instance** *i* : *ADT*; **var** *f* : *filedADT*);

A program that retrieves an initial value for an *ADT* instance from a file *oldADT*, and saves its final value in a file *newADT*, would then have the form:

> **program** *p* (*oldADT, newADT*);
>
> **envelope** *ADT* **in** *library*;
>
> **envelope module** *filedADTpackage* **in** *library*;
>
> **instance** *i* : *ADT*;
>
> **var** *oldADT, newADT* : *filedADTpackage.filedADT*;
>
> **begin**
>   *filedADTpackage.retrieve* (*i, oldADT*);
>   . . .
>   {*use and update i*}
>   . . .
>   *filedADTpackage.save* (*i, newADT*)
> **end** {*p*}.

This approach has the benefit that the overheads of the save and retrieve facilities are not carried within the *ADT* envelope itself, and need be incurred only by those programs that actually require them. The approach assumes, however, that the *save* and *retrieve* procedures can be implemented solely in terms of the available *ADT* operators, without any knowledge of the internal representation involved.

For some *ADT*s, expressing the *save* and *retrieve* procedures in terms of the exported operators may be either inefficient or impossible. In such cases an alternative strategy is to imbed *save* and *retrieve* operators within the *ADT* abstraction itself, again providing an exported file type which enables the user program to create the actual files required.

With this approach, the interface of any *ADT* envelope is extended as follows:

> **envelope** *ADT*;
>
> {*assumptions as before . . .*}
>
> **type** **filedADT* = **file of** . . .;
>
> **procedure** **save* (**var** *f* : *filedADT*);
>
> **procedure** **retrieve* (**var** *f* : *filedADT*);
>
> {*remaining interface as before*}

The program that retrieves and saves initial and final values of an *ADT* instance is then as follows:

> **program** *p* (*oldADT*, *newADT*);
>
> **envelope** *ADT* **in** *library*;
>
> **instance** *i* : *ADT*;
>
> **var** *oldADT*, *newADT* : *i.filedADT*;
>
> **begin**
>   *i.retrieve(oldADT)*;
>   . . .
>   {*use and update i*}
>   . . .
>   *i.save* (*newADT*)
> **end** {*p*}.

With this approach a simpler user program results, but every program using the *ADT* envelope includes the implementation of the *save* and *retrieve* operators whether it needs them or not. We could, of course, provide alternative versions of the *ADT* envelope, with and without these operators, but this in turn creates a larger library of envelopes with duplicate code and increased maintenance costs.

In practice, we shall illustrate both approaches in providing storage and retrieval facilities for the abstract data types defined in previous chapters.

STORING AND RETRIEVING SEQUENCES

For the abstract types that are themselves sequential in form, namely stacks, queues and lists, storage as a sequential file is trivial. The following package implements the storage and retrieval of lists as defined in Chapter 8.

```
envelope module filedlistpackage;

    {assumes envelope list in library;
                type itemtype as assumed by list}

    type *filedlist = file of itemtype;

    procedure *save (instance l : list; var f : filedlist);

        procedure writeitem (i : itemtype);
            begin write (f,i) end;

        begin
            rewrite (f);
            l.traverse (writeitem)
        end {save};

    procedure *retrieve (instance l : list; var f : filedlist);
        var i : itemtype;
        begin
            if not l.empty
            then error ('retrieval to non-empty list')
            else begin
                    reset(f);
                    while not eof (f) do
                    begin
                        read (f,i);
                        l.precede (i)
                    end
                end
        end {retrieve};

    begin *** end {filedlistpackage};
```

The method is obvious and has already been illustrated in the editor program developed in Chapter 8. As such it barely merits inclusion as a library package. Note, however, that the *retrieve* procedure flags an error if the list *l* is not empty, rather than disposing of the existing list contents. This design choice helps to prevent the inadvertent overwriting of an existing list, and is not unduly restrictive since the user program can itself detect and dispose of such lists when it means to do so.

STORING AND RETRIEVING TREES

The tree structures defined in Chapter 10 are examples of non-linear recursive structures which cannot be directly expressed in sequential form. In primary storage we represent the tree structure by storing two pointer values in each tree node, but such pointers must not be written to secondary storage since a pointer value created during one program execution is meaningless if read back during another. The tree structure must therefore be represented in a sequential file in some other way.

In principle, primary storage pointers can be simulated in file store by numbering the components written to a file, and using these numbers as 'pointers' to represent the non-linear relationship between components. Generating such a file store representation requires a preliminary traversal of the structure to determine the order in which its components will be filed, and hence their ordinal numbers. The components are then written to the file in this order, replacing pointer references within them by the known ordinal numbers of the components they point to.

For hierarchic recursive structures such as binary trees, however, this component numbering approach is unnecessary. Such a recursive structure can be represented in a sequential form by imbedding the values of recursive substructures within the representations of their parents.

Using a Pascal sequential file this may be achieved most conveniently as follows. Each tree node is written to the file, starting from the root node, as a record containing the item value at that node, and two Boolean flags indicating whether its left and right subtrees are empty. If non-empty, the subtrees are then written as the following records in the file in a similar manner, in left–right order.

If we denote a record containing an item value *i* and Boolean flags *emptyleft*, *emptyright* as:

   (*i*,*emptyleft*,*emptyright*)

then the tree shown in Fig. 13.1 would be written to the file as the following sequence of records:

$(X1,T,T)$ $(X2,F,T)$ $(X3,F,F)$ $(X4,T,T)$ $(X5,F,F)$ $(X6,F,F)$

where T denotes true and F denotes false.

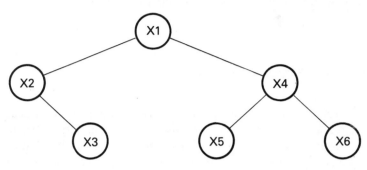

Figure 13.1   A binary tree

The above approach is well-suited to Pascal sequential files, which are usually represented using fixed-length records, in that each record contains a similar amount of information. It has the disadvantage, however, that it relies on the *eof* condition to represent an empty tree. This means that a single file cannot be used to store more than one tree, if any of the trees can be empty.

An alternative approach is to use file records, each of which represents a subtree by a single Boolean flag which indicates whether the subtree is empty, and an item value which is the value at the root node if the subtree is non-empty. The left and right subtrees are again represented by the immediately following file records. With this approach file records have one of two forms:

(false,i)   or   *(true)*

and the tree in Fig. 13.1 would be filed as the following sequence:

*(false,X*1) *(false,X*2) *(true)* *(false,X*3) *(true)* *(true)* *(false,X*4)
*(false,X*5) *(true)* *(true)* *(false,X*6) *(true)* *(true)*

An empty tree is now represented by a single record *(true)*, and any number of trees, empty or non-empty, can be stored as a single file. Note, however, that the number of records used to represent each tree is approximately double that used with the first approach, and half of these records represent empty subtrees as a single bit of information (*true*). If fixed-length file records are in use, as is usually the case with implementations of Pascal, and the node items themselves are of significant size, the file store overheads of this second approach are extremely high.

We will illustrate the implementation of the first approach as imbedded *save* and *retrieve* operators for the general binary tree implementation given in Listing 21. Similar code could be added to the ordered list implementation given as Listing 20, with similar effect.

The file type to be exported from the tree envelope is defined as follows:

```
filednode = record
              nodevalue : itemtype;
              emptyleft,emptyright : Boolean
            end;


*filedtree = file of filednode;
```

The *save* operator is then implemented using a recursive procedure which implements a pre-order traversal of the tree as follows:

```
procedure *save (var f : filedtree);

  procedure savenode (n : node);
    begin
      if n <> nil then
      begin
        f↑.nodevalue := n↑.nodevalue;
        f↑.emptyleft := (n↑.left = nil);
        f↑.emptyright := (n↑.right = nil);
        put(f);
        savenode (n↑.left);
        savenode (n↑.right)
      end
    end {savenode};

  begin
    rewrite (f);
    savenode (root)
  end {save};
```

The *retrieve* operator rebuilds the tree using a similar recursive procedure. Note, however, that an extra parameter is used to recreate the parent pointer in each node, and that care must be taken to read all necessary information from the current file record before making the recursive calls that create its subtrees, since these advance the file.

```
procedure *retrieve (var f : filedtree);

    procedure retrievenode (var n : node; p : node)
        var fn : filednode;
        begin
            read (f,fn);
            new (n);
            with n↑ do
            begin
                nodevalue := fn.nodevalue;
                if fn.emptyleft
                then left := nil
                else retrievenode (left, n);
                if fn.emptyright
                then right := nil
                else retrievenode (right, n);
                parent := p
            end
        end {retrievenode};

    begin
        reset(f);
        retrievenode (root,nil)
    end {retrieve};
```

STORING AND RETRIEVING OTHER STRUCTURES

Where more complex structures, such as the graphs discussed in Chapter 11, have to be stored in secondary storage, some means must be found to denote the structural relationships that exist between components. This may involve the identification of node labels which exist within the node data itself, as was suggested for graph input in Chapter 11, or the use of the ordinal positions of components within a file as secondary storage 'pointers'. The latter is in effect equivalent to the construction of a contiguous or positional representation in backing store. Where a contiguous representation is already in use in primary storage, an obvious expedient is to write the entire contents of the contiguous 'array' storage straight to a sequential file.

Thus, with the contiguous representations of graphs described in Chapter 11, the entire *nodes* array can be written, element by element, to a sequential file, and retrieved in a similar manner. This gives a simple and effective means of graph storage and retrieval which must be embedded in the graph abstraction itself. Likewise, as described in Chapter 12, a hash table can be stored simply by writing the *table* array, element by element, to a sequential file.

One disadvantage of this simple approach to filing contiguous representations is that unused elements within the contiguous representation array now occupy permanent secondary storage, at some cost. In some cases, this cost may be insignificant, in others it may not.

For the contiguous array representation of a graph this unused storage overhead can be avoided by applying a preliminary compaction process that shifts graph nodes from high index array elements to unused low index positions. For each node shifted, all references to it in the *successors* (and *predecessors*) sets of other nodes must be located and adjusted. Depending on how node set processing is implemented, the computational cost per node shifted may thus be proportional to the maximum number of nodes in the graph, to the highest index of the node being shifted, or to the actual number of successors and predecessors that it has. In principle this compaction cost must be weighed against the storage savings achieved, though for many graph applications the actual compaction that is possible may not involve either significant storage saving or significant compaction overheads. More significantly, it must be remembered that any such compaction in principle invalidates all node references held with the user program, and thus adds to the node reference security problem if graph compaction and storage is anything other than the final action of a graph processing program.

For hash tables the unused storage overhead that arises from filing the entire table array can be avoided by converting the table back to an (unordered) list of significant entries, filing these in sequence, and then recomputing their hash table positions at retrieval time. This has the advantage of allowing the retrieved table to be of a different size (and thus have a different hash function) to that from which the entries were filed. This is in fact one means of dealing with hash table overflow when it occurs—by filing the table entries and then retrieving them to a table of increased size. Again, it must be noted that the entries may take up new positions in the retrieved table. This is true even if the same table size and hash function as before are used, since the arbitrary order of filing and re-insertion of table entries is in general different from their original order of insertion. (The hash table abstraction defined in Chapter 12 does not allow the user program to obtain and store references to hash table positions, and thus precludes the invalid reference errors that could otherwise arise through deletion or through the saving and retrieval of tables while references persist.)

The implementation of save and retrieve operators for graphs and for hash tables, using the techniques described above, are left as exercises for the reader.

SUMMARY

In this chapter we have seen how various data structures that are manipulated in primary store can be held in secondary store between manipulations. We have seen that the storage and retrieval for data structures can and should be separated from the programs that use them, either as auxiliary packages used in association with the primary data abstractions, or as additional operators embedded in the abstractions themselves. We have seen that, in designing the storage and retrieval mechanisms, due consideration must be given to error security if hard-to-diagnose programming errors are to be avoided. Finally, we have seen that, in choosing how to store the data structures in secondary storage, trade-offs between storage utilization and program efficiency arise, in this case between the amount of secondary storage needed to store the structure and the computation involved in the save and retrieve operations.

Thus our final topic of consideration remains consistent with the theme that has developed throughout the book, from the initial programming goals identified in Chapter 1. We have seen that program correctness is enhanced by a logical separation of concerns during program design, using abstraction as the basic conceptual tool within the concrete framework of a modular programming notation. We have seen that program flexibility also stems from such separation, and that an awareness of the general utility of many program components, coupled with a library mechanism that encourages the storage and retrieval of such general-purpose modules, enables a variety of application programs to be assembled with relative ease from a library of modules such as those we have developed. Finally, we have seen that for programs of significant complexity manipulating data structures of significant scale, overall program efficiency depends on an awareness of the order of magnitude variations in efficiency that arise from different algorithms and data representations available. It is awareness of such variations, rather than the detail of how any chosen algorithm is coded, that determines whether basic efficiency requirements are met. By adopting an approach to programming based on

(a)   logical separation of concerns through modular abstraction,

(b)   exploitation of existing library modules as available, and

(c)   awareness of the order of magnitude variations in efficiency that alternative algorithms may imply,

the objectives of program correctness, flexibility and efficiency can be achieved to an appropriate degree.

EXERCISES

13.1   Implement packages to provide for the storage and retrieval of stacks
and queues, respectively.

13.2   Extend the animal guessing program shown in Listing 22 to store its
knowledge of animals at the end of each run, and to retrieve it at the
start of the subsequent run, using the tree filing operators defined in
this chapter.

13.3   Implement the alternative method of storing and retrieving binary
trees, using variant records, outlined on page 354.

13.4   Implement the *save* and *retrieve* operators for the *hashtable* envelope
given in Listing 25.

13.5   Write a program to check the spelling of each word in a text file using
an existing dictionary organised as a retrieveable hash table. The
dictionary should be extended if any new, correctly spelt, words are
encountered during the text analysis.

13.6   Implement the *save* and *retrieve* operators for one of the graph
implementations given in Listings 23 and 24

(a)   by filing the complete *nodes* array;

(b)   by first applying a compaction process to reduce the secondary
storage required.

Appendix 1

The language Pascal Plus is used throughout this book to illustrate and reinforce the style of programming advocated. Pascal Plus is a well-defined superset of ISO standard Pascal, providing facilities for modular and parallel programming. A variety of implementations of Pascal Plus are available, including several compilers for mainframe computers and a portable implementation which is easily installed within UNIX and other environments. Further details of the available implementations may be obtained from Dave Bustard, Department of Computer Science, Queens University, Belfast, BT7 1NN, Northern Ireland.

A complete definition of Pascal Plus together with a tutorial guide to its use is also available from Dave Bustard. In this Appendix a concise summary of the Pascal Plus features used within this book is provided. All language features referenced but not defined explicitly in the summary have the same definition as in ISO standard Pascal.

1. Blocks

The syntax of a Pascal Plus block is:

> *block : declaration-part statement-part.*

where declaration-part has the form:

360

declaration-part =
  {label-declaration-part |
  constant-definition-part |
  type-definition-part |
  variable-declaration-part |
  procedure-or-function-declaration "*;*" *|*
  envelope-definition "*;*" *|*
  instance-declaration-part }.

The component parts of a declaration-part may appear in any order, subject to the normal declare-before-use requirement for identifiers. Each kind of component part (label-, constant-, type-, etc) may occur zero or more times.

2.   Procedure and Function Declarations

In Pascal Plus new procedure or function identifiers may be defined to denote existing program-defined procedures and functions. A procedure or function declaration may also be held in a system library and included in a program by using a retrieval declaration.

   The definition of a function-declaration thus becomes:

function-declaration =
  function-heading "*;*" *directive |*
  function-identification "*;*" *function-block |*
  function-heading "*;*" *function-block |*
  function-equivalence-declaration |
  function-retrieval-declaration.

The syntax of a function-equivalence-declaration is as follows:

function-equivalence-declaration =
  "**function**" *identifier* "*=*" *function-identifier.*

The function-equivalence-declaration

   function $A = B$;

defines A as a function-identifier. The function which A denotes has

(a)   a parameter list congruous with the parameter list of the function denoted by B,

(b)   the same result-type as the function denoted by B, and

(c)   an effect which is identical to that of the function denoted by B as determined on entry to the block that contains the equivalence declaration.

The required (i.e. standard) procedures and functions of the language may not be renamed or equivalenced in this way.

The syntax of a function-retrieval-declaration is as follows:

function-retrieval-declaration =
   "function" *identifier* [*" =" library-identifier*]
   "in" [*library-path-name "in"*] *"library"*
   [*environment-specification*].

A function-retrieval-declaration is equivalent to its replacement by a function-declaration retrieved from a library of such declarations.

The resultant function is denoted in the block that contains the retrieval-declaration by the identifier that immediately follows the word **function** in the retrieval-declaration. This identifier is thus defined as a function-identifier in the block containing the retrieval-declaration.

The identifier that appears in the function-heading of the function-declaration in the library is called its library-identifier. If it differs from the function-identifier being defined it must be cited as the library-identifier in the function-retrieval-declaration.

library-identifier = *identifier*.

If no library-identifier appears in a function-retrieval-declaration the library identifier of the retrieved function must be the same as the function-identifier defined by the function-retrieval-declaration.

The function-declaration to be retrieved from the library is selected in an implementation-defined manner. A library-path-name, which is a string of implementation-defined form, may be used to specify a particular selection

library-path-name = *string*.

If no library-path-name is specified the selection is based on the library identifier cited or implied by the function-retrieval-declaration.

The identifier that appears in the function-heading of the function-declaration retrieved from the library (i.e. its library-identifier) may be used to denote (recursive references to) the function within itself.

Since a retrieval-declaration is equivalent to the inclusion of the retrieved function-declaration at the same point, the latter may refer to identifiers whose scope encloses the retrieval-declaration. In addition, however, the retrieved function-declaration may refer to identifiers defined in the environment-specification, if any, of the retrieval-declaration.

environment-specification =
    "(" "where" environment-section {environment-section} *")"*.

environment-section =
    constant-definition-part |
    type-definition-part |
    function-equivalence-declaration *";"* |
    procedure-equivalence-declaration *";"*.

The scope of constant-, type-, function- and procedure-identifiers defined in the environment-specification is the environment-specification itself and the function-declaration retrieved from the system library.

The extensions to the definition of a procedure-declaration for Pascal Plus are identical to those given above for function-declaration, with the word **function** replaced by the word **procedure** throughout.

3.   Envelope Definitions

An envelope is a set of definitions and declarations defined by the envelope-block of an envelope-definition.

An envelope instance is the set of variables, procedures and functions that result from instantiation of an envelope.

The syntax of an envelope-definition is:

envelope-definition =
    envelope-heading *";"* *envelope-block* |
    envelope-retrieval-declaration.

envelope-heading =
    envelope-type-heading | *envelope-module-heading*.

envelope-type-heading =
    *"**envelope**" identifier* [*formal-parameter-list*].

envelope-module-heading = *"**envelope**" "**module**" identifier*.

envelope-identifier = *identifier*.

envelope-block = *block*.

The identifier in an envelope-type-heading is defined as an envelope-identifier. Instances of the envelope it denotes may be declared as explained in Section 4, with properties which are determined by the associated envelope-block, as explained in Sections 6 and 8.

The identifier in an envelope-module-heading is defined as an envelope-instance-identifier. It denotes the only instance of an anonymous envelope whose properties are determined by the associated envelope-block.

The envelope-block must not contain any references to the envelope-identifier or envelope-instance-identifier defined by the envelope-heading, i.e. an envelope must not refer to itself.

An envelope-retrieval-declaration has the following syntax:

> *envelope-retrieval-declaration* =
>   *"**envelope**" ["**module**"] identifier ["=" library-identifier]*
>   *"in" [library-path-name "in"] "library"*
>   *[environment-specification].*

An envelope-retrieval-declaration is equivalent to its replacement by an envelope-definition retrieved from a library of such definitions.

If the word **module** is absent from the retrieval-declaration the retrieved envelope-definition must have an envelope-type-heading.

In this case, the identifier following the word **envelope** in the envelope-retrieval-declaration is defined as an envelope-identifier, and denotes the envelope defined by the retrieved envelope-definition.

If the word **module** is present in the retrieval-declaration the retrieved envelope-definition may have either an envelope-module-heading or an envelope-type-heading without a formal-parameter-list. In this case the identifier following the word **module** in the envelope-retrieval-declaration is defined as an envelope-instance-identifier, and denotes the only instance of an anonymous envelope defined by the envelope-block of the retrieved envelope-definition.

Other aspects of envelope-retrieval-declarations are identical to those of function- or procedure-retrieval-declarations.

4.   Instance Declarations

Envelope instances are declared in an instance-declaration-part, the syntax of which is as follows:

> *instance-declaration-part* =
>   *"**instance**" instance-declaration ";"*
>   *{instance-declaration ";"}.*

> *instance-declaration* =
>   *simple-envelope-declaration | envelope-array-declaration.*

A simple-envelope-declaration declares one or more envelope-instance-identifiers, each of which denotes one instance of the specified envelope:

> *simple-envelope-declaration =*
> *identifier-list ":" envelope-specification.*
>
> *envelope-specification =*
> *envelope-identifier [instance-parameter-lists].*
>
> *instance-parameter-lists =*
> *actual-parameter-list {"," actual-parameter-list}.*

Each identifier in the identifier-list of a simple-envelope-declaration is defined as an envelope-instance-identifier, and denotes a corresponding instance of the envelope denoted by the envelope-identifier.

If that envelope is defined without a formal-parameter-list the envelope-specification must not contain any actual-parameter-lists. If the envelope is defined with a formal-parameter-list the envelope-specification must contain exactly one actual-parameter-list for each identifier in the identifier-list. Each actual-parameter-list must correspond to the formal-parameter-list of the envelope, as defined for actual-parameter-lists of procedures and functions in Pascal and extended in Section 5. Each actual-parameter-list is used in the instantiation of the corresponding envelope instance as explained in Section 8.

An envelope-array-declaration declares one or more envelope-array-identifiers, each of which denotes an array of instances of the specified envelope.

> *envelope-array-declaration =*
> *identifier-list ":" envelope-array-specification.*
>
> *envelope-array-specification =*
> *"array" "[" index-type "]" "of" envelope-identifier*
> *[instance-array-parameter-lists].*
>
> *instance-array-parameter-lists =*
> *instance-array-parameter-list*
> *{"," instance-array-parameter-list}.*
>
> *instance-array-parameter-list =*
> *"[" instance-parameter-lists "]".*

Each identifier in the identifier-list of an envelope-array-declaration is defined as an envelope-array-identifier, and denotes a corresponding array of instances of the envelope denoted by the envelope-identifier.

If the envelope is defined without a formal-parameter-list the envelope-specification must not contain any actual-parameter-lists. If the envelope is defined with a formal-parameter-list the envelope-specification must contain exactly one instance-array-parameter-list for each identifier in the identifier-list. Each instance-array-parameter-list must contain one actual-parameter-list for each value of the index-type. Each actual-parameter-list must correspond to the formal-parameter-list of the envelope, as defined for actual-parameter-lists of procedures and functions in Pascal and extended in Section 5. Each actual-parameter-list is used in the instantiation of the corresponding envelope instance as explained in Section 8.

Use of an envelope-instance is denoted by an envelope-access:

envelope-access =
  envelope-instance-identifier | indexed-envelope.

indexed-envelope =
  envelope-array-identifier ''['' index-expression '']''.

The index-expression of an indexed-envelope must be assignment-compatible with the index-type of the envelope-array-specification used to declare the envelope-array-identifier.

5. Instances as Parameters

Envelope instances may be passed as parameters to other blocks. The extension to formal-parameter-list is:

formal-parameter-section =
  value-parameter-specification |
  variable-parameter-specification |
  procedural-parameter-specification |
  functional-parameter-specification |
  conformant-array-parameter-specification |
  envelope-parameter-specification.

envelope-parameter-specification =
  *''***instance***'' identifier-list '':'' envelope-identifier.*

Each identifier in the identifier-list of an envelope-parameter-specification is defined as an envelope-instance-identifier in the block, if any, of which it is a formal parameter. The corresponding actual parameter must be an envelope-access to an instance of the same envelope. Thus the syntax of actual-parameter becomes:

    actual-parameter =
        expression | variable-access | procedure-identifier |
        function-identifier | envelope-access.

Envelope instances are passed by reference. Thus the actual parameter is accessed before activation of the block to which it is passed. The corresponding formal parameter denotes the accessed envelope instance during the activation.

6.   Envelope Interfaces

An identifier defined within an envelope-block may be made visible outside the block by prefixing the identifier by a star (″*″) in its declaration or definition.

    Such identifiers are referenced outside the block using the dot or "with" notation applied to Pascal records. To integrate these starring and access conventions into the existing definition of Pascal a distinction must be made between the roles played by identifier occurrences, which in the standard definition of Pascal are classified as either "defining" or "applied" occurrences. As the name implies, a defining occurrence is where an identifier appears in its own definition or declaration. All other occurrences are applied occurrences corresponding to some defining occurrence.

    In the definition of Pascal defining occurrences are represented in the syntax by the direct use of the meta-identifier "identifier", as in these examples:

    type-definition = identifier ″=″ *type-denoter.*

    procedure-heading =
        ″**procedure**″ *identifier [formal-parameter-list].*

For these occurrences of identifier the appropriate definition in Pascal Plus may be thought of as:

    identifier = [″*″] *letter {letter | digit}.*

where the optional star applies only to defining occurrences within an envelope-block.

    A ″starred identifier″ is one which has been declared with a star in this way. It is visible to other blocks, and can have applied occurrences outside the block in which it is declared. In the definition of Pascal all applied occurrences of identifiers are denoted by meta-identifiers which specify the role of the identifier, such as "variable-identifier". Such meta-identifiers all have trivial definitions such as:

variable-identifier = identifier.

In Pascal Plus, however, a variable-identifier may either be an identifier whose declaration as a variable is currently in scope, or it may be a reference to a starred variable-identifier declared in an envelope-block of which an instance is currently in scope. In that case the envelope instance concerned must be specified as part of the variable-identifier, thus:

variable-identifier =
    identifier | envelope-access "." starred-variable-identifier.

starred-variable-identifier = variable-identifier.

The above rules apply not just to variable identifiers. In general they apply anywhere that the Pascal syntax refers to an identifier of a specific variety (variable-identifier, type-identifier, function-identifier etc.) Thus, using the term "x-identifier" to refer to any one of these possibilities, the general rules are:

x-identifier =
    identifier | envelope-access "." starred-x-identifier.

starred-x-identifier = x-identifier.

where the x specified must be the same on both sides of any production in which it appears.

A starred-x-identifier referenced in this way may be used in any way appropriate to an x-identifier, with the single restriction that starred variables are "read-only" to external blocks. That is, a starred variable may be inspected by other blocks, but it may only be modified by the code of the envelope in which it is declared.

Conversely, an envelope may use variables declared in blocks which enclose their definition, by the normal rules of scope, but may not directly assign values to such global variables.

7.   Simple Statements

Pascal Plus introduces an additional simple statement, the inner-statement, with the following syntax:

simple-statement = *empty-statement* |
assignment-statement |
procedure-statement |
goto-statement |
inner-statement.

inner-statement = ''***''.

The executable effect of an inner-statement is explained in the following section.

Pascal Plus imposes two restrictions on the use of goto-statements, which are as follows:

(a)   An envelope-block must not contain a goto-statement that refers to a label defined in a block enclosing the envelope-block.

(b)   If execution of a goto-statement within the execution of an inner-statement (as defined in the following section) causes the execution of the inner-statement to be interrupted, an error occurs.

8.   Activations, Instantiations and Inner Statements

In Pascal Plus the activation of a block B is defined as follows:

If block B contains no defining points for envelope-instance-identifiers or envelope-array-identifiers the activation of block B involves execution of the statement-part of B, as defined in Pascal. Otherwise activation of B involves the instantiation of the envelope instance or envelope array denoted by the first envelope-instance-identifier or envelope-array-identifier defined in B.

Instantiation of an envelope-array involves the instantiation of the first envelope instance contained by the array. Instances contained by an envelope array are ordered according to the corresponding values of the index-type.

Instantiation of an envelope instance involves the evaluation of the corresponding actual-parameter-list, if any, followed by the activation of the corresponding envelope-block, E.

The execution of an inner-statement contained by the statement-part of a block E, which has been activated by instantiation of an envelope instance I within the activation of a block B, is defined as follows:

If I is an element of an envelope array then the next element contained by that array, if any, is instantiated. Otherwise the envelope instance or envelope array denoted by the next envelope-instance-identifier or envelope-array-identifier defined in B, if any, is instantiated. Otherwise the statement-part of B is executed.

Appendix 2

Pascal Plus is an established programming language which may be used for direct implementation of programs written in modular form. It is, however, also an effective design notation which may be used for the modular design of programs to be implemented in other languages, such as Pascal itself. In this appendix we give a simple set of transcription rules by which programs using Pascal Plus envelopes can be converted to standard Pascal. Similar transcription rules can be devised for other target languages.

TRANSCRIBING ENVELOPE MODULES

Consider first the simple case of an envelope module E defined in some block B as follows:

```
procedure B . . . ;
   . . .
envelope module E ; . . .
   . . .
begin
  {body of B}
end ;
```

The block for B may include a variety of other definitions and declarations for constants, types, variables, procedures, functions, envelopes and instances. As we shall see, however, these affect the transcription of module

370

E only by the potential name clashes they create, and by any necessary ordering of definitions and declarations that must be preserved.

Let us now suppose that module *E* defines starred and unstarred identifiers as follows:

    envelope module *E* ;

        const **c*1 = {*value of c*1} ;
              *c*2 = {*value of c*2} ;

        type **t*1 = {*type for t*1} ;
              *t*2 = {*type for t*2} ;

        var **v*1 : {*type of v*1} ;
              *v*2 : {*type of v*2} ;

        procedure **p*1 ; {*block for p*1} ;

        procedure *p*2 ; {*block for p*2} ;

    begin
    {*initialization of E*} ;
    *** ;
    {*finalization of E*}
    end ;

In transcribing the block *B* to standard Pascal each component part of the envelope module *E* is transcribed to a corresponding position in *B* as follows:

(a)   Constant definitions

    Constant definitions within *E* are transcribed to the constant definition part of the block *B* in a way that preserves the overall order of constant definitions throughout *B* and its embedded envelope definitions. Thus we get a constant definition part of *B* of the form

    const {*constants in B before E*}
        *c*1 = {*value of c*1} ;
        *c*2 = {*value of c*2} ;
        {*constants in B after E*}

Note that any stars on identifiers are omitted, and that *c*1 and *c*2 are now equally accessible within *B*. Note also that *c*1 or *c*2 may clash with existing identifier usage in *B* and that such clashes must be eliminated by systematic renaming when they occur.

(b)   Type definitions

Type definitions within *E* are transcribed in a manner similar to that for constant definitions. Thus we get an overall type definition part for *B* of the form

type   {*types in B before E*}
    *t*1 = {*type for t*1} ;
    *t*2 = {*type for t*2} ;
    {*types in B after E*}

Again stars on type identifiers are eliminated and any resulting identifier clashes must be resolved by systematic renaming.

(c)   Variable declarations

Variable declarations within the module *E* could also be transcribed directly to the variable declaration part of block *B*, but a more effective reflection of their modular grouping can be achieved by declaring them as the fields of a single record variable *E* declared in *B*, thus:

var {*variables in B before E*}

    E : **record**
        *v*1 : {*type of v*1} ;
        *v*2 : {*type of v*2}
     end ;

    {*variables in B after E*}

(d)   Procedure declarations

Each procedure or function declaration within *E* is transcribed to the procedure declaration part of block *B*, but the procedure body, and the bodies of any nested procedures or functions, are prefixed by a with statement referencing the record variable *E*. With this convention all references to constant, type, variable, procedure and function identifiers within the transcribed procedure remain unaltered.
    Thus, if procedure *p*1 of *E* has the simple form

procedure **p*1 ;
  begin {*action for p*1} **end** ;

it is transcribed as

procedure $p1$;
  begin
    with E **do**
      begin {*action for* $p1$} **end**
  end ;

(e)   Module bodies

The body of a Pascal Plus envelope module in general consists of an initialization sequence, an inner statement *******, and a finalization sequence. In standard Pascal the initialization sequence and finalization sequence must be transcribed as two additional procedures, which are then called from appropriate points in the enclosing block. Thus the envelope module E results in two additional procedures for block B as follows:

procedure *initializeE* ;
  begin
    with E **do**
      begin {*initialization of* E} **end**
  end ;

procedure *finalizeE* ;
  begin
    with E **do**
      begin {*finalization of* E} **end**
  end ;

Again, the with statements allow the actual initialization and finalization code for E to be transcribed without alteration.

Having transcribed the envelope module E into the definition and declaration parts of block B, corresponding changes are required within the text of B itself where references to E occur. In practice the changes required are simple, and are as follows:

(a)   References to the starred constants or types of E, such as $E.c1$, $E.t1$, are simply transcribed without the prefix $E.$, since $c1$ and $t1$ are now corresponding constant and type identifiers in B.

(b)   References to starred variables of E, either using the dot notation $E.v1$, or via a with statement **with** E **do** . . . $v1$ . . . are left unchanged as the same notations are valid for the corresponding fields of record E.

(c)   References to starred procedures and functions of E, such as $E.p1$, are simply written without the prefix E.

In addition, however, the body of the block B must be augmented with explicit calls to the initialization and finalization procedures introduced for E. Thus the body of B becomes

> **begin**
>   *initializeE* ;
>   {*body of B*} ;
>   *finalizeE*
> **end** ;

When a block B contains two or more embedded modules care must be taken that the initialization procedures for these modules are called in the order of their appearance within B, and that the finalization procedures are called in the inverse order, if precise equivalence with Pascal Plus is to be maintained.

TRANSCRIPTION OF ENVELOPES AND INSTANCE DECLARATIONS

By definition an envelope module is equivalent to an envelope of which only a single instance is declared in any program using it. The more general case of an envelope with multiple instances poses greater difficulty in transcription to Pascal because of the multiplicity of variable copies it implies and because of possible use of envelope parameters.

Consider first the case of a *parameterless* envelope E embedded in some block B which declares two or more instances of E, thus

> **procedure** B ;
>
>   . . .
>
>   **envelope** E ; . . .
>
>   . . .
>
>   **instance** $i1, i2 : E$;
>
>   **begin**
>   {*body of B*}
>   **end** ;

We will again assume that envelope E defines the same range of starred and unstarred identifiers as the envelope module E used earlier. Transcription of each component part is then carried out as follows:

(a) Constant and type definitions within E are transcribed in exactly the same way as for envelope modules, as are references to starred constant or type identifiers within B.

(b) Variable declarations within E are transcribed to the type definition part of B as the definition of a record type E, thus

```
E = record
      v1 : {type of v1} ;
      v2 : {type of v2}
    end ;
```

Instance declarations within B are then transcribed to the variable declaration part as variable declarations using type E.

Thus

instance . . . $i1, i2 : E$;

becomes

var   . . . $i1, i2 : E$;

This creates a separate set of variables (or fields) $v1, v2$ for each instance, and references to the starred variables of any instance via the dot or with notations remain valid.

(c) Procedures and functions within E are again transcribed to the procedure declaration part of B, but with an additional variable parameter of type E to denote the particular instance to which each particular call is applied. Thus procedure $p1$ would now become

```
procedure p1 (var i : E) ;
  begin
    with i do
    begin {action for p1} end
  end ;
```

and a procedure call $i1.p1$ in B becomes $p1(i1)$.

(d)   The initialization and finalization sequences of the envelope body are again transcribed to additional procedures in B, but with a variable parameter of type E denoting the instance to be initialized or finalized. Thus the body of E is transcribed as

```
procedure initializeE (var i : E) ;
  begin
    with i do
    begin {initialization of E} end
  end ;
```

```
procedure finalizeE (var i : E) ;
  begin
    with i do
    begin {finalization of E} end
  end ;
```

Each instance declared in B then requires an appropriate call to each procedure at the beginning and end of the body of B. Thus the body of B, as illustrated earlier, would become:

```
begin
  initializeE (i1) ;
  initializeE (i2) ;
  {body of B} ;
  finalizeE (i2) ;
  finalizeE (i1)
end ;
```

Again the ordering of the calls for different instances must be determined carefully to maintain exact equivalence with Pascal Plus.

With these modifications to the transcription rules for envelope modules, multi-instance envelopes can also be transcribed easily, even mechanically, to standard Pascal.

DEALING WITH ENVELOPE PARAMETERS

In transcribing Pascal Plus envelopes to Pascal significant problems arise only when the envelopes concerned have parameter lists. This follows from the fact that envelopes with parameters represent an effective increase in power of Pascal Plus over Pascal, rather than a more elegant and secure way of exploiting the same power. A parameter passed to an envelope instance remains accessible throughout the ensuing sequence of calls on its starred procedures and functions. This effect is not generally expressible in Pascal.

If the envelope parameters are value parameters the effect can be simulated by declaring corresponding fields within the record type that represents the variables declared within the envelope and passing the actual parameters for each instance to the corresponding call of the initialization procedure, which copies their values to the fields of the record variable concerned.

For example an envelope of the form

> **envelope** E (vp : {*type of vp*}) ;
>
> **var** $v1$: . . .
> . . .

would be transcribed to a record type

> E = **record**
> vp : {*type of vp*} ;
> $v1$: . . .
>   . . .
>   **end** ;

and an initialization procedure

> **procedure** *initializeE* (**var** i : E ; vp : {*type of vp*}) ;
>   **begin**
> $i.vp := vp$;
>   **with** i **do**
>   **begin** {*initialization of E*} **end**
>   **end** ;

Subsequent references to vp within any procedure of the envelope will access the record field vp by the transcription already defined.

The same technique cannot be used for variable or procedural parameters, since Pascal provides no means of storing a reference to an arbitrary variable or procedure in a record field. In general this problem can be overcome only by transcriptions that are not strictly semantically equivalent to the original. For example one technique is to require the user block B to repass the variable or procedural parameter to each call of an envelope procedure that uses it.

Thus for example the *wordinput* envelope defined in Listing 4, which takes a text file as parameter, could be transcribed into an initialization procedure of the form

> **procedure** *initializewordinput* (**var** *i* : *wordinput* ;
> > **var** *f* : *text*) ;

and a *getword* procedure of the form:

> **procedure** *getword* (**var** *i* : *wordinput* ;
> > **var** *f* : *text*) ;

For many programs that use the *wordinput* envelope the consequences of this transcription would be quite acceptable. However, in the transcription of calls to *getword,* the file parameter from the instance declaration must be transcribed in a way that is valid and equivalent at each point of call. This depends on the semantics of the program surrounding these calls and can not in general be handled by any mechanical transcription.

SUMMARY

Apart from the minor problems arising from envelope parameters, the transcription rules given in previous sections show that the features of Pascal Plus used in this book are semantically equivalent to features already in Pascal. (This is not necessarily true of those Pascal Plus features that are not considered in this book). The major advantage of the envelope is not any increase in semantic power, but the elegance and security that it provides for modular programming. If Pascal Plus is used as the implementation language this elegance remains in the final program text, and the security is guaranteed by the language compiler. If, however, Pascal Plus is used only as a design notation, the resultant designs can be transcribed easily, even mechanically, into Pascal or some equivalent language, using the transcriptions outlined in this appendix.

Bibliography

The role of abstraction in the construction of programs is described in Hoare's "Notes on Data Structuring" in

Dahl, O. J., Dijkstra, E. W., Hoare, C. A. R., *Structured Programming* (New York: Academic Press, 1972).

Those not familiar with Pascal are referred to two introductory texts

Welsh, J., Elder, J., *Introduction to Pascal,* 2nd Edition (London: Prentice-Hall International, 1982).
Findlay, W., Watt, D., *Pascal: an Introduction to Methodical Programming,* 2nd Edition (Potomac, Md.: Computer Science Press, 1982)

The Quicksort algorithm discussed in Chapter Eight was first described in

Hoare, C. A. R., "Quicksort", *Computer Journal,* 5, 1(1962), pp 10–15.

A detailed exposition of the most important list sorting methods appears in

Wirth, N., *Algorithms + Data Structures = Programs* (Englewood Cliffs: Prentice-Hall, 1976).

The official definition of Ada is

American National Standards Institute, *The Programming Language Ada Reference Manual,* ANSI/MIL-STD-1815A-1983, February 1983 (Springer-Verlag, 1983).

Further details of graphs and graph manipulation algorithms appear in

Sedgewick, R., *Algorithms,* (Reading, Mass.: Addison-Wesley, 1983).

Abstractions of sequential and random access files held on backing store (and their implementations) are studied in

Elder, J., *Construction of Data Processing Software* (London: Prentice-Hall International, 1984).

For a further example of modular programming in practice, and the use of Pascal Plus, read the description of the model compiler implemented in

Welsh, J., McKeag, R. M., *Structured System Programming* (London: Prentice-Hall International, 1980).

Index